OFF THE BEATEN PATH®
TENNESSEE

Help Us Keep This Guide Up to Date

We would love to hear from you concerning your experiences with this guide and how you feel it could be improved and kept up to date. Please send your comments and suggestions to:

editorial@GlobePequot.com

Thanks for your input, and happy travels!

TENTH EDITION

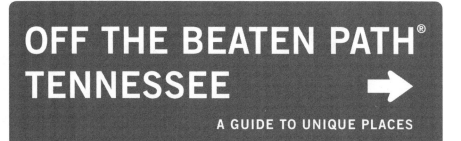

OFF THE BEATEN PATH®
TENNESSEE
A GUIDE TO UNIQUE PLACES

JACKIE SHECKLER FINCH

gpp®
travel

Guilford, Connecticut

All the information in this guidebook is subject to change. We recommend that you call
ahead to obtain current information before traveling.

Editor: Kevin Sirois
Project Editor: Lauren Szalkiewicz
Layout: Joanna Beyer
Text Design: Linda R. Loiewski
Maps by Equator Graphics © Rowman & Littlefield

ISSN 1539-8102
ISBN 978-0-7627-9208-5

Printed in the United States of America

Distributed by NATIONAL BOOK NETWORK

To my parents, Jack and Margaret Poynter,
for instilling in me the desire to travel.
And to my first traveling buddies—my sisters:
Elaine Emmich, Jennifer Boyer, Juliette Maples, and Jeanine Clifford;
and my brothers: Jim Poynter and Joe Poynter.

Contents

Acknowledgments

Many thanks to Tennessee residents, public relations officials, and business owners who took the time to help me update this book. Thanks especially to Cindy Dupree of Tennessee Tourism who shared little nooks and crannies in this wonderfully diverse state. I'm grateful to my editors Kevin Sirois and Lauren Szalkiewicz and the friendly and professional staff at Globe Pequot Press.

My gratitude to my family for their encouragement: Kelly Rose; Sean, Devin, Dylan, and Emma Rose; Stefanie, Will, Trey, and Arianna Scott; and Logan, Olivia, and Grayson Peters. And a special remembrance to my husband, Bill Finch, who taught me how to value every day on this earth.

—Jackie Sheckler Finch

About the Author

An award-winning journalist, Jackie Sheckler Finch has covered a wide array of topics—from birth to death, with all the joy and sorrow in between. She has written for numerous publications and has been named the Mark Twain Travel Writer of the Year by the Midwest Travel Writers Association a record five times, in 1998, 2001, 2003, 2007, and 2012. She has also won many photography awards. Finch shares her home with resident guard and entertainer, a black dog named Pepper. One of her greatest joys is taking to the road to find the fascinating people and places that wait over the hill and around the next bend.

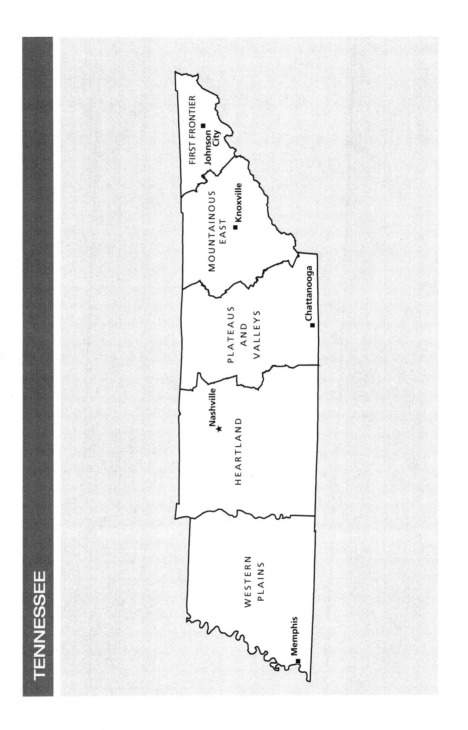

TENNESSEE

Introduction

The word "Tennessee" conjures up many different images. To the lover of country music, Nashville comes to mind when Tennessee is mentioned. To the blues aficionado or the Elvis fan, it's Memphis. To whitewater buffs, it's more than likely the Ocoee River. To conservationists and outdoors lovers, it's probably the Great Smoky Mountains or West Tennessee's Reelfoot Lake. To football fans, it's definitely the University of Tennessee's Volunteers.

As with any state, Tennessee is many things to many people. It's a fun and funky state to explore. From the mountainous east to the delta plains of the Mississippi River in the west, the variety of natural and man-made wonders and attractions the state has to offer is awesome.

Once you drive across the back roads of this long and narrow state, you'll never again think of it in the same way. I'm here to help you do just that. In reality it would take volumes to detail all that can be done and seen in Tennessee. However, in the book you now hold in your hands, I have narrowed your choices considerably by taking you off the interstates and onto the side roads, where the unique character of the state truly shines through.

My philosophy is important to understand here because I stayed true to it while writing this book. First of all, to me off the beaten path is more of an attitude than a place. I can enjoy something that's offbeat, funky, and unusual and consider it off the beaten path—even if it's on a major highway or in the middle of the city. Even though I may view it as off the beaten path, you may not. Don't worry; I'm sure we'll agree on something else.

Second, there are two types of people who will use this book: tourists and explorers. The tourists will bring home souvenirs; the explorers will bring home experiences. I'm an explorer, so don't expect too many stops at gift shops.

The state has a great highway system that is easy to follow, and while I won't be taking you down too many of the major highways, it is reassuring to know that they are usually nearby—in case you need to make a quick escape back to civilization.

As you drive along, look for signs that sport the image of the mockingbird, the state's official bird. They are mounted directly above the state highway designation numbers and signify that you are on a stretch of the

2,300 miles of the Tennessee Scenic Parkway System. Consisting primarily of two-lane roads, it connects the state's parks, major lakes, and historical sites, as well as this book's lesser-known attractions.

Along the way you'll definitely meet whittlers and collectors, and you might meet Dolly Parton. You'll meet ladies with hair higher than a church steeple and a hip guy who gives tours from a pink Cadillac. By the time you finish your journey, I'll have you floating on a lake 300 feet below the Earth's surface, playing miniature golf on the side of a mountain, cruising on a lake created by the strongest earthquake on record, and eating the world's sweetest-tasting, vilest-smelling vegetable.

Don't overlook some of the state's better-known tourist traps. Sometimes our trip down the less-traveled paths of Tennessee will intersect with the well-worn trails in order to highlight an event, an attraction, or a person worth visiting. I have found that sometimes it's worth fighting a crowd to see or do something that you'll probably never get a chance to see or do again.

Music is a big attraction as well as a big industry in Tennessee. From the birthplace of the blues in Memphis to the birthplace of the Grand Ole Opry in Nashville to the songs of the Appalachian mountain folk in East Tennessee, music is an important part of the heritage of our state.

Our tour will touch on much of that heritage and the people who have contributed to it. We'll visit the commercial monuments that honor Elvis Presley, Carl Perkins, Dolly Parton, and Loretta Lynn, among others. We'll also take a hike back into the woods to see the monument erected where Patsy Cline lost her life in a plane crash. We'll visit a museum honoring the best soul singers of the 1950s and 1960s, and we'll sit back and enjoy Sunday services at a Cowboy Church that passes a Stetson hat instead of the plate.

Southern hospitality is more than a myth in Tennessee, and our people may well be the state's friendliest attraction. There is one thing you'll never have to worry about as you travel through the state: You'll never truly be lost. Knock on any door or stop by any store, and chances are you'll get the directions you need, plus a whole lot more. Just when you think you've met the world's most colorful person, you'll meet one just a bit more fun. That's the way it is in Tennessee.

The state is full of crossroad communities with colorful and descriptive names. Usually the community has little more to offer than a gas station–general store combination, but here's where you'll usually find the most intriguing characters of the area.

In the summer these folks will be sitting on the porch of that store solving the world's problems. In the winter you'll find them sitting around the potbellied stove. There are more than 100 such communities with colorful names around the state, including Fly, New Flys Village, Defeated Creek, Ugly Creek, Pretty Creek, Dull, Soddy Daisy, Bell Buckle, Gilt Edge, Finger, Frogjump, Nutbush, Bucksnort, Only, Who'd A Thought It, and Skullbone.

This book has been broken down into five major areas:

The First Frontier. More than 200 years ago this part of the state was America's new frontier. Explorers, including Daniel Boone, blazed paths across the Appalachian Mountains, establishing some of the first settlements outside the original 13 colonies.

Much of the area is heavily forested, with the extreme east and southeast parts quite mountainous. Davy Crockett was born here, and the state of Franklin, which never quite made it to statehood, was formed here several years before Tennessee became a state.

The Mountainous East. As the name implies, this area is probably the most rugged of all Tennessee terrain. The 500,000-acre Great Smoky Mountains National Park and its foothill communities provide beauty incomparable to what you'll find elsewhere in the southeast US.

Throughout the area several museums have dedicated their collections and grounds to the preservation of mountain life, and many communities have preserved that lifestyle by their very existence.

Plateaus & Valleys. Forested and rugged, the Cumberland Plateau rises like a gigantic wall that spans the width of the state, forming the western boundary of the Tennessee Valley.

Although relatively flat, the area has many spectacular streams that have carved out deep gorges in the sandstone, making it one of the best areas in the state for whitewater enthusiasts. In fact, the 1996 Olympic Games whitewater events took place here.

The Heartland. Also known as Middle Tennessee, the area is a region of gently rolling hills, sloping green meadows, and miles of river and lake frontage.

At the heart of the area lies Nashville, "Music City," the home of the Grand Ole Opry. Musical attractions are popular in this area, as are

Tennessee walking horse farms, sour mash whiskey distilleries, and the homes of two US presidents.

The Western Plains. An area of fertile bottomlands and dense hardwood forests, the Western Plains region is bordered on the east by the Tennessee River and on the west by the Mississippi.

A few of the state's most colorful folk heroes—frontiersman Davy Crockett, train engineer Casey Jones, and *Walking Tall* sheriff Buford Pusser—have strong roots here, as do *Roots* author Alex Haley and the King of Rock 'n' Roll, Elvis Presley.

The 520-mile-long state is divided into six telephone area codes, 423, 731, 865, 901, 931, and 615; about half of it lies in the eastern time zone and half in the central zone.

Although care has been taken to ensure accuracy in all listings in this book, visitors are advised to call ahead before traveling any great distance. Life throughout Tennessee is slow-paced and mellow, so if a day appears to be going a bit slow, it isn't uncommon for a proprietor to close early and go fishing. Phone numbers, websites, and admission prices have been included in listings where appropriate.

Most of the attractions are open on a year-round basis, but some cut operations a bit during the winter months.

Before venturing forth, you may want to contact the state tourism bureau and load up on brochures and maps of the areas you plan on visiting. In the material you receive from the state, there will be a list of local tourism bureaus that will be able to provide even more specific information.

Contact the ***Tennessee Department of Tourist Development*** (Wm. Snodgrass/Tennessee Tower, 312 Rosa L. Parks Ave., Nashville, TN 37243; 615-741-2159; tnvacation.com).

Tennessee Facts

STATE SYMBOLS

- **Bird:** Mockingbird

- **Insects, two of them:** Firefly and ladybug

- **Gem:** Tennessee river pearls

SELECTED TOURISM WEBSITES & TELEPHONE NUMBERS

Chattanooga
(800) 453-8366
chattanoogafun.com

Cherokee National Forest
(800) 832-1355
fs.fed.us/cherokee

Gatlinburg
(800) 588-1817
gatlinburg.com

Historic Rugby
(423) 628-2441
historicrugby.org

Knoxville
(865) 523-7263
knoxville.org

Memphis
(901) 543-5300
memphistravel.com

Middle Tennessee Visitors Bureau
(888) 852-1860
antebellum.com

Nashville
(800) 657-6910
visitmusiccity.com

Northeast Tennessee Tourism Association
(423) 913-5550
netta.com

Pigeon Forge
(865) 453-8574
mypigeonforge.com

Smoky Mountains and Townsend
(800) 525-6834
smokymountains.org

State of Tennessee Tourism
(615) 741-2159
tnvacation.com

Tennessee Department of Environment and Conservation
(888) 891-8332
state.tn.us/environment

Tennessee Farm Winegrowers Association
tennesseewines.com

Tennessee Overhill Heritage Association
(423) 263-7232
tennesseeoverhill.com

Tennessee State Parks
(423) 881-5298
tn.gov/environment/parks/

Tourism Association of Southwest Tennessee
(866) 261-7534
tast.tn.org

Upper Cumberland Tourism Association
(931) 537-6347
uppercumberland.org

- **Tree:** Tulip poplar

- **Rock:** Limestone

- **Wildflower:** Passion flower

- **Flower:** Iris

- **Songs, five of them:** "My Homeland, Tennessee," "When It's Iris Time in Tennessee," "My Tennessee," "Tennessee Waltz," and "Rocky Top"

- **Animal:** Raccoon

- **Amphibian:** Tennessee cave salamander

- **Reptile:** Box turtle

- **Butterfly:** Zebra swallowtail

Bed-and-Breakfast Inns

Bed-and-breakfast inns can be found throughout the state. Many are listed in this book. Here are two contacts to call for information on more locations:

- **Natchez Trace Bed & Breakfast Reservation Service** (800-377-2770; natcheztracetravel.com), information on lodging along the Natchez Trace Parkway

- **Bed and Breakfast Association of Tennessee** (931-924-3869; tennessee-inns.com)

THE FIRST FRONTIER

➡️

Corner of the Frontier

Bristol is about as far north as one can go in the state and stay in Tennessee. In fact, about half the city is in Virginia. The state line runs down the middle of State Street in the heart of the downtown shopping district. But other than the small state markers embedded in the street between the double yellow lines, there's little evidence that the city has two mayors, two city councils, and two telephone area codes.

A big, old-fashioned neon sign forms an archway across State Street, near Randall Street, and proclaims Bristol is a good place to live. It was erected in 1910 as a symbol of unity between the two Bristols. Arrows point to the Tennessee and Virginia sides.

Although Nashville, about 300 miles to the west, gets credit for being the center of country music, it was here in Bristol that the **Carter Family** and **Jimmie Rodgers** recorded the first country-and-western music that was distributed nationwide. That recording took place on August 2, 1927, and put the area on the musical map. A monument

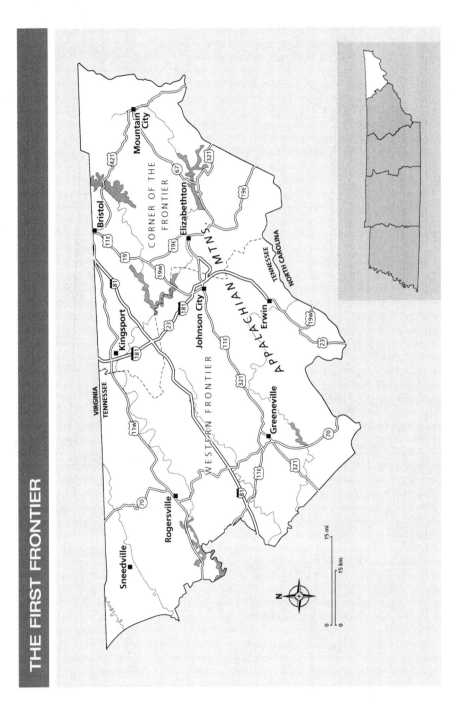

THE FIRST FRONTIER

honoring those musical pioneers stands at Edgemont Avenue and State Street. Farther down State Street, a large mural on the side of a building presents a visual memorial to that event.

The performing arts are alive and well in Bristol at the historic **Paramount Center for the Arts** (518 State St.; 423-274-8920; theparamount center.com). It's a circa 1931 theater restored to its original art deco style and is now listed on the National Register of Historic Places. Theatre Bristol calls the Paramount home for its own productions, and the venue is the site of other touring shows and concerts, as well as local meetings and seminars. It's a great place to watch a show.

Tennessee Ernie Ford was born Ernest Jennings Ford on February 13, 1919, in Bristol, and before he became the booming voice behind many hit country songs, including "Sixteen Tons," "The Shot Gun Boogie," and "Mule Train," he was a radio staff announcer and a bombardier during World War II. He was elected to the Country Music Hall of Fame in 1990 and died in October 1991.

Today the house where Ernie Ford was born has opened as a lasting memorial to the city's favorite son. Located on Anderson Street, the home is garnished with memorabilia of his long musical and television career. The home isn't open on a regular basis; contact the **Bristol CVB** (423-989-4850; bristolchamber.org), for hours and more information.

Southwest of Bristol, Johnson County is surrounded by the hills of the Appalachian Mountains, and the businesses and attractions reflect that way of life quite nicely. Throughout the county you'll see small handwritten signs hanging from mailboxes advertising handmade quilts or birdhouses for sale.

AUTHOR'S TOP TEN PICKS

Appalachian Fair	Kissing Bridge
Archie Campbell Days	Tennessee Ernie Ford Home
Bays Mountain Park	Tennessee Wilderness Road
Cooper's Gem Mine	Trade Days
Heritage Days (Rogersville)	Unicoi County Heritage Museum

In **Mountain City** about the only thing you won't find are crowds. Within a few-block area of the downtown section, you'll come across numerous antiques and gift shops selling a variety of neat things.

A great place to start your East Tennessee mountain trek is at the **Johnson County Welcome Center & Museum,** located on US 421 in Mountain City. In addition to maps, brochures, and great stories from the attendants, there's a historical museum with a large selection of Native American and pioneer artifacts. One of the coolest exhibits is Jessie Murphy's wedding gown. Jessie married Robert Ferdinand Wright on June 7, 1905, in Mountain City. Along with the dress are her shoes and pictures of the church and wedding party. The center is open 9 a.m. to 5 p.m. daily year-round, weather permitting. For information call (423) 727-5800, or log on to johnsoncountychamber.org.

South of Mountain City on US 421 is **Trade,** the oldest unincorporated community in the state. It's the spot where, in 1673, the first English-speaking white man set foot on Tennessee soil. Situated on an old buffalo trail, the community flourished as a resting place for those traveling the three major paths through the wilderness that crossed at this point.

By the 1790s the area had a country store, a post office, a blacksmith shop, and a handful of cabins, and today it's about as low-key as it was then—no big signs and no souvenir shops. **Trade Days** are held each June, when the entire county comes out to celebrate the heritage of the area.

Wilderness Road, one of the three major paths that converged at Trade, continues through East Tennessee to Cumberland Gap, where it heads northward into Kentucky and on to the "Great American West." Today the **Tennessee Wilderness Road** tour follows as closely as possible the original trail of the pioneers. The leisurely drive along the path takes you through a landscape of spectacular valleys dotted with church spires, old towns, and, if you take the time to explore on your own, plenty of unique experiences. Use the designated roads as your main route, but don't hesitate to follow a few side roads now and then to experience even more. There is also a full-color brochure and map, America's First Frontier tour, available for this part of the state. For more information contact the **Northeast Tennessee Tourism Association** (800-468-6882; netta.com).

In **Kingsport** early travelers through the area exchanged their Virginia currency for Tennessee money at a stagecoach stop known as the **Exchange**

Place (423-288-6071; exchangeplace.info). Today the small farm-like village and crafts center is open Sat and Sun May through Oct. Admission is free during regular events. A small admission is charged for festivals and other special events. The ***Fall Folk Arts Festival*** and an open-house celebration take place during the last weekend of Sept. There are a lot of really neat traditional Christmas events here as well, including a Yule log burning. The village is located just off US 11W at 4812 Orebank Rd.

Unlikely as it may seem, a major US boatyard was in operation along the Holston River in Kingsport in 1802. William King's boatyard had a reputation for quality that stretched as far as New Orleans. On the hill across the stagecoach road from the yards was the always busy ***Netherland Inn*** (423-247-3211; netherlandinn.com), an inn and tavern where the likes of the state's three presidents, Andrew Jackson, Andrew Johnson, and James K. Polk, whiled away hours with their friends. The inn has been restored and is open to the public as a museum. Several other buildings on the property, including a shop and wagon shelter, have also been restored. A log cabin that was moved here from Virginia and served as Daniel Boone's home from 1773 to 1775 is now a children's museum; it is a must if there are any small travelers with you. Start your visit at the Log Cabin Visitors Center and Gift Shop, located behind the inn. The former boatyards are now a city park that stretches for miles down the river. Open weekends only, May through Oct. Admission is charged.

Within the city limits of Kingsport, tucked away between Holston River Mountain and Bays Ridge, is the secluded and tranquil ***Bays Mountain Park*** (423-229-9447; baysmountain.com). The 3,550-acre city-owned facility has a wildlife park, a planetarium, a wildlife tour on the 44-acre lake, a natural history museum, 38 miles of hiking trails, an Adventure Ropes Course complete with a 300-foot zip line, and the unique ***Harry Steadman Mountain Heritage Farmstead Museum.***

The museum contains a collection of old tools and implements the founders of the area used in their

yumyum

The first Cracker Barrel Old Country Store and Restaurant opened in Lebanon on September 19, 1969, and there are now more than 600 stores in 42 states, with 50 of those in our own state. That means you're never far from a great plate of country cookin'!

daily lives. Donated by local families, the museum's collection gives a glimpse into the difficult challenges faced by the early pioneers. In the park there's an unusual gray wolf habitat and a snake habitat.

The park is a great way to spend a quiet, laid-back afternoon away from the crowds usually associated with natural parks of this size. The park is located 3 miles off I-181 at Bays Mountain Road, and it is open daily year-round. Check the website for current hours. Their entrance fee is $4 per car.

The city fathers of **Blountville** say that there are more original log houses along their city's main street than in any other town in the state. Whether that's true or not, there are a great many vintage buildings to see here. One of those, **The Deery Inn,** played an important part in the frontier era of this part of the state. Built during the late 1700s, the building is actually three structures: a 2-story hewn-log house, a 3-story cut-stone house, and a 2-story frame structure, all built adjacent to one another and joined together. Now known as the **Deery Inn Museum,** it offers group tours. Contact the museum at (423) 323-4660, historicsullican.com/tourism_deeryinn/html.

Everyone gets a chance to relive the old panning days when they stop by **Cooper's Gem Mine** (423-323-5680; coopersgemmine.com). Here you can buy a bucket of ore starting at $4 and take it out back to the stream, step up to the flume, wash away the sand and dirt, and what you find, you can keep! The shop is open year-round and sells specialty crafts and jewelry; the sluice at 1138 Big Hollow Rd. is usually open Mar through Oct. Closed Sun.

A walking-tour map of Blountville is available, and most of the buildings are decorated and open to the public around Christmas.

Perhaps one of the most historically significant structures in the state is **Rocky Mount,** a 2-story log cabin in **Piney Flats** near Johnson City. Built in 1770, Rocky Mount is the oldest original territorial capitol in the US and one of the oldest buildings in the state.

It was the capitol of "The Territory of the United States south of the river Ohio" from 1790 until a new capitol was built in Knoxville. With 2 stories and 9 rooms, pine paneling, and real glass windows, the structure was a mansion by frontier standards, and it quickly became a gathering place for people across the entire frontier.

Today the house is open to the public, as is the adjoining **Overmountain Museum** (888-538-1791; rockymountmuseum.com), which shows the early life of the area. First-person interpretation provides visitors with a true

OTHER ATTRACTIONS WORTH SEEING

Bristol Caverns
Bristol
(423) 878-2011
bristolcaverns.com

Dickson-Williams Mansion
Greeneville
(423) 787-7746

Farmhouse Gallery & Gardens
Unicoi
(423) 743-8799

Hands-On! Regional Museum
Johnson City
(423) 928-6509
handsonmuseum.org

Museum of Ancient Brick
Johnson City
(800) 414-4661
generalshale.com

Tipton-Haynes State Historic Site
Johnson City
(423) 926-3631
tipton-haynes.org

Wetlands Water Park
Jonesborough
(888) 662-1885
wetlandsjonesborough.com

sense of what was taking place in 1791. Guides talk with you as they would have in that year and stay in character for your entire visit. The museum is on US 11E and open Tues through Sat, Mar through Dec. 20. Admission is $8 adults, $7 senior citizens, and $5 children.

Sycamore Shoals (on US 321 in Elizabethton; 423-543-5808; sycamore shoalstn.org), the first permanent settlement outside the 13 colonies, was a muster point for the Overmountain Men on their way to the battle of King's Mountain. Today it is a State Historic Area and offers a reconstructed Fort Watauga that interprets the role this area played in the early settlement of what is now Tennessee and in the expansion of America's western boundary. An outdoor drama, *The Wataugans,* is presented during mid-July. A new interpretive museum was opened in the summer of 2013, telling the story of the area through three-dimensional interactive exhibits. Open year-round with free admission, the museum also has a new theater with a new film.

There are plenty of hiking trails here among the park's 45 acres, and there are several boat launch ramps for the lake. Beautifully shaded and peaceful, this is truly an off-the-beaten-path mixture of history and recreation.

One of the state's remaining original covered bridges crosses the Doe River in downtown **Elizabethton** and is the focal point for the city's riverside park. Built in 1882, **The Kissing Bridge** (423-547-3852; tourelizabethton.com) is the oldest such structure in the state. The **Covered Bridge Celebration** takes place in June. Activities include concerts, a crafts show, an antique car show, and kids' games and contests.

For many years a tall Fraser fir tree on Elk Street near downtown Elizabethton was considered the tallest such tree in the world. Then the gloomy day came when officials found it was only the second tallest. But since the tallest is never decorated at Christmas, they now decorate the fir in Elizabethton, making it the tallest decorated Fraser fir in the world. While you are in the area, pick up a free walking tour map of downtown Elizabethton; there are some great buildings here. Maps are available at the chamber of commerce on East Elk Avenue, (423) 547-3850, elizabethton chamber.com.

About 20 miles southeast of Elizabethton on Route 143 is **Roan Mountain State Park.** The park itself lies at the foot of Roan Mountain, one of the highest peaks (6,285 feet) in the eastern US, but that's not what makes this park so special. On the side of that mountain is one of the largest rhododendron gardens in the country. More than 600 acres of color bloom each June, making the area a striking display of pinks and purples. The **Rhododendron Festival,** held in mid-June, features native arts and crafts, mountain music and dancing, local food festivals, and wildlife tours. The park is also the best place in the area to view fall foliage. A campground and cabins offer overnighters grand vistas of the mountains.

agreatname

The name "Tennessee" originated from the old Yuchi Indian word *tana-see*, meaning "the meeting place." White men traveling the area in the 1700s associated the word with the name of a Cherokee village and as the name of a river in Cherokee Territory.

Walking and hiking trails line the mountain with numerous scenic overlooks. The **Dave Miller Homestead** (800-250-8620), a preserved farm, is tucked in a hollow atop Strawberry Mountain. The Miller family first settled in the area around 1870 and for generations lived in virtual seclusion. Today the farm is preserved intact and serves as a model of early

Appalachian life. The park is open year-round; the homestead is open 9 a.m. to 5 p.m. Wed through Sun Memorial Day to Labor Day. Admission is free.

Farther down US 321 toward Johnson City is the **Sinking Creek Baptist Church** (423-928-3222; sinkingcreek.org), the oldest church congregation in the state, having been established in 1773. Next to its new church building, built in the 1960s, is the congregation's former place of worship, a log church built in 1783. It has been renovated, but many of the logs are from the original church. Occasionally the old log church is host to weddings and Sunday services, weather permitting. Reece Harris, pastor of the congregation for 51 years, once told me that the sight of the log church provokes "a sense of pride knowing that Christians have been on this creekbank for a long time."

Johnson City resident John Tipton was a participant at the 1776 Constitutional Convention, and today the home he built in 1784 is a significant piece of restored history. At the **Tipton-Haynes State Historic Site** (423-926-3631; tipton-haynes.org), 10 original and restored buildings still stand on the property. A cave and a spring here were resting places for the early white explorers, and it is believed that Daniel Boone set up a hunting camp near the spring. The cave can be visited today. The site is open year-round at 2620 S. Roan St.

While walking through Johnson City, notice the great brick sculptures, created by Johnny Hagerman, a brick sculptor for General Shale Brick. The company, headquartered here, has plants throughout the South and Midwest and is the nation's leading brick maker.

Make sure you're in town when it's time for lunch, and make your way over to 3301 N. Roan St. to the **Dixie Barbeque Company** (423-283-7447; dixiebarbecue.net). What a selection of smoked meat meals and sandwiches you'll find here! Owner Alan Howell is quite the host and is willing to tell you everything you need to know in order to enjoy the meat he serves, which ranges from sliced pork and pork ribs to smoked chicken. Try the smoked chicken sandwich with Howell's own East Tennessee sauce. Wow!

At any one time, there will be eight sauces to choose from—most of them made by Howell himself. "If it doesn't have a label on it, that means I made it," he said. Open Mon through Sat, 11 a.m. to 9 p.m.

South of I-81, on Highway 36 headed toward Johnson City, is the little community of **Boone's Creek.** Daniel Boone loved this area, and he came back often to hunt. On one of his trips he brought along William Bean, who liked the area so much he decided to settle his family here in 1769, thus making them the first permanent white settlers in Tennessee. He built his first cabin on the site of Boone's hunting camp next to Boone's Creek. A monument now marks that spot.

Inside the chapel at **Boone's Creek Christian Church** (corner of Highway 354 and Christian Church Road; 423-282-0248; boonescreekcc.org) are several rooms of artifacts from Boone, Bean, and other pioneers of the area. The **Boone's Creek Museum** is not open on a regular basis.

Out on Old Gray Station Road, off Highway 36, is a small waterfall that Boone once hid under to escape the Indians. The waterfall has eroded over time, but you can still see it right after you turn onto Old Gray Station Road. Approximately 2 miles farther down the road, you'll find a historic marker showing where Boone carved his own monument into a beech tree: D. BOON CILLED A BAR in 1760. The tree is now dead, but a short walk off the highway will take you to the spot, which is fenced in.

Western Frontier

The Unicoi County seat community of **Erwin** probably holds the distinction of being the only town ever to put an elephant on trial for murder, find it guilty, and carry out the death penalty.

"Murderous Mary," a circus elephant who trampled her owner to death, was hanged from a railroad derrick before 5,000 spectators in 1916. Newspaper clippings and photos of that event are but a few of the interesting items in the **Unicoi County Heritage Museum** (423-743-9449), housed in a century-old home on the grounds of the **National Fish Hatchery** (423-743-4712) on US 23.

The hatchery was established in 1894, and the 10-room superintendent's residence was constructed in 1903. By the early 1980s the house wasn't being used by the superintendent, so the federal government signed an agreement allowing the county to use it as a museum. In addition to the story of Murderous Mary, various displays highlight local pottery production and the history of local railroading. On the second floor is a replica of the city's Main Street as it looked a century ago. "Grandmother's Attic" holds a collection of quilts, antique dolls, and children's toys, all displayed as they might be in your own grandma's attic.

TOP ANNUAL EVENTS

JUNE

Covered Bridge Celebration
Elizabethton
(423) 547-3850
coveredbridge.elizabethtonchamber
.com

Rhododendron Festival
Roan Mountain State Park
(800) 250-8620

JULY

The Wataugans **Outdoor Drama**
Elizabethton
(423) 543-5808

SEPTEMBER

Fall Folk Arts Festival
Kingsport
(423) 288-6071
exchangeplace.info/

OCTOBER

Apple Festival
Erwin
(423) 743-3000
unicoicounty.org

Heritage Days
Rogersville
(423) 272-1961
rogersvilleheritage.org

National Storytelling Festival
Jonesborough
(800) 952-8392
storytellingcenter.net

Outside, the fish hatchery is still in operation and produces about 10 million rainbow trout eggs each year. Free tours are available at the hatchery as well as at the museum. Bring your lunch; the entire area is a beautiful parklike setting, complete with a picnic pavilion and restrooms.

A fun event to catch in Erwin each fall is the ***Apple Festival*** (423-743-3000), held the first full weekend in Oct. There is continuous music, dancing, handmade crafts, the famous Blue Ridge Pottery Club Show and Sale, and various local food vendors.

The 16 counties that now make up the eastern tip of Tennessee were at one time united in an effort to become a state by themselves. The framework for the would-be state of Franklin was set when about 30,000 white settlers crossed the Appalachian Mountains and founded several settlements in this area, which was a part of North Carolina at the time.

Leaders met in ***Jonesborough*** and created a bill of rights for their new state and requested that the lawmakers of North Carolina allow its creation.

They refused, but Franklin, under the leadership of John Sevier, continued the battle for several years, until 1788. Several skirmishes between Franklin and North Carolina militia took place in the area.

Although never recognized as an official state, Franklin operated like a sovereign government with an assembly, administered justice, and negotiated treaties with Native Americans.

Eight years after the fight for the quasi state ended, Sevier became the first governor of the state of Tennessee, which incorporated the former boundaries of Franklin. Jonesborough, chartered in 1779, 17 years before there was a Tennessee, holds the distinction of being the oldest incorporated area in the state. And thanks to an ambitious restoration effort, much of the city appears as it did more than a century ago. Jonesborough was the first Tennessee town placed on the National Register of Historic Places.

There are more than 27 points of interest on the walking tour map of the historic downtown area, including the historic ***Chester Inn Museum*** (423-753-4580; storytellingcenter.net), where a young Andrew Jackson stayed while working on his law degree in 1788. Now owned by the state of Tennessee, the inn is a museum and houses the International Storytelling Foundation. A gift shop on the first floor offers a wide variety of storytelling tools, including books and tapes.

Many of the old buildings along the main streets now house a wide array of specialty shops. One particular structure, the ***Old Town Hall,*** at 144 E. Main St., was restored in 1982 and contains about 50 crafts-oriented shops.

The Bad-Shot President

Once, a long time ago, a small crowd of onlookers followed a fiery lawyer named Andrew Jackson from a courtroom in Jonesborough to a nearby meadow, where Jackson and his opponent, attorney Waightstill Avery, squared off, and a duel began.

Crack! A pistol shot rang out. Crack! Another shot.

Yet both men still stood, unharmed. Each dueler, it seems, had fired into the air, and a deadly conclusion was avoided. Moments later, the two adversaries shook hands.

Jackson went on to become the seventh president of the US.

The ***Hawley House Bed & Breakfast*** (800-753-8869; megtrott.com/hawleyhouse) on Lot #1 at 114 E. Woodrow Ave. is the oldest house in the state's oldest town! Built in 1793, the house offers 3 bedrooms with private baths and a full breakfast. Prices range from $105 to $150.

The ***Jonesborough History Museum*** (866-401-4223; historicjonesborough.com) is inside the visitor center at 117 Boone St. and a good place to begin your visit to this historic area. Brochures, maps, and a short film will get you started in the right direction. The museum is open daily.

There are two great festivals in town you won't want to miss. An old-fashioned, family-oriented July 4 celebration known as ***Historic Jonesborough Days*** features arts and crafts, southern cooking, and clogging. In early Oct, the ***National Storytelling Festival*** is a celebration of the country's top storytellers. Call (423) 753-2171 or (800) 952-8392; their website is storytellingcenter.net. For information about Historic Jonesborough Days, contact the Jonesborough Visitors Center at historicjonesborough.com, (866) 401-4223.

If you're in this part of the state during late Aug, be sure to visit the ***Appalachian Fair*** (423-477-3211; appalachianfair.com), which is held at the fairgrounds in Gray. This 6-day event is the largest fair in East Tennessee and features one of the best carnival companies in operation today, the Great James H. Drew Exposition. There are all kinds of live Appalachian crafts demonstrations, farm and home exhibits, and various agricultural exhibits and competitions. This is truly an old-time country fair, complete with demolition derbies, mud drag racing, baby shows, baking contests, and top-name country music entertainment.

Contrary to the myth promoted by Walt Disney, Davy Crockett was not born on a mountaintop in Tennessee; he was born along the banks of the Nolichucky River, near the mouth of Limestone Creek. Today that birth spot, just outside the small community of Limestone, is preserved as the ***Davy Crockett Birthplace State Historic Park*** (423-257-2167).

Born in 1786, David (he never signed his name Davy) went on to become the "King of the Wild Frontier." His name and legend can rightfully be claimed by many areas in the state. He was born here in the east, he ran a gristmill in middle Tennessee, and he was elected to Congress from western Tennessee.

But here is where it all began. A reproduction of his birthplace cabin has been constructed, with the cornerstone of his original cabin on display.

Probably the most unusual aspect of this park is the monument erected in the late 1960s by a local civic organization. In honor of Crockett's stature as a national hero, each of the 50 states is represented in the wall of the monument. Stones native to each state are incorporated in the wall and engraved with the respective state's name.

The park, located off US 11E, has a campground, swimming pool, picnic facilities, and a visitor center. Open year-round.

Fifteen minutes down US 321 is the county seat city of **Greeneville,** which happens to be the only Greeneville in the US that uses that third "e" in its name.

It was to this city that an 18-year-old boy moved in 1826 to establish a tailor business for himself. Several years later that boy, Andrew Johnson, became the country's 17th president. Today Johnson's Greeneville years are highlighted at the **Andrew Johnson National Historic Site** (423-638-3551; nps.gov/anjo), in the downtown section. His small tailor shop has been preserved and is inside the site's visitor center. Across the street is the brick home in which Johnson lived from the early 1830s to 1851. On Main Street is the Homestead, his home from 1851 to 1875, during which time he was vice president and then president of the US. The cemetery where he and his family are buried is a few blocks away. All four attractions are open every day except Christmas, Thanksgiving, and New Year's Day. The visitor center is located at the corner of College and Depot Streets. The visitor center and Homestead are free.

A walking tour map of Greeneville is available that highlights 36 historic areas or structures of the community.

Greeneville's **Tusculum College** (423-636-7300; tusculum.edu), founded in 1794, is the oldest college south of the Ohio River and west of the Allegheny Mountains. It was the 28th college founded in America, is the oldest college in the state, and is the oldest coed college associated with the Presbyterian Church. Eight buildings on the campus were constructed between 1841 and 1928 and make up the college's historic district. A walking tour of the campus is included in the city's walking tour brochure.

trivia

The nation's 17th president was laid to rest on a high hill known as Monument Hill in Greeneville. President Andrew Johnson was buried with his beloved American flag and his personal copy of the US Constitution.

The college's ***Andrew Johnson Library and Museum*** (800-729-0256, ext. 5251) is the state's largest presidential library and houses a great many of the president's books, papers, and manuscripts, as well as those of his family. In addition, the library houses almost 200 original Civil War–era newspapers from throughout the country.

On US 11W, look for ***Pal's Sudden Service*** (palsweb.com) drive-through restaurant. You can't miss any of the 21 Pal's drive-throughs, all of which are located in East Tennessee and southwestern Virginia. While the restaurants probably don't stand out if you see them every day, those of us from outside the area should surely appreciate the unique architecture.

In fact, each location is vernacular architecture at its finest. There is no doubt what the restaurant sells: Huge hot dogs, fries, hamburgers, and soft drink containers bedeck each of the little square buildings. Colorful and fun, the buildings stand out from the urban clutter. The food and service are pretty good, too.

Tennessee's first newspaper was printed in Rogersville in 1791, and to celebrate that fact, the ***Tennessee Newspaper & Printing Museum*** (423-272-1961) has been established in the city's old railroad depot, just down the street from the Hale Springs Inn at 415 S. Depot St.

Most of the old structures in downtown ***Rogersville*** have been restored, and the entire district is listed on the National Register of Historic Places. A walking tour of the historic district includes the Hawkins County Courthouse. Erected in 1836, the building is the oldest original courthouse still in use in the state. You can view the entire walking tour, including information on each site, online at rogersvilleheritage.org.

Most of the Main Street retail businesses now sell antiques or crafts, but there are still a few old-time offices and clothing stores along the way.

There's a fascinating natural phenomenon a few miles outside Rogersville on Ebbing & Flowing Spring Road that you won't want to miss. The ***Ebbing & Flowing Spring*** is one of only two known springs in the world to flow and stop at regular intervals. The underground hollow is filled slowly with water. As it nears the surface of the ground, a suction is formed and the water begins to be siphoned out of the ground into the spring basin. The siphon continues to drain the hollow until it dries up, breaking the siphon and stopping the flow. It then fills up and starts all over again. This has happened for at least the past 200 years at 2-hour-and-47-minute intervals. The water remains at a constant 34 degrees.

Legend claims that any couple drinking from the spring at the height of its flow will marry within the year. The flat rock nearby was a favorite courting spot and the site of many marriage proposals.

The ***Ebbing & Flowing Spring School*** (423-272-1961; rogersville-heritage.org) was built in the early 1800s by families of its first students. Generations of the Amis family, the original land grant owners, were taught here until the dismissal bell rang for the last time in 1956.

The Ebbing & Flowing Spring United Methodist Church met in the school when it was organized in 1820 until a permanent church was built between the school and the cemetery in 1898. It still stands today with its original timbers and interior and is used regularly by the congregation.

taxmoney atwork

There are 54 Tennessee state parks, with 932 miles of hiking trails to walk, 394 species of birds to watch, 18 waterfalls, and 3,119 campsites. For specifics, phone them at (888) 867-2757 or go to tn .gov/environment/parks.

From the center of Rogersville, head east on old US 11W (not the bypass) for about a mile to Burem Road. Bear right at the Amis House historical marker, and go a little more than 2 miles and turn left on Ebbing & Flowing Spring Road, a narrow country road. You'll go by ruins of a stone mill on your right. In less than a half mile, you'll come to a stream crossing the road. Immediately to your left is the spring. The road on your right leads to the church and school.

Plan your visit to Rogersville in mid-Oct. That's when the popular ***Heritage Days*** take place. All the activities are reminiscent of a harvest celebration at the turn of the 20th century.

Out on US 11E at Highway 66 is the little community of ***Bulls Gap.*** Named after local gun maker John Bull, who settled here in the mid-1790s, this natural gap in Bays Mountain later became a strategic location when the railroad through here was completed in 1858. During the Civil War both the North and South wanted to control the railroad through the mountains; as a result, Bulls Gap was the site of several skirmishes.

Even though the area has more than 200 years of history and architecture going for it, the event that put it on the map more than anything else was the birth of comedian Archie Campbell, who went on to become a member of the Grand Ole Opry in Nashville and to star on the long-running television show *Hee Haw*. He died in 1987.

Today a reconstruction of his birthplace is open in the town park alongside the ***Bulls Gap Railroad Museum.*** A fun time to visit is during Labor Day weekend, when ***Archie Campbell Days*** take place. In addition to the Campbell complex, there's an Old Town historic district walking tour featuring nearly 30 structures. Campbell's birthplace is 2.5 miles off exit 23 of I-81, at 139 S. Main St. Call (423) 235-5216 for further information, or visit bullsgaptn.us.

Off Highway 31, 7 miles south of Sneedville, is ***Elrod Falls*** (423-733-4341), one of the great hidden treasures of this sparsely populated county. Flat Gap Creek cascades more than 100 feet to the lower pool, where swimming is permitted in the cool, deep water. Take the unnamed gravel road off Highway 31 at the sign for the falls and follow it approximately 1 mile to a small picnic area. Park there; the walk is a very short, easy one to the lowest of the three falls.

Places to Stay in the First Frontier

BLOUNTVILLE

Rocky Top Campground
496 Pearl Ln.
(423) 323-2535
rockytopcampground.com
Cable TV; pets allowed

BRISTOL

Travelodge
111 Holiday Dr.
(423) 968-1101
travelodge.com
Restaurant, lounge,
exercise, pool

ERWIN

Nolichucky Gorge Campground
1 Jones Branch Rd.
(423) 743-8876
nolichucky.com
Showers, flush toilets,
fishing, cabins, RV sites

GREENEVILLE

General Morgan Inn
111 N. Main St.
(423) 787-1000
generalmorganinn.com
Restaurant, room service,
fireplaces

JOHNSON CITY

Carnegie Hotel & Spa
1216 W. State of Franklin Rd.
(423) 979-6400
carnegiehotel.com
Hotel built to match elegance of original Carnegie Hotel, circa 1891

Doubletree Hotel
211 Mockingbird Ln.
(423) 929-2000
doubletreejohnsoncity
.com
Restaurant, lounge, pool

JONESBOROUGH

Hawley House Bed & Breakfast
114 E. Woodrow Ave.
(423) 753-8869
megtrott.com/
hawleyhouse
Built in 1793; private
baths, full breakfast

Historic Eureka Inn
127 W. Main St.
(423) 913-6100
eurekajonesborough.com
Private baths, continental
breakfast, private garden
terrace

KINGSPORT

Fox Manor B&B
1612 Watauga St.
(423) 378-3844
foxmanor.com
In old neighborhood;
private baths, full
breakfast

LIMESTONE

**Davy Crockett
Birthplace State Historic
Park** (camping)
Off US 11E
1245 Davey Crockett Park
Rd.
(423) 257-2167
Hiking trails, playground,
scenic riverside

Home Place Bed & Breakfast
132 Church Ln.
(423) 921-8424
Quiet, private in small rural
town; run by historic local
family

MOUNTAIN CITY

Prospect Hill Inn Bed & Breakfast Inn
801 W. Main St.,
Highway 67
(423) 727-0139
prospect-hill.com
Circa 1889 mansion;
private bath, fireplace,
Jacuzzi; balcony with
mountain view

Places to Eat in the First Frontier

HAMPTON

Captain's Table
2285 Hwy. 321
(423) 725-2201
Overlooking Lake
Watauga; specialty is
seafood, also steaks and
chicken. Open seasonally.

JOHNSON CITY

**Dixie Barbeque
Company**
3301 N. Roan St.
(423) 283-7447
dixiebarbeque.net

Selection of smoked
meats and sandwiches.
Open Mon through Sat,
11 a.m. to 9 p.m.

**The Firehouse
Restaurant**
627 W. Walnut St.
(423) 929-7377
thefirehouse.com
In circa 1900 building,
firefighting memorabilia;
pit-cooked barbecue, ribs,
steaks. Lunch and dinner
daily.

Gourmet & Company
214 E. Mountcastle Dr.
(423) 929-9007
gourmetandcompany.com
Fresh croissants, pasta,
salad, and sandwiches.
Lunch and dinner daily.

Harbor House Seafood
2510 N. Roan St.
(423) 282-5122
harborhousejc.com
Seafood, chicken, steak.
Open daily 11 a.m. to 9
p.m.

JONESBOROUGH

The Dining Room
148 E. Main St.
(423) 753-6400
American dining with a
Cuban flair. Open Sun
11 a.m. to 2 p.m., Tues
through Thurs 11 a.m.
to 4 p.m., Fri and Sat 11
a.m. to 8 p.m.

Of Lincoln & Boone

The quaint little village of **Cumberland Gap** rests just a few miles away from one of the most historic natural passageways of all time. Much of the westward movement of early America came through this V-shaped indentation in the Appalachian Mountains, a wall of rock that stretches from Maine to Georgia.

It was 1775 when Daniel Boone and his 30 axmen hacked out the Wilderness Road through the gap to open up the "western frontier" and the fertile farmlands on the other side. It was the first road platted by a white man in the state. That byway became a major thoroughfare and later was a 4-lane paved highway for decades.

Now the Cumberland Gap Tunnel, which opened October 18, 1996, takes US 25E through the mountain instead of up and over the top.

At the top of the gap, a marker in the **Cumberland Gap National Historical Park** (606-248-2817; nps.gov/cuga) shows where the states of Kentucky, Virginia, and Tennessee meet. It is said that from the top, those three

Cumberland Gap

KY.
TENN.

VA.
TENN.

Huntsville

75   25W

63

25E

La Follette

FORESTS AND CLIFFS

27

11W

Morristown

11E

Norris

OF LINCOLN
AND BOONE

81

THE DREAM
COUNTIES

Clinton

25W

441

Oak Ridge

61

62

Knoxville

441

Newport

25E

321

70

25

40

70

140

411

321

40

27

GATEWAY TO THE SMOKIES

Pigeon Forge

75   11

Loudon

321

Maryville

Gatlinburg

129

441

Sweetwater

GREAT SMOKY MTNS.

411

COUNTRY
LIFESTYLE

TENN.
N.C.

N

0   25 mi
0   25 km

states, plus Georgia and North Carolina, can be seen on a clear day. A visitor center and museum are part of the park.

To reach the park's visitor center, go through the tunnel to Middlesboro, Kentucky. Inside the center is an informative museum about the park, the gap, and early life in the area. A good way to see the terrain of the mountains is to drive 4 miles up to the Pinnacle, where you'll park in Kentucky, walk into Virginia, and overlook the village of Cumberland Gap in Tennessee. You can look down on the actual gap where Daniel Boone came through, and you'll see the old highway that follows the original Wilderness Road.

When old US 25E was built over the gap, much of it followed the Wilderness Road and was paved. Now that the tunnel takes all the traffic, that portion of 25E has been closed, all the paving removed, and the road restored to a primitive condition. The original dirt Wilderness Road, which can be seen from the Pinnacle, was reopened to foot traffic in mid-2002; we can all now walk exactly where those early settlers trekked in the late 1700s.

A fun, albeit somewhat tiring, side trip while you're in this area takes you to the mountaintop village where Sherman Hensley lived until 1951.

In 1904 he decided to get away from it all and moved, along with several relatives, to the mountaintop a few miles from Cumberland Gap. They all became self-sufficient when the rest of America was learning to rely more on one another for basic needs.

Since 1965 the National Park Service has restored parts of the **Hensley Settlement** (606-248-2817), including 12 homestead log cabins, several barns, many of the fences, the schoolhouse, and the cemetery. The public

AUTHOR'S TOP TEN PICKS

Davy Crockett's marriage license	Moonshine Capital of the World
Dollywood	Museum of Appalachia
Hensley Settlement	Ripley's Davy Crockett Mini-Golf
The Lost Sea	Rugby's Utopian Community
Mel's Diner	World's Largest Stalagmite

is invited to visit. It's not an easy place to get to, but what an adventure it is. The most popular way of coming in is on foot via a 3.5-mile path up the side of the mountain, or you can be shuttled there by park-operated vehicles, leaving from the visitor center daily from May through Oct. Tours are $10 adults, $5 senior citizens and children (ages 12 and under). Call for directions and a schedule of special events.

Deep in the mountain, directly underneath the historic Wilderness Road, is *Cudjo's Caverns* (606-248-2817), the home of the *"Pillar of Hercules,"* one of the world's largest stalagmites. The formation is 65 feet high and 35 feet in circumference, and it is still growing. It's estimated to be 85 million years old. The National Park Service oversees the caverns.

The village of Cumberland Gap was founded by English settlers and today shows a strong English influence in its architecture. The downtown section has been virtually untouched by modernization for more than 50 years. The opening scene of a movie was filmed here in 1988, and according to one of the downtown businessmen, only one sign had to be removed to make the village look like a small town of the 1930s.

On Wilderness Trail at the edge of town is the historic *Newlee Iron Works* iron furnace, built in the early 1820s. It was used to make iron that was shipped off to Chattanooga and to blacksmiths throughout the region. At its peak the furnace created more than 35 tons of pig iron a week. To the left of the furnace is a path that is part of the original Wilderness Road, which you can follow to get up to the historic gap itself.

There's a great website for Cumberland Gap and the surrounding Claiborne County area. Log on at claibornecounty.com, or call the Chamber of Commerce at (423) 626-4149.

A few miles south on US 25E is Harrogate, the home of *Lincoln Memorial University* (423-869-3611; lmunet.edu). The school's mascot is the Railsplitters. Founded in 1896 as a living memorial to President Abraham Lincoln, the school's charter mandated the establishment of a museum to house memorabilia of the Lincoln era. Today the *Lincoln Library and Museum* (423-869-6235) on the campus houses the third-largest collection of Lincolniana and Civil War items in the world.

One of the most significant historic items in the museum is the ebony cane the president was carrying on the night he was assassinated. A lock of Lincoln's hair is also on display. The *Lincoln General Store* is a fun

OTHER ATTRACTIONS WORTH SEEING

Farragut Folklife Museum
Farragut
(865) 966-7057
townoffarragut.org

Forbidden Caverns
Sevierville
(865) 453-5972
forbiddendcaverns.com

Great Smoky Mountains National Park
Gatlinburg
(865) 436-1200
nps.gov/grsm

James White's Fort
Knoxville
(865) 525-6514
jameswhitesfort.org

Museum of East Tennessee History
Knoxville
(865) 215-8830
easttnhistory.org

stop where visitors can try out 19th-century games like pick-up sticks and checkers. Replica soldier items for sale include caps, haversacks, and canteens.

The school itself is beautiful and is a nice tribute to mountain life in East Tennessee. Take time to walk through the campus. Admission is charged for the museum.

High atop Clinch Mountain, about 5 miles out of Bean Station on US 25E, you'll find *Clinch Mountain Lookout Restaurant* (865-767-2511; clinchmountainlookout.com). It's not much to look at and the signs are falling down, but don't let any of that scare you away. The eatery is home to the famous vinegar pie. What a taste sensation. As the story goes, lemons were hard to get during the Depression, so vinegar was substituted for lemons in pie making; some liked the taste so much, they never switched back.

Joining vinegar pie on the menu are ostrich burgers from a local farmer, hamburgers, and steaks. Breakfast is served all day. The outside tables have an astounding view of the valley and the Clinch River far below. It's open 7 days a week at 7 a.m.

When Andrew Johnson came to Tennessee to establish a tailor shop, he spent a few months in Rutledge before relocating to nearby Greeneville.

TOP ANNUAL EVENTS

APRIL

Dogwood Arts Festival
Knoxville
(865) 637-4561
dogwoodarts.com

Townsend in the Smokies Spring Festival
late Apr/early May
Townsend
(865) 448-6134

MAY

Christy Fest
end of May
Townsend
(865) 448-6134
christyfest.org

Festival of British & Appalachian Culture
Rugby
(888) 214-3400
historicrugby.org

WINTER

Winterfest
Nov through Feb
Pigeon Forge, Gatlinburg & Sevierville
(800) 251-9100
mypigeonforge.com

A reproduction of Johnson's first shop has been built and is located in front of *Grainger County Courthouse,* on the original site.

A few blocks away is the circa 1848 *Grainger County Jail,* the oldest standing brick jailhouse in Tennessee. Restored by the county's historical society, the facility now houses the society and serves as a public meeting-house for the area's clubs and organizations. Inside, the original metal stairs and wall partitions are intact.

In the 1790s Davy Crockett's dad opened a small 6-room tavern near present-day *Morristown.* That's where little Davy spent his early years. In the 1950s a reproduction of that tavern was built on the original site, and today the *Crockett Tavern and Museum* (423-587-9900; crocketttavern museum.org) serves as a frontier museum honoring the Crockett family and other early Tennessee pioneers. The tavern is full of period utensils and furnishings. It's located at 2002 Morningside Dr. Open Tues through Sat, 11 a.m. to 5 p.m., May through Oct. Admission $5 adults, $1 students, and free for children under 5.

The first patented flying machine in America was developed by Melville Murrell, a Morristown preacher. Patented in 1877, a good while before the Wright brothers' flight, the **Murrell Flyer** flew several hundred yards under bicycle-type power. Parts of the original flyer, including its wings and some of the frame, are on display at the city's Rose Center. A video presentation features interviews with some of Murrell's descendants and several photos of the plane itself.

Built in 1892 and saved from destruction in 1975 by a community action group, the **Rose Center** (442 W. Second St. North; 423-581-4330; rosecenter .org) was the area's first school. It now serves as a community cultural center and includes a history museum, art gallery, exhibit space, and gift shop.

Each Oct, the **Mountain Makins Festival** is held on the grounds of the Rose Center and features one of East Tennessee's finest juried crafts shows. Two music stages spotlight various forms of local mountain music and other activities. Admission is $5 adults, $1 children (ages 6–12), and free for children under 6.

Downtown Morristown is a busy business center, and there are several antiques and collectibles shops along Main Street.

Cosby was settled in 1783 by a corn farmer searching for a quiet, peaceful life. Corn remained the main crop for many years, and it didn't take long before the discovery was made that it was easier to transport corn in the liquid form known as moonshine. For many years the area was known as the **Moonshine Capital of the World.**

Apples are now considered one of the area's biggest cash crops, and there are five or six major orchards that sell directly from their farms. Also, many smaller orchards have been planted and produce excellent crops. Look for APPLES FOR SALE signs along the roads.

One of the most popular year-round apple producers of the area is the **Kyle Carver Orchards** (423-487-2419; carversappleorchard.com), located on US 321 South at 3462 Cosby Hwy., about 5 miles from I-40. The best time to visit is between mid-Aug and Dec—that's when most of the action takes place. They grow and sell many different varieties of apples on the

doubleletterduo

Tennessee and Mississippi are the only two states having three sets of double letters in their names. And they border each other!

farm and are known widely for their fresh fried apple pies. For a couple of bucks, you get a huge, tasty, magnificent, and hot fried treat. Forget your diet. You can't find pies of this quality just anywhere.

Along with their apples, the Carvers also sell grapes, peaches, fresh vegetables, honey, jellies, jams, apple butter, molasses, cider, and other seasonal items. Ice cream and several apple products, including both fried and baked apple pies, are available. A candy store features locally produced chocolate candies and other homemade delicacies. The barn is open daily year-round 8 a.m. to 6 p.m.

The Tales of a Quilter's Husband

John Holloway is a quilter's husband. His wife, Maria, is owner of Holloway's Country Home quilt shop on US 321 near Cosby. John defines his position as "a sad individual whose only outlet is driving from quilt shop to quilt shop—except when the grass needs cutting." We don't know if he really feels that way, but maybe he does.

In any case, he certainly has a sense of humor. When Maria wrote a cookbook containing her favorite recipes and short stories about her special quilts, she asked John to put in a few of his own favorite recipes. He contributed 19 to her book, *Windows of My World*. The names alone are wonderful, but John's true humor comes out in his instructions for each. He admits about halfway through that all the recipes aren't his; some came from Jake, the resident squirrel who visits him in his workshop each day.

In addition to A Quilter's Husband's Groundhog Stew, where he explains how to catch a groundhog, he recalls how he learned to make A Quilter's Husband's Raccoon and Corn. "Walking through the woods one day, I came upon this raccoon. While holding him at gunpoint, I demanded that he tell me why he had been stealing my corn. He complied by giving me his recipe."

He explains how to gather mushrooms in his Mushrooms a la Jake. "An elf told me once that the best time to pick mushrooms is when you can walk under them. I guess that works great for elves, but we big people need another standard. Mine is when they are big enough to eat, go for it."

Maria includes an eclectic mix of recipes in the book, including a nice selection from her family's Portuguese heritage. The book is available at the shop or by calling (423) 487-3866. Visit their website at hollowaysquilts.com for more information.

Carver's Apple House Restaurant (423-487-2710; carversappleorchard.com) is located in the barn. According to Irene Carver, who runs the eatery for the family, the menu is "great country cooking," and "everything" is made from secret recipes and "that's why it's all so good." Well, secret or not, the chicken potpies are exceptional. Of course there are a lot of apple products on the menu, including apple fritters, apple pie cake, fried apples, and baked apple pies. The restaurant is open daily 8 a.m. to 8 p.m.

Down the road from Carver's is a historical log cabin that houses ***Holloway's Country Home*** (423-487-3866; hollowaysquilts.com). It is said to have the largest selection of vintage quilts in the area. If you're a quilt maker, the shop carries a full line of fabrics, quilt kits, and supplies.

Headed up by Maria Holloway, the shop employs 40 full-time quilters to help keep her custom-made quilt inventory to more than 50 hand-sewn quilts at any one time. Next to the rustic log cabin store, Maria has created a quilter's getaway, a kind of bed-and-breakfast for quilters. "It's a retreat where people can come and concentrate on nothing but quilting," she said. This refuge is located at 3892 US 321, just a few miles off I-40. Take exit 435 for Newport, and head toward Cosby. The shop is open Mon through Sat 9 a.m. to 5 p.m. Call first during winter, as they may close at times.

The ramp is an onion-like vegetable native to the foothills of the southern Appalachian Mountains. The odd-looking plant has been described as the "vilest-smelling, sweetest-tasting vegetable in the world." Early settlers attributed special medicinal qualities to the ramp.

Raw, parboiled, fried, or scrambled in eggs, it was regarded as a necessary spring tonic to ward off the sluggishness of winter. In the 1950s Cosby introduced the ramp to the rest of the world when it established its first annual spring festival in the plant's honor. Each May thousands come here for the annual ***Cosby Ramp Festival*** to enjoy activities and eat truckloads of ramps.

In the county seat of ***Newport,*** the ***Cocke County Museum*** (423-623-3382) is located upstairs in the Community Center building. Among items on display are many from Grace Moore, an internationally known opera singer and movie star who was born in the southern part of the county. The museum is open only on Wed 1 to 5 p.m. Downstairs are the chamber of commerce and tourist information offices. This is a good place to start a tour of the county—at 433B Prospect Ave., where access is free; call the chamber at (423) 623-7201 or go to cockecounty.org.

One of the classiest bed-and-breakfast inns in this part of the state is just outside Newport off English Mountain Road at 1500 Pinnacles Way. ***Christopher Place*** (423-623-6555; christopherplace.com), which classifies itself as an "Intimate Resort," is a true Four Diamond Smoky Mountain resort. *Vacations* magazine named the inn "one of the Top 10 romantic inns in America." Great views of the mountains, big and hearty breakfasts, and a nightly four-course dinner by candlelight are only a few of the amenities. Others include a heated pool, tennis courts, billiard room, fitness room, and a library filled with books, music, and movies.

Nine different rooms, all with private baths and luxurious furnishings, range in price from $150 to $330 per night. If you're looking for the best mountain view the inn has to offer, ask for the Roman Holiday Room.

If you're looking for more of a rustic, off-the-beaten-path place to stay, you're only 15 miles away when you're in downtown Newport. To find ***Meadow Creek Mountain Rustic Resort*** (423-623-7543; meadow creekmountain.com), head out on US 321 to Parrotsville, the state's third-oldest town. Then you'll turn left, then right, then left, and then at the fork, you'll . . . well, you get the picture. You're better off calling first. This place is way out there in the proverbial boonies. It's located deep in the beautiful Cherokee National Forest on 100 acres of pristine mountain property.

There are 4 individual cabins, sleeping anywhere from 2 to 10 per night, plus a 6-bedroom, 6-bath lodge with kitchen. These are full-size cabins, each with bedrooms and private baths, air-conditioning, fireplaces, a gas grill and a hot tub on a private deck, satellite TV, and a kitchen. You can bring your own horse, or you can rent one from Diane and Charlie Phillips, the proprietors of this fun, unique getaway and giddy-up resort.

In-season prices per cabin start at $110. You can grab some grub at the resort's ***Crazy Horse Cafe*** or create some fixin's in your own kitchen. The ***General Store*** sells basic merchandise, plus it has a lending DVD and book library and wireless Internet.

Located next to the popular Lake Douglas, ***Dandridge*** holds the distinction of being the only town in the US named for ***Martha Dandridge Washington,*** George's wife, and today has a well-preserved downtown historic district to be quite proud of. Self-guided tour maps are available throughout town and at the *Jefferson County Museum* (865-397-4904), located on the first level of the circa 1845 county courthouse. One of the unique holdings of this regional history museum is Davy Crockett's marriage license. Admission is free, and the museum is open during courthouse hours.

This community was quite the crossroads through the years. It was a regular stop for boats carrying provisions up and down the French Broad River, it was a major stage stop, and it was a road traveled by the stock traders operating between Tennessee and the Carolinas. As we know, wherever travelers gather, there will always be an abundance of taverns. Today three are still standing in Dandridge.

Almost swallowed by the waters when the Tennessee Valley Authority (TVA) dammed the river to create Lake Douglas in the early 1940s, Dandridge was saved thanks to local protests and the intervention of President Franklin D. Roosevelt. The million-dollar dike of native stone that holds back the waters today serves as backdrop to many of the historic buildings along Main Street. The lake dominates the outdoor activities in Dandridge as well as the entire county. The yacht club holds a July 4 boat parade, various fishing tournaments run throughout the year, and the lake is always dotted by the colorful sails of pleasure boaters enjoying themselves.

As a result of the dam and the abundance of water, the TVA built a hydroelectric plant that is still in operation today.

If possible, plan your visit to the area for the first Sat in Oct. That's when Jefferson City's *Old Time Saturday* (865-475-7367; oldtimesaturday .org) festival takes place. This one-day event mixes entertainment and food with a festive open-air market featuring local arts and crafts.

The *Glenmore Mansion* (865-475-5014; glenmoremansion.org) is considered by many architects as an almost perfect example of Second Empire architecture. Built in 1869, the 27-room, 5-story mansion is fully furnished with antiques of the period. In eastern Tennessee, where most historical preservation efforts are saved for pre-1850 architecture, it's good to see something from the Victorian era. The mansion is located at 1280 N. Chucky Pike in Jefferson City. It's open Sat and Sun afternoons 1 to 5 p.m., May through Oct and for special events. Admission is $5 adults and $3 children under 12.

Great Smoky Mountains National Park

As the most visited national park in the country, with 10 million visitors a year, the **Great Smoky Mountains National Park** (865-436-1200; nps .gov/grsm) is hardly off the beaten path. But the 500,000-acre facility is so large and has so many nooks and crannies that it isn't difficult to get away from the madding crowds.

There are established camping areas throughout the park, but camping is also permitted in the undeveloped regions. Special backcountry permits are needed for that.

The Sugarland Visitors Center, located 2 miles inside the park from Gatlinburg, has maps and other information about the entire park, as well as exhibits on what one will most likely see during a visit.

Featuring more species of plants than any other area on our continent, this official **International Biosphere Reserve** is a true gem in Tennessee travel opportunities.

Within the boundaries there are 16 peaks towering above 6,000 feet, including **Clingman's Dome,** which, at 6,643 feet, is the highest point in Tennessee.

One of the park's most unusual attractions is **LeConte Lodge** (865-429-5704; lecontelodge.com), a great (but rugged and rustic) place to stay while in the mountains if you enjoy walking. In fact, that's the only way you can get there, and it's not the easiest walk you'll ever make. The lodge rests atop the third-highest peak in the park, making it the highest guest lodge in the eastern US. The shortest (and steepest) hike to the lodge is 5.5 miles long, which is about a 4-hour hike for a person in good condition. Once

Be(ar) Aware

The Great Smoky Mountains National Park is home to about 1,800 black bears. Here are a few bear facts: During the spring and summer, bears are most active in early morning and late evening. Momma bears and their newborn cubs leave their winter dens in late March or early April. Bears usually mate in July. Bears are good tree climbers and swimmers. They also can run about 30 miles per hour. Do not approach a bear if you see one. Black bear attacks are rare, but they have happened.

there you'll find no electricity, phones, or showers—just a great view and wonderful food. The lodge can host up to 60 guests per night housed in one of the seven rough-hewn cabins or the three multiroom lodges. All units are equipped with kerosene lanterns for light and propane heaters for warmth. It does get quite chilly in the mountains. Rates start at $126 per adult and $85 per child ages 4–12, per night, and include dinner and breakfast. Wine is available with dinner at $10 per person for those 21 and older. The lodge is open late Mar through late Nov.

Gateway to the Smokies

The tourist destination city of **Gatlinburg** is near the main entrance to the park and considered its main gateway. Souvenir and craft shops and various attractions line the main streets, while honeymoon houses and motels line the backstreets.

Gatlinburg officials have put together one of the most helpful tourism websites in the state: gatlinburg.com. You can also call (800) 588-1817 for information. Among the attractions here you'll find something to please everyone. The parkway strip is lined with fun, colorful, and often macabre things to see and do. Don't miss **Ripley's Believe It or Not!,** up from the **Guinness World Records Museum,** across from the **Sky Lift,** and under the **Space Needle.**

High atop Mt. Harrison, overlooking Gatlinburg is the **Ober Gatlinburg Amusement Park and Ski Resort** (800-682-4386; obergatlinburg.com). It's a fun, year-round facility that has a mountain resort feel to it even though it's just up the mountain from Gatlinburg's touristy downtown area.

In the summer there are amusement rides, an alpine slide, a water ride, miniature golf, go-karts, and other outdoor fun. In the winter there is skiing. Indoors, and open year-round, is a large ice-skating rink, shops, a lounge, restaurants, and a wonderful little fudge maker!

Gatlinburg's **Municipal Black Bear Habitat** is located here and provides some great close-up views of the bears. There is also a Black Bear gift shop, museum, and a short film on the species.

A quick but somewhat expensive way to get to the top is via the celebrated tramway. It's free if you have ski lift tickets, and it takes you directly to the top of the mountain. If you have a car full and want to save some money, you can drive to the top and park directly adjacent to all the activity.

The tram is at Traffic Light #9. If you want to drive, go to the end of the parkway; just before you enter the national park, turn right for Ski Mountain Road.

If you're looking for some of the best fine artwork and crafts the state has to offer, a drive through the ***Great Smoky Arts & Crafts Community*** (gatlinburgcrafts.com) is a must. It's an 8-mile auto loop that features more than 120 independent artists and craftspeople with cafes, restaurants, and lodging sprinkled throughout. Many shops are grouped with others in large complexes, while some are set off by themselves.

Designated as a Tennessee Heritage Arts & Crafts Trail, the community was established in 1937. Along the route, artisans whittle, paint, sew, cast, weave, and carve to create original pieces of art, such as candles, baskets, quilts, brooms, pottery, jewelry, dolls, ceramics, scrimshaw, leather, stained glass, fine photography, and just about anything else you can think of. In all, there are 78 stops. Most of the shops are open daily during the summer usually from 10 a.m. to 5 p.m. They may close completely during the winter or at best have reduced hours of operation. Call first—individual shop numbers are available on the group's website. (Speaking of calling, you're in the mountains here and there's a very good chance your cell phone won't work, so plan accordingly.)

For a relaxing and environmentally friendly ride, park the car in town and go green. Take an old-fashioned trolley to the Gatlinburg Arts & Crafts Loop for only $1. The trolley can be boarded at the Gatlinburg Mass Transit Center at Traffic Light #5. The trolley runs daily Apr through Oct and Mon through Sat in Nov and Dec. Exact change is required for the trolley, and it takes about an hour for the trolley to run the entire loop. A good place to start (and finish) the loop is 3 miles out of Gatlinburg from Traffic Light #3, on US 321. You'll see a big green sign with GREAT SMOKY ARTS & CRAFTS COMMUNITY printed in white letters with arrows pointing the way. Turn left onto Glades Road near McDonald's, and the art-venture begins.

You'll definitely want to stop at the ***Glades Arts & Crafts Center,*** one of the first major complexes on the right, at King Road. There are nine shops here, and across the street in the Morning Mist Village, there are nearly 25 more arts and crafts shops.

However, before you start your journey through all the shops, stop by the **Mountain Visions Gallery** (600 Glades Rd., No. 6; 865-430-1994; mountainvisionsgallery.com), owned by Steve and Terri Shoemaker. Steve is a nationally known nature photographer who now specializes in unique scenes of the Smoky Mountains. Some great stuff on the walls in this shop! Steve is also a good one to know if you're looking for some expert advice on quiet hiking trails; he'll be glad to point the way.

What started as a co-op for female artists, the **Cliff Dwellers Gallery** (668 Glades Rd.; 865-436-6921; cliffdwellersgallery.com) is now owned by five women who represent approximately 60 other local artists, both male and female. Their building was originally built in downtown Gatlinburg in 1933 and moved to its current location in 1993. On special days you might find a craft demonstration by a participating artist in anything from glass working and painting to creating wooden bowls on a lathe. This is one of the most interesting stops along the trail.

At the end of Glades Road, just around the corner on Buckhorn Road, is Hemlock Village, with several different shops. The largest is **Highland Craft Gallery** (865-430-8951), which represents more than 70 different artists offering an eclectic selection of fine crafts. By the way, a photo of many of the represented artists hangs on the wall, so you can see whom you're buying from!

And if you're still hungry, check out the charming **Wild Plum Tea Room** (865-436-3808) in a log cabin setting, just past Hemlock Village at 555 Buckhorn Rd. Open only for lunch, this popular eatery, known for its signature chicken salad and Wild Plum Tea, is a peaceful and relaxing stop along the way as you ponder what great art must find its way into your suitcase. Farther down the road, on your left just before you get back to US 321, be sure to stop at **Turtle Hollow Gallery** (865-436-6188) and **J. Alan Gallery** (865-430-5904)—both of whose art offerings could go up against any big city gallery. They represent unique, top-quality artisans featuring traditional and contemporary crafts—many of them a one-of-a-kind. Turtle Hollow Gallery showcases bronze and stone sculptures made by Ross Markley. The gallery features contemporary jewelry, glass, wind chimes, wood, and ceramics. J. Alan Gallery offers work by the contemporary painter as well as pottery, metal sculptures, wood, and jewelry.

The community sponsors three annual shows, all held at the Gatlinburg Convention Center at Traffic Light #8 in downtown Gatlinburg, with free admission. For more information check out the community's website: arts andcraftscommunity.com.

Since parking is at such a premium in Gatlinburg, perhaps the best deal in town is the 50-cent ride on its rapid transit system, **the trolley** (865-436-3897; gatlinburgtrolley.com). During peak season the entire city can become one large parking lot, so find a place to park on the edge of town or at your hotel and rely on the trolley. The trolley has more than 100 boarding stops.

The nation's earliest Fourth of July parade takes place on the streets of Gatlinburg each year at 12:01 a.m. July 4. Floats, bands, and huge helium balloons go by as more than 80,000 annually gather for the **"Midnight Parade."**

The **Hillbilly Golf Course** (865-436-7470) may well be one of the most unusual miniature golf courses in the world. To get to the first hole, you must ride an incline up to a point 300 feet above the city. Two 18-hole courses, with all sorts of mountaineer hazards, including a genuine outhouse and a moonshine still, are carved out of the mountainside. It's near Traffic Light #2 at 340 Parkway.

If you happen to be a Ripley's fan, Gatlinburg is heaven. Five of the company's top attractions are located in the city, including its newest, the high-tech and high-fun **Davy Crockett Mini-Golf** course (865-430-8851), located at Traffic Light #1 at 188 Parkway. Here you'll find two 18-hole courses with animated figures and interactive holes. Where else can you be chided by a couple of old crows if you miss a putt? This neat place stands out from all the other miniature golf courses in the area! Open year-round, weather permitting.

Moving on down the parkway toward the Great Smoky Mountains National Park, on your right at Traffic Light #5 at 88 River Rd. you'll find the world-acclaimed **Ripley's Aquarium of the Smokies** (865-430-8808; ripleysaquariumofthesmokies.com). The fun starts here as you drive up. It's one of the most amazing structures in the state, and there's a real sense of arrival. Inside, there are many great exhibits, including a moving walkway under a large habitat that houses sharks (some up to 11 feet) and thousands of colorful tropical fish. Another fascinating exhibit contains jellyfish highlighted by special lighting and classical music. You'll rarely see anything more calming and surreal in your life! Open daily, year-round.

At Traffic Light #7 at 800 Parkway is **Ripley's Believe It or Not! Museum** (865-436-5096; ripleys.com/gatlinburg) of the weird and unusual. From shrunken heads and matchstick sculptures to vampire killing kits and pieces of the Berlin Wall, the odditorium has one-of-a-kind items. There are original Robert Ripley cartoons, and you'll get a chance to see clips of the *Ripley's Believe it or Not!* television show featuring Dean Cain. A fun place for everyone in the family! Open daily, year-round.

Ripley's Moving Theater (865-436-9763) and **Ripley's Haunted Adventure** (865-430-9991) are located next to each other at Traffic Light #8. Both are open daily, year-round. You'll ride along with the 3-D film at the Moving Theater, which is quite fun. Remember to hold on, and eat lunch afterward, not before! Get a chance to explore your nightmare at the Haunted Adventure. Created on the site of the old Grimsby & Streaper Casket Company, the haunted house has live actors and classy scare techniques and is quite a long walk through. They suggest you hold hands to keep from getting lost. Not a bad suggestion.

The **Peddler Steakhouse** (865-436-5794; peddlergatlinburg.com) has the best view, the best ambience, and the best salad bar (can you say smoked oysters?) of any restaurant in town. Located at 820 River Rd., the restaurant and bar are on the edge of the river, and even if you're not lucky enough to get a window table, you still have a lot to look at. The Peddler is actually constructed on history. The restaurant was built around the C. Earl Ogle cabin. Ogle was the descendant of one of the first pioneer families. Materials from four other original homesites were used to complete the structure. People come from all over for the steak, huge salad bar, and grilled fresh salmon. The place is always busy, and although they don't take reservations, you can call ahead and get your name placed on the waiting list. If you get there and there's a long list, go back to the lounge, which also offers great river views. If you find a table you like there, go ahead and order and enjoy your meal in the bar. It's the same menu as the dining room. The locals love this place, and it has been locally owned and operated since 1977.

Known for romantic wedding chapels, Gatlinburg and the Smoky Mountains offer plenty of opportunities for those looking for a memorable wedding. If you're on the market for something quite different and a bit funky and fun, call the Hillbilly Minister (865-436-3817) and he'll arrange

a true ***Hillbilly Wedding*** for you. The minister says he offers a "nontraditional and no-frills approach, yet with reverence and dignity." Wearing bib
overalls, the minister will perform "a simple basic Christian ceremony" for
$75. He'll come to your hotel or cottage, or he can suggest a great location
in the mountains.

And speaking of memorable, a great home base while you're enjoying
the area is one of the nearly two dozen bed-and-breakfasts in the Smokies.
They are all unique, with different amenities, and all offer spectacular breakfasts. Find a listing of the best at smokymountainbb.com.

With hundreds of nationally known craftspeople living and working
around the Smoky Mountains region, you can only imagine the scope of
arts and crafts, paintings, furniture making, and wood carvings you'll find
at the ***Gatlinburg Craftsmen's Fair,*** held twice a year at the Gatlinburg
Convention Center (Traffic Light #8). There's a weeklong summer event in
late July and a 2-week fair in mid-Oct.

In addition to local and regional craftspeople, the best from around the
country also take part in these events, and there is always live music, from
bluegrass to mountain music, being performed on the trade show floor.
Admission is charged. Find out more at (865) 436-7479 or craftsmensfair.com.

Head north on US 441 out of Gatlinburg, go through a part of the
national forest, and 5 miles later you'll be in ***Pigeon Forge,*** where a
50-cent trolley ride with 50 stops helps you avoid traffic congestion. Similar
to Gatlinburg in its attractions, this city's main draw is country singer Dolly
Parton's theme park, ***Dollywood*** (865-428-9488 or 800-Dolly-wood; visit
dollywood.com). Country music prevails in the park, as do country crafts
and good country cooking.

Even if you're one who doesn't like theme parks, chances are very good
you'll love this place, which is more of a trip into mountain culture than it is
an amusement ride park. Craftsmen's Valley offers a shady walk through a
genuine holler past all sorts of working craftspeople, chefs cooking in huge
cast-iron skillets over open fires, and a winding brook. The steam train takes
you on a 5-mile journey to the top of the ridge and back and is one ride
you definitely need to take. The Thunderhead wooden roller coaster offers
a 100-foot drop at speeds of 55 mph. Whew!

Opened in 2012, America's first wing coaster, the Wild Eagle soars 21
stories above Dollywood to give riders the sensation of flying. With nothing

but air above and below them, riders are seated on either side of the track rather than in a train directly on the rails. Definitely a "wind-beneath-your-wings" feeling.

There are plenty of other great rides, but most people don't come to Dollywood for the rides. The live shows, as you can imagine, are quite well done, with many of Dolly's relatives performing. Food? Did I mention that the food here is about the best you'll find at any theme park in the world? Great southern cooking at its finest! Throughout the year there are special festivals inside the park, including a traditional Smoky Mountain Christmas celebration and a fall Harvest Festival. A summer concert series features more than 40 top names in country music.

"In after 3, next day free" is the policy here. Travel into the area, pay to get in after 3 p.m., and have a nice relaxing dinner at one of the park's restaurants. Leave, get a good night's rest, and come back the next day for free!

Next door is ***Dolly's Splash Country,*** a water park that opened in 2001. You won't find a tropical theme here. No pastels or palm trees. Instead you'll find a re-created Smoky Mountains watering hole, complete with waterfalls, winding streams, and plenty of earth tones and rustic architecture. It's a fun and laid-back way to cool off. Opened in May 2013, the new RiverRush is Tennessee's first and only water coaster. An impressive 4 stories high with a 25-foot drop, the RiverRush "launches" 4-person rafts on a merry ride over 1,175 feet of hairpin curves, tunnels, and hills. RiverRush travels on a track that covers more than an acre in a newly developed area near the park's Big Bear Plunge.

Dollywood is open from spring through the first week of Jan; the water park is open from May through Labor Day. A money-saving combo pass is available if you want to go to both parks.

If you haven't driven through Pigeon Forge lately, you're in for a surprise. Where the Music Mansion used to be at 100 Music Rd., there is now an upside-down building. That's right. ***WonderWorks*** (865-868-1800; wonder worksonline.com) looks as though it has been picked up and tossed upside down. Sure makes you wonder. And that's the whole point. Everything in WonderWorks is fun and has some sort of educational purpose.

Opened in June 2006, WonderWorks mixes fantasy and reality. It's a place where the unexplainable comes to life and natural mysteries are explored. This is all done with sophisticated graphic and audio techniques.

WonderWorks even has a tale to explain how it came to be. The story is pure fantasy, of course. Legend has it that an experiment on a remote island off the Atlantic coast went awry. During an attempt to harness the power of a man-made tornado, the giant swirling vortex spun out of control and took on a life of its own. The energy vortex was so powerful that it sent the entire structure skyward, hundreds of miles away, where it landed upside down in the heart of Pigeon Forge. The attraction has more than 100 interactive, hands-on exhibits.

It also offers a great magic show. Enjoy ***The Wonders of Magic*** as Terry Evanswood uses comedy, music, impersonations, sleight of hand, illusions, and Houdini-type escapes in a 75-minute magical variety show for all ages. He tops off his show with a message that proclaims hope and love to be the real magical wonders of the world. The show is $14.99 for all ages.

An iceberg in the heart of Pigeon Forge? And a huge cruise ship? Folks have been known to stop and stare. No wonder. Opened in April 2010, the ***Titanic Museum Attraction*** (800-381-7670; titanicattraction.com) towers 100 feet above the parkway and holds 400 priceless artifacts in 20 galleries. Built half scale to the original, the eye-catching building is a permanent 2-story museum shaped like *Titanic* herself. The structure is "anchored" in water to create the illusion of *Titanic* at sea. A 2-hour self-guided tour is designed to give guests the feeling of actually being a passenger on *Titanic*'s 1912 maiden voyage.

When they come aboard, visitors are given a boarding card with the name of an actual passenger. At the end of the tour, they discover whether their character survived or perished. The museum does an excellent job of helping visitors get to know real passengers through their stories, personal memorabilia, photos, cards, and letters. Everything on display once belonged to a *Titanic* passenger or crew member. The memorabilia was either taken off the ship at the time of the sinking or was found floating in the debris field. Save time for the gift shop. One of my favorite items is the *Titanic* "survival kit"—a box of chocolates which are quite good.

Located at 2134 Parkway, the Titanic Museum Attraction is open daily 9 a.m. to 9 p.m. Advance purchase is suggested as tickets sell out quickly. Tickets are $21.39 plus tax for adults, $11.14 for children (ages 5–12, and free for ages 4 and under).

Sounds of "Silent Night" fill the air. Santa Claus greets children of all ages. Stockings are hung by the chimney with care. And glittering Christmas trees brighten the winter night. Scenes like this are familiar during the holiday season. But at ***The Inn at Christmas Place*** (888-465-9644; innatchristmasplace.com), it is Christmas every day. Opened June 15, 2007, the Smoky Mountains destination at Traffic Light #2A on the Parkway has been drawing visitors no matter the season. The Inn at Christmas Place is open year-round and filled with all the joys of the holiday season—no matter what the weather may be outside. Featuring the mountain village architecture of the European Alps, the inn offers luxurious old-world charm including copper-crowned turrets, a stone-terraced courtyard, two large ponds with natural stone waterfalls, and landscaped gardens.

Uniformed bellmen and caroling figurines welcome guests through custom-etched glass doors into a holiday wonderland. Guest rooms are also clad in holiday finery, including 2- and 3-room suites with full-size decorated trees, fireplaces, 2-person whirlpools, and private balconies overlooking the courtyard. A stay at the inn includes a complimentary breakfast with country-style buffet items and an omelet bar. Located across the parkway from ***The Incredible Christmas Place and Village*** shops, the inn is within easy walking distance of many Pigeon Forge attractions. For guests who appreciate the inn's decor so much that they would like to add it to their own homes, most of the items on view are sold at The Incredible Christmas Place and Village shops. Not surprising, since the Biggs family who started The Incredible Christmas Place more than 2 decades ago are also owners of The Inn at Christmas Place.

If you're a real Elvis fan, you can get a good fix by visiting the ***Elvis Museum*** (865-428-2001), where you'll see the King's last limousine, his Double Trouble tuxedo, and the one-of-a-kind "TCB" (Taking Care of Business, his motto) ring he designed and wore throughout his career. The ring alone is valued at more than $250,000. Of course there is a full line of the wonderfully kitsch Elvis souvenirs in the gift shop, along with plenty of CDs, cassettes, videotapes, and DVDs. There is an admission fee for the museum but none for the gift shop.

As interesting to me as the exhibit was the story of how one man acquired such a huge collection of Elvis memorabilia. Mike L. Moon was a Georgia entrepreneur and former owner of the Stamps Quartet. One evening in 1971, Moon accompanied J. D. Sumner, bass singer and leader of the Stamps Quartet, to a party that Elvis hosted after a Las Vegas performance. When Moon was introduced to Elvis that evening, he complimented "The King" on a black leather belt he was wearing. True to form, the generous Elvis took the belt from his waist and gave it to Moon. Moon was so impressed that he became an avid Elvis fan, collecting authentic Elvis memorabilia whenever he could.

When Elvis died in 1977, Sumner told Moon he should share his collection with a grieving public. He suggested that that Moon open the first Elvis Presley Museum beyond the gates of Graceland. Members of Elvis's entourage, including Charlie Hodge, Ed Enoch, Buck Buckles, Billy Smith, Marty Lacker, and Sonny West, shared their personal items with Moon for the museum.

The original museum in Pigeon Forge opened in 1979. For the next 2 decades, Moon expanded his collection to earn the prestigious title of "World's Largest Private Collection of Elvis Memorabilia." The collection now belongs to Moon's daughter, Lynn Moon McAllister, her husband Donald, and their children Sunni and Skyler. It's located at 2638 Parkway, 1 block south of Ogle's Waterpark. A TCB Theatre in the Elvis Museum complex features a live show nightly with several Elvis tribute artists. (For much more on Elvis see the Memphis listing in the last chapter of this book.)

The **Dixie Stampede** (865-453-4400 or 800-356-1676; dixiestampede .com) has an interesting concept for a dinner theater. While eating a southern feast, patrons watch a live show in the central dirt-covered arena. The Western Show features 32 horses, Conestoga wagons, pig racing, bull riding, steer wrestling, and a bunch more good-old-boy activities. For added flavor, a friendly competition divides the audience into the northerners on one side, the southerners on the other. Reservations are sometimes necessary. The Dixie Belle Saloon opening act begins 50 minutes prior to Dixie Stampede and is well worth arriving early to see.

Another feature of the Dixie Stampede is the **world's largest stick-horse collection,** which is displayed throughout the venue. An offhand comment is what started it all. Dan Cavanah had a friend in Seattle with many fine horses. When he retired, Cavanah told his buddy that he would gather an even larger herd, the biggest in all of Florida. When he got home from visiting Seattle, Cavanah received a gag gift from his pal—a stick horse to get him started on his herd. That was in 1990. Since then, Cavanah has collected more than 500 stick-horse pieces. In November 2002 he was honored by the *Guinness Book of World Records* for having the world-record stick-horse collection.

As his collection increased, Cavanah decided he wanted to display his stick horses where others could enjoy them. After checking out various places, Cavanah settled on the Dixie Stampede in Pigeon Forge. With its horse-related show, Cavanah figured his make-believe mounts would fit right in. The stick horses were delivered to the Dixie Stampede in April 2004. The amazing collection is displayed everywhere inside the Dixie Stampede, from the theater to the entrance hall to the carriage room and from the lobby to the gift shop. There's a Davy Crockett stick horse, an orange one autographed by country singer Tammy Wynette, a Lone Ranger stick horse, Gumby's horse Pokey, Roy Rogers's Trigger, and many more. Some have wheels that make a galloping noise, while others have reins with bells, yarn manes, and moving mouths. A 1950s model is battery operated to make a whinnying sound.

Another unique dining opportunity in Pigeon Forge is **Mel's Diner** (865-429-2184; melsdinerpf.com), where the good ole days of rock 'n' roll are featured on the menu, on the walls, and on the jukebox. Located at 119 Wears Valley Rd., one road west of the parkway, in an authentic stainless-steel diner, Mel's features a fun, tasty menu. The half-pound burgers are called Jukebox Heroes, and among the offerings are the Beach Boy Basic Burger, the Chubby Checker Cheeseburger, Marilyn's Mushroom Burger, and the Little Deuce Coupe Cajun Burger. The Sandwich Favorites include

A Veterans' Thank-You

Pigeon Forge throws a big party each August to say "thank you" to our country's military veterans. The city is loaded with activities, including a land and air parade, lectures, educational forums, keynote speeches by well-known American veterans, a military history book fair, static aircraft displays, canteen dances, war story storytelling, and a huge picnic. The 2-week **Celebrate Freedom** event is sponsored by the city of Pigeon Forge, with help from the University of Tennessee and the Center for the Study of War and Society. Contact them at (800) 251-9100 or mypigeonforge.com.

the Hot Diggity Dog, the Bette Davis B.L.T., James Dean Grilled Chicken, and the Doo Wah Diddy Philly Chicken Cheese. Starters include Fonzarelli Cheese Sticks, Potsy's Potato Salad, Ralph Malph Nachos, and Chachi's Cheese Nachos. The kid's menu is called Little Anthony's, and the wonderful thick and creamy milk shakes can be found under the Shake, Rattle & Roll heading.

Next to the vintage jukebox is a sign that reads IF MUSIC IS TOO LOUD, YOU'RE TOO OLD, and near the cash register a sign proclaims IF YOU THINK YOU HAVE A RESERVATION, YOU'RE IN THE WRONG PLACE. This is a fun, quality eatery. Open daily.

The country's first indoor skydiving simulator, *Flyaway Indoor Skydiving* (865-453-7777 or 877-293-0639; flyawayindoorskydiving.com), bills itself as America's "most unique" sports attraction. You suit up and ride in a vertical wind tunnel with wind speeds up to 115 mph, and as you float and fly in the air current, you're never more than 5 or 6 feet from a padded landing spot or from the arms of your personal flight attendant. Each flyer receives training, and the entire experience will last about an hour. A video machine is running so that you can take your experience home with you and impress your friends. The flight costs $34, plus tax, and anyone under 18 must be accompanied by a parent. Located at Traffic Light #5, 3106 Parkway.

Imagine climbing into a huge balloon and bouncing down a hill. That's the basic idea behind an attraction known as Zorb (865-428-2422; zorb .com). These heavy-duty balloons, however, are 12 feet high and 12 feet round. Riders roll down a 700-foot-long hill just along the Smoky Mountains. Choose the adrenaline rush that suits you: one of four track options and eight ride variations. Adding even more excitement, the Smoky Mountains Zydro Double Trouble Ride mixes two people with water inside the orb and sends them down the hill. The result is a lot of slipping, sliding, spinning, and hilarious laughs as the action-filled wet ride careens down the slope. Located at 203 Sugar Hollow Rd., Zorb is open year-round, and rides start at $35.

Applewood Farms is located just off US 441 at 230 Apple Valley Rd., right where Pigeon Forge and Sevierville meet. Part of a working apple orchard, the barn was converted into a cider mill in 1981, just in time to attract people from 45 different states and 10 foreign countries who were in the area visiting the 1982 World's Fair in nearby Knoxville. Today, in addition to the cider mill, they have a bakery, a winery featuring apple and other fruit wines, an apple butter kitchen, a fudge kitchen, a candy factory, an ice-cream factory specializing in apple-flavored ice cream, a smokehouse, a Christmas and candle shop, and a gift shop featuring crafts, gifts, and souvenir items. In 1987 their old farmhouse home was turned into the ***Applewood Farmhouse Restaurant*** (865-428-1222; applewood farmhouserestaurant.com). On the menu you'll find traditional items such as prime rib and steaks, but you'll also find a local favorite, fresh Smoky Mountains trout. One of the favorites is trout cake, made from crumbled trout mixed with cheese and onions. But save room for some wonderful apple dessert. The homemade apple pies are always a favorite, but the apple fritters, accompanied by homemade apple butter, are also high on the list for apple lovers. Located across the road from the Little Pigeon River, there are plenty of huge shade trees to sit under while you wait your turn. There was such a demand for their food that the owners decided to build a second eatery on the property in 1995 so that they wouldn't have to turn away so many hungry friends. Now the ***Applewood Farmhouse Grill*** (865-429-8644) offers the same menu, plus some lighter options for those who want to sample the different foods without digging into a full meal. Open daily for breakfast, lunch, and dinner. There are special meals and hours for Thanksgiving and Christmas.

Hike with a Personal Guide

If you've thought about hiking in the Smokies but felt you didn't know enough about the mountains or about hiking, here's a unique opportunity to enjoy the area on foot. Liz Domingue, owner of **Outdoor Adventures,** located in the Wears Valley area of Sevierville, is a noted naturalist and wildlife biologist who has hiked the world over in the name of environmental science. Give her a call and she'll custom-fit a hike to your interests and skill level. She is an expert on the salamanders, frogs, and birds of the Great Smoky Mountains and can talk with you about the cultural as well as the natural history of the mountains as she points out all the various flora and fauna. She also knows where all the neatest views and waterfalls are located. Prices start at $85 per day per person for groups of two to four, $65 per person for 4 hours for groups of two to four. Reach them at (865) 977-4453, or visit justgetoutdoors.com.

About 4 miles north on US 441, or the **Dolly Parton Parkway,** as they call it around here, is the downtown section of Dolly's hometown, **Sevierville.** Stop and ask about her and you'll be amazed at how many "good friends" this lady has. Less commercial than the other communities along US 441, the downtown section has retained most of its small, mountain atmosphere. On a walking tour of 26 historic landmarks, you'll get to see a life-size bronze statue of Dolly.

Billing itself as the World's Largest Live Reptile Zoo, the **Rainforest Adventure** (865-428-4091; rfadventures.com) takes you on a fun journey into the mysteries of the world's rain forests. In here you'll find hundreds of cool-looking species in natural habitats. Look close, because they'll be looking back at you. There are snakes, gators, amphibians, spiders, and scorpions and several live shows daily. Open daily year-round, 9 a.m. to 5 p.m. Located in Governor's Crossing, across from Wal-Mart at 109 Nascar Dr.

Heading to **Knoxville** from Sevierville on US 441/411, you'll pass an abundance of antiques and craft shops, potteries, and souvenir and gift shops. When the highways split, continue on US 441 into Knoxville until you cross the Tennessee River. That big golden ball you see high in the air to your left as you cross the river is the **Sunsphere,** the 300-foot-tall centerpiece of the 1982 World's Fair.

Adjacent to the fair site at 1050 Worlds Fair Park Dr. is the **Knoxville Museum of Art** (865-525-6101; knoxart.org), with a fine permanent collection as well as 12 exhibitions a year to choose from. On most Friday nights during the year, a special Alive After Five program features jazz and blues music from 6 to 8:30 p.m. The $8–10 admission gets you the music and access to the exhibits. A cash bar and light appetizers are available. The museum is open Tues through Sun.

A great way to start a visit in Knoxville is at the **Knoxville Visitor Center** (800-727-8045; knoxville.org), located downtown at 301 S. Gay St. The Knoxville Visitor Center has four different areas in one location. It's the place to pick up printed information or get questions answered at the visitors' desk. Then there's the gift shop which carries locally made products such as candles, pottery, and paintings. The Parlor offers snacks and drinks. And a stage inside the visitor center is the site of live music at noon every day, except Sun. The music is broadcast live on the WDVX radio station. Open daily.

See the Warbirds

The **Tennessee Museum of Aviation** is home to resident warbirds and is intended to be patriotic, educational, and entertaining. It certainly achieves all three! Even if you're not particularly interested in aviation or war history, this is a compelling, emotional stop. We guarantee you'll end up with a couple of lumps in your throat.

Located in a 50,000-square-foot hangar next to the Gatlinburg–Pigeon Forge Airport, along Dolly Parton Parkway in Sevierville, the museum has a collection of functional warbirds, including two rare P-47D aircraft, a P-47 Thunderbolt, a Mig-17, and a T-6 trainer. Planes will be flown in, flown out, and rotated in the exhibit lineup.

Exhibits include a comprehensive historical timeline, uniforms, memorabilia, plane engines, and jeeps. Among the prized possessions is the Congressional Medal of Honor presented to aviator general Jimmy Doolittle in 1942. Also on display is an in-depth look at the roots of flight through the eyes of the Wright Brothers; it showcases their first 10 years of flying experimentation, complete with models of nine of the planes they built during that time.

The mission of the privately owned museum is to preserve an understanding and appreciation for the aircraft and those who flew them to change the course of American history. There is a gift shop, and the museum is also home to Tennessee's Official Aviation Hall of Fame. Open daily, year-round. Just call (866) 286-8738, or visit tnairmuseum.com.

The **Women's Basketball Hall of Fame** (865-633-9000; wbhof.com) is easy to find. Just look for the big basketball. Located at 700 Hall of Fame Dr., the facility sits under a huge 30-foot-wide, 20,000-pound orange basketball. Although I have never counted them, officials say there are 96,000 pebbles on that ball. I'll take their word for it. Inside the entranceway is a spectacular 17-foot-tall, 3-player bronze sculpture. There are exhibits, videos, and memorabilia from all facets of women's basketball—from collegiate to professional. The Hall of Fame is open Tues through Sat Labor Day through Apr 1 and Mon through Sat May 1 to Labor Day. Closed major holidays. Admission is $7.95 for adults, $5.95 for seniors and children ages 6 to 15.

Knoxville is the site of the main campus of the **University of Tennessee,** where the Volunteers play their football games in the 95,000-plus-seat **Neyland Stadium.** It's only natural that tailgate partiers would adapt to the unique position of the stadium next to the Tennessee River. The Volunteer

Navy, as it is called here, starts gathering as early as the Thurs before a Sat game, and by game time as many as 300 boats have tied up. The only traffic these folks have to contend with is walking across the street to the stadium. Washington State has the only other major college stadium in the nation accessible by water.

Colorful "Big Orange" football is king in the fall, but the pinks and whites of flowering dogwood dominate the city's attention each spring. City officials estimate that about a million such trees bloom in their city each year. Why is Knoxville so decked out in beautiful trees? The story goes that it is all the result of a perceived insult. Seems that in 1947, New York newspaper reporter John Gunther came to town and looked around. Then he returned to his New York home and wrote a scathing article.

"Knoxville is the ugliest city I ever saw in America, with the possible exception of some mill towns in New England. Its main street is called Gay Street; this seemed to me to be a misnomer." Understandably, those words riled some Knoxville folks tremendously. They not only got riled, they decided to do something about living in "the ugliest city." Members of the Knoxville Garden Club, led by Betsey Creekmore, Martha Ashe, and Betsy Goodson, joined with other concerned citizens to begin a civic beautification project—the Dogwood Trails. Today the city has seven designated dogwood trails for self-guided tours. A **_Dogwood Arts Festival_** is held annually during late Apr with arts, crafts, and other activities. Bus tours for $5 a seat leave from the festival grounds at Market Square Mall.

You won't find any chain stores or nationally known restaurants in the **_Old City area_** (800-727-8045; knoxville.org) of Knoxville. What you'll find instead is a several-block area of one-of-a-kind shops, restaurants, bars, and music clubs that feature everything from jazz to reggae.

The hub of the Old City is at the junction of Jackson Avenue and Central Street in the northeastern section of downtown Knoxville. The area is a product of the period when the railroad made the city a center for commerce by delivering merchandise to the many huge 19th-century brick warehouses in the neighborhood.

The Old City's charm adds a perfect backdrop to various festivals and events during the year. Don't miss the fun.

In Morningside Park, near downtown, is the largest statue of an African American in the US. The 13-foot-tall bronze statue honors Tennessee's own

Alex Haley, author of numerous novels, including **Roots.** Designed for interaction, the statue depicts Haley with an open book as if he's reading to children; it's a popular setting for photos.

Dedicated in 1998, the *War Dog Memorial* commemorates all the dogs that served during World War II. It's located in front of the University of Tennessee's Veterinary Hospital at 2407 River Dr. A touching memorial, the sculpture features a Doberman pinscher to represent the hundreds of dogs that served.

The *Bijou Theatre* (865-522-0832; knoxbijou.com), Knoxville's third-oldest building, is on the National Register of Historic Places and is a fun place to attend a concert or a live stage production. Located at 803 S. Gay St., the restored relic houses all sorts of events, plays, and concerts throughout the year.

The *Three Rivers Rambler* train excursion (865-524-9411; threerivers rambler.com) is one of the best in the South. The 90-minute trip aboard a vintage train pulled by a 1925 Baldwin steam engine, affectionately known as Lindy, runs parallel to the Tennessee River, providing some great views. It passes through the historical areas of the city, past industrial plants, and through farmland.

Where the Holston and French Broad Rivers converge to form the head of the Tennessee River, the train crosses the Holston River on the historic Three Rivers Trestle. On the way back, the engineer will usually slow way down or stop on the trestle, allowing passengers to take in a fabulous view.

There is food and drink in the club car, and passengers are permitted to bring a picnic lunch if they desire.

birthplaceofa phrasemaker

"Damn the torpedoes! Full speed ahead." That well-known command was given by David Farragut, a Civil War admiral of the Union navy during the battle of Mobile Bay. He was born in Knoxville, and today the community where he grew up is named for him.

You can choose to ride in a plush circa 1925 Pullman car, a circa 1932 enclosed passenger car, or an open-air gondola car. Adult rates are $26.50, senior citizens $25.50, and children (ages 3–12) are $15.50. The train loads at Volunteer Landing, downtown on the Tennessee River, and runs Sat and Sun from late Mar through Dec, except for Sat home football games.

East Tennessee's preeminent fair, the ***Tennessee Valley Fair*** (865-215-1470; tnvalleyfair.org), takes place in early Sept each year in Chilhowee Park, 4 miles east of downtown. There's top-name entertainment, livestock and agriculture shows, carnival rides, and plenty of great old-time fair flavor. Admission is charged.

Another example of the old-time company town is found along US 129 south of Knoxville. Incorporated in 1919, the city of ***Alcoa*** was created by the Aluminum Company of America (ALCOA). Corporate offices are in Pittsburgh, but the southern plant opened in 1913 in a town called North Maryville. Six years later, with the financial help of the corporation, the city was created and its name changed.

Sam Houston, Davy Crockett's good friend, came to Blount County with his family when he was 14 years of age and in due time developed a fascination for the lifestyle of the neighboring Cherokee Indians. Soon he was adopted by the Cherokees, who called him The Raven.

He left the Indians to take a teaching position in a one-room schoolhouse near Maryville. He had little formal education but had read every book he could get his hands on, had won every spelling contest he entered, and could recite large portions of Homer's *Iliad* from memory. His teaching career lasted one term. In March 1813 he gave up teaching to enlist in General Andrew Jackson's army to fight the Creek Indian War.

The schoolhouse where he taught still stands and is considered the oldest original schoolhouse in the state and the only building left having a close association with this famous soldier and statesman. Built in 1794, the school now houses many Houston artifacts, including a pair of lead knuckles with his name carved in the soft metal. The guide at the ***Sam Houston Schoolhouse*** (865-983-1550; blountweb.com/samhouston) speculates whether he used them to keep order in the classroom.

The site also includes a visitor center and museum exhibits. It's located 6 miles north of Maryville on Sam Houston Schoolhouse Road, off Highway 33. Open year-round 10 a.m. to 5 p.m. Tues through Sat and 1 to 5 p.m. Sun. Admission for adults, $1; children under 10, free.

Before the Smoky Mountains became a national park in 1935, the little community of ***Townsend*** was a major lumbering center. The ***Townsend***

Visitor Center (800-525-6834; townsendchamber.org) on Lamar Alexander Parkway is the place to start your visit to this part of the state. In addition to having just about all the information you need, the Carl Koella Exhibit Center has local artists and craftspeople demonstrating their skills most every day.

The Little River Railroad and Lumber Company, headed by Colonel W. B. Townsend, set up mills and harvested logs from the rich, fertile forests that are now federal lands. Today very little of that heritage exists except in memory and old photos. In the center of town you'll find the *Little River Railroad and Lumber Company Museum* (865-448-2211; littleriverrailroad.org) at 7747 E. Lamar Alexander Pkwy. Among its memorabilia are a restored Shay Engine No. 2147 that was used locally during the early 1900s and an L&N Class NE Little Woody vintage caboose.

A restored train depot serves as a museum that's filled with memorabilia and photos of the early railroad and lumbering industries. It's open daily during the summer; weekends Apr, May, and Sept. Admission is free.

Sandy Headrick is one of the dedicated group members that run the museum, and she can be found across the street at the resort facility she owns and operates with her husband, Don. The Tudor-style *Highland Manor Inn* (865-448-2211 or 800-213-9462; highlandmanor.com) has a classy country inn atmosphere. The views from the balconies offer a spectacular vista of the Smokies, and several rooms have private whirlpool baths. It's located up on a hill, off US 321, near the center of town at 7766 E. Lamar Alexander Pkwy. In-season room rates start at $79.50.

Townsend calls itself "The Peaceful Side of the Smokies," referring to the fact that it is still quite laid-back and low-key, while the cities on the other side of the mountain, Pigeon Forge and Gatlinburg, are bustling tourist magnets. However, there is still a great deal to do here, especially if you love the outdoors.

You're only 8 miles from one of the national park's premier attractions when you're in Townsend. *Cades Cove* was a thriving mountain community in the 1850s with about 685 residents and 15,000 acres of usable farmland under cultivation. Today the area remains as it was then, with original buildings in original locations, so visitors can get a true sense of the spaciousness of early mountain life. An 11-mile self-guided auto loop tour gives the best idea of the culture of the region. Most homes, churches, and stores are open to the public.

The **Foothills Parkway,** which runs from US 321 near Walland for 17 miles, is a magnificent stretch of road that provides some great scenic pull-off opportunities that give you superb panoramic views of the mountains.

While it's always beautiful around here, our favorite time to visit is in the spring. Wildflowers seem to be growing everywhere you look. The mountains and valleys are carpeted with mountain phlox, dwarf irises, trilliums, and pink lady's slippers. Dogwoods, redbuds, and azaleas also add their color. The temperatures are usually comfortable, and the hiking and biking are superb. If you're interested in hopping on a horse and doing some trail riding in the mountains, contact the expert horsemen at the **Davy Crockett Riding Stables** (865-448-6411; davycrockettridingstables.com). They are located at 505 Old Cades Cove Rd.

Billing itself as the "greatest sight under the Smokies," the **Tuckaleechee Caverns** (865-448-2274; tuckaleecheecaverns.com) is a fun diversion if you get tired of always going up into the mountains. Here's your chance to go under things. It's always 58 degrees, and some of the formations and cave rooms are quite spectacular. These lovely caverns are open daily 10 a.m. to 6 p.m. and located off US 321. Admission is $15 adults, $7 children (ages 5 to 11), and free for children under 5.

Country Lifestyle

Sequoyah was an uneducated, crippled Cherokee half-breed who was shunned by his peers for much of his life until, in 1821, he introduced an alphabet to his people. It was so easy to learn that soon thousands were using it. Before long the Cherokees were more literate than most of the white men living in the area.

Sequoyah is the only man to single-handedly develop and perfect an alphabet. In doing so he endowed an entire nation with learning. The story of Sequoyah is told in the **Sequoyah Birthplace Museum** (423-884-6246; sequoyahmuseum.org), which is located south of Vonore on Highway 360 and is owned and operated by the Eastern Band of Cherokee Indians. The only Indian-operated historical attraction in Tennessee, it's found on the shores of Tellico Lake, 37 miles south of downtown Knoxville.

The museum is dedicated to this brilliant Native American, but it also tells a great deal about the Cherokee as a nation. Displays range from

Native American artifacts to a present-day *Blondie* comic book written in the Cherokee alphabet. An adjacent gift shop offers a wide variety of Cherokee crafts, works of art, and related books. Open daily, year-round; admission for adults, $3; children under 12, $1.50.

Along US 11 a few miles from Sweetwater lies the little town of **Niota,** which you may remember from national news reports a few years back. It was put on the map when the town was run by an all-female government. Coincidentally, this was the home of Harry Burn, the Tennessee legislator who cast the deciding vote to ratify the amendment to the US Constitution that gave women the right to vote.

The main attraction here is the **Niota Depot** (423-568-2584; niotatn .org), the oldest standing railroad depot in the state. Built in 1853, the building now houses the town offices. If you'd like a tour, stop by and someone will take you on a guided walk through the historic building, or contact them in advance for more tour information.

Along Highway 68, just outside Sweetwater, you'll find something quite amazing "under the beaten path." It's the **Lost Sea** (423-337-6616; thelostsea.com), an attraction that the *Guinness Book of World Records* calls America's largest underground lake. It's a 4.5-acre "bottomless" lake 300 feet underground.

The 55-minute tour is an easy walk down to the lake. There's not a single step to concern yourself with, since all paths are sloping and include handrails. Glass-bottomed boats take you out onto the water, and white trout will gather around the boat as you approach their end of the lake. The tour guides are local and have quite a few interesting stories to tell. They might even try to scare you a few times as you walk along.

The Lost Sea has been designated as a Registered Natural Landmark by the US Department of the Interior because of the lake phenomenon and the abundance of rare crystalline formations throughout the cavern system. Open year-round; admission for adults, $17.95; children (ages 5 to 12), $7.45.

Eugene Morgan is in the museum business now and he loves it. The **Museum from the Past** (423-442-4833) is his creation and is regularly open on weekends during the warmer months and during the week by chance. On display is his personal collection of 20 years' worth of acquiring everything from South American pottery to a 5.3-foot-long chain saw to a genuine Tennessee moonshine still.

Trade Faire Follies

Trade fairs were the commercial centers of an English community during the 18th century. Streets were filled with vendors and craftspeople selling all sorts of essentials. Puppet shows were presented for the kids and theatrical plays for the adults. Farmers would bring their oxen to trade and their handiwork to sell.

In America trade fairs were abundant throughout most of the colonies and were originally set up to resemble those in Britain. However, it wasn't long until Americans came up with their own version of this annual social event. Sporting challenges, including fistfights and running races were held; fortune-tellers foretold ladies' dreams for the coming year; and circus performers and gypsies would appear for both fun and profit.

It's not often in today's society that one gets the opportunity to walk among the sights, sounds, and smells of those early social gatherings. However, early each September, more than 100 reenactors regularly gather at Fort Loudoun State Historic Area to put on an early trade fair, both for their own fun and for the public's education.

At the *18th Century Trade Faire,* you can sample the foods and the crafts of the 1700s, enjoy period musical entertainment, and see how good we really have it today! You'll have the opportunity to interact with costumed reenactors—from British and French soldiers to ladies with small children—all of whom will be more than happy to talk with you and explain the way of life they are re-creating.

It all takes place at the 1,200-acre **Fort Loudoun State Historic Area,** one of the earliest British fortifications on the Western Frontier, built in 1756. Today the area houses an interpretive center offering information and artifacts excavated from the ruins prior to the fort's reconstruction. Numerous other unique events take place on the grounds during the year, including a warm and wonderful Christmas celebration. Located 30 miles south of Knoxville, off US 441 in the town of Vonore. Call (423) 884-6217, or go to fortloudoun.com for more information.

Most of his collection of 1,300 items is out on tables and shelves, and he encourages you to touch them or pick them up. He'll even show you how the things worked.

"I had to get special permission from the government to put up the still. I think they thought I might want to put it in action," he laughed as he told the story of how he acquired it. The permission letter is tacked to the door of the still, located down a short path from the museum in deep woods. Morgan is a cordial host, and he'll be more than happy to spend time with you explaining every item inside and outside his main building. He has built his own blacksmith shop and has devised an old-time round pump to pump water out of the creek up to his bathrooms.

The museum is 4 miles south of Madisonville, on Highway 68. Watch for signs along the road and the old stoplight in his front yard.

Back in 1958, members of the Tellico Plains Kiwanis Club started talking about the lack of roads from Monroe County across the mountains into North Carolina. That put plans in motion, and in 1996 The **Cherohala Skyway,** also known as the Ribbon in the Sky, opened as a $100 million, 43-mile scenic stretch of pure, uninterrupted mountain beauty. It runs along the ridge for a portion, down into the valleys for a while, and provides amazingly colorful vistas from 5,000 feet up, from the dogwoods and redbuds in the spring to the oranges, reds, and browns of the fall.

The road is one of only 20 National Scenic Highways in the US and gets its unusual name from a combination of the two national forests where it begins and ends, the Cherokee in Tennessee and the Nantahala in North Carolina.

In **Tellico Plains,** enter the Skyway via Highway 165. There are plenty of brochures out about the road, and you can see some stunning photographs of the highway at monroecounty.com. Or call (800) 245-5428.

The **Tellico Ranger Station** of the Cherokee National Forest (423-253-8400; fs.usda.gov/cherokee) is located just off the Skyway. Sited at an old Civilian Conservation Corps camp, the visitor center is located in a building built by the CCC in the 1930s. An exhibit area has a display of CCC items, including photos, caps, coats, and equipment. The folk here know the area quite well and can help you custom-build a day in the forest. There are plenty of maps and brochures, as well as a gift shop. Open Mon through Fri 8 a.m. to 4:30 p.m.

To reach the ranger station, take the Skyway out of town; the river will be on your right. Approximately 5 miles out of town, you'll see Forest Service Road 210 forking off to the right and continuing along the river. Take it; the station is less than half a mile down the road on your left. The river will still be on your right.

As a little boy, Charles Hall used to love to listen to tales told by local men around the old potbellied stove at his father's country store. Hall became fascinated with area history. Even as a child, he began collecting memorabilia that might have been lost over the years. Today, we are all the richer for this man's vision.

Opened in 2003, the **Charles Hall Museum** (423-253-8000; charleshall-museum.com) at 229 Cherohala Pkwy. in Tellico Plains has grown to more than 6,000 artifacts and thousands of historical pictures and documents. The huge collection contains coins and currency, guns, historic equipment, telephones, and much more. It is now showcased in two museum buildings. Among the first white settlers in the area, Charles's mother's family settled in Tellico Plains in 1830. His father's family settled in the area in 1908. Hall has spent his life serving the community he loves. His list of offices held is quite impressive—mayor for 31 years, alderman-recorder for 2 years, justice of the peace for 6 years, and county commissioner for 6 years. Hall and his wife Billie Nell were also former owners of the Tellico Telephone Company.

Close to celebrating a century of life, Hall can often be found at the museum sharing his wealth of stories. He is the true treasure here. Open Mon through Sat 10 a.m. to 5 p.m., Sun noon to 5 p.m. Free admission.

It may be wise to fill up your tummy before heading to the mountains, and in Tellico Plains, the popular **Tellihala Cafe** (423-253-2880) is the place to do it. There's an enormous selection, but if you're stopping for lunch, try the country-ham sandwich or the chicken-fried steak. You'll find them on the menu under "Luncheon Favorites." Located at 128 Bank St., it's open every day but Mon for lunch and dinner.

herewecome

Tennessee earned its nickname, the Volunteer State, by its remarkable record of furnishing volunteers in the War of 1812 and the Mexican War.

For more information on this area, call (800) 245-5428, or you can log on at monroecounty.com.

The people of the Coker Creek area are still shouting, "There's gold in them thar hills!" The community has been celebrating the **Autumn Gold Festival** each October since 1968 to highlight the area's two forms of gold—the golden color of the leaves as they turn each fall and the gold that can still be found in the creeks of the area. The festival salutes the gold-mining heritage of the region, which goes back to the late 1820s.

Organizers bring down a few truckloads of dirt from the mountain gold mines so that festivalgoers have a better chance of finding some real gold when they participate in one of the major events, panning for gold. There are also board splitting, syrup making, gospel and country music, and arts and crafts. The festival is held at Coker Creek Elementary School at mile marker 34 on Highway 68 south of Tellico Plains.

Coker Creek Crafts Gallery (423-261-2157; cokercreekgallery.com) is 1 block off Highway 68 on Hot Water Road. Turn onto Hot Water across from the fire station in town. Owned by Ken and Kathleen Dalton, the business specializes in high-quality crafts and visual arts. The Daltons' baskets are widely known and are in craft collections and museums all over the country. Closed Jan through Mar, it's open the rest of the year Tues through Sat.

The **Crosseyed Cricket** (865-986-5435; crosseyedcricket.com) advertises that it's more than "just a place to stay." Located on Country Lane a few miles from exit 364 on I-40, about 20 miles southwest of Knoxville, the Cricket is a campground in a beautiful rural setting and open year-round.

From Thanksgiving through Christmas, the Christmas Tree Plantation is open. You can choose from several thousand trees to cut down. Bone saws are provided, or you may bring your own.

Roane County is dominated by the Tennessee Valley Authority's (TVA) **Watts Bar Lake.** With 783 miles of lakefront, water-oriented activities are quite popular. Numerous marinas with boat rentals are scattered throughout the county. Once on the lake, island hopping is a popular activity. Hundreds of small islands make perfect secluded areas for picnicking and swimming.

Watts Bar Lake is one of several TVA lakes throughout the state that make up the chain called the **Great Lakes of the South.** Many families live on the lake in houseboats. One colony is located just west of Kingston off US 70.

A driving tour of the county has been developed, as has a backcountry trail driving tour. Brochures and maps for both are available from the **Roane County Visitors Bureau** (865-376-4201 or 800-FUN-INTN; roanetourism .com), 1209 N. Kentucky St., 1 block north of I-40.

The **Old Courthouse Museum** (865-376-9211; roanetnheritage.com), located, as you can imagine, in the old county courthouse, features local and state history from prehistoric time to World War II. The building, with tall white columns, is only one of the seven remaining antebellum court-houses in the state. Located at the corner of Kentucky and Cumberland Streets in Kingston, it is open Mon through Fri 8:30 a.m. to 4:30 p.m. for free.

Fort Southwest Point (865-376-3641; southwestpoint.com) in Kingston is the only fort in the state that has been reconstructed on its original foundation. The completed sections of the fort so far include the barracks, blockhouse, and more than 250 feet of palisade walls. A separate building houses the welcome center and the *Fort Southwest Point Museum.* Work began on the site in the early 1970s, with a lot of construction still to do, according to officials.

The fort is located on a 30-acre hill overlooking Watts Bar Lake. Take Highway 58 south out of town; go 1 mile and the fort is on your right.

West of Rockwood off US 70, high atop "the mountain" (as locals call it), is a Forest Service–run fire tower. Although visitors are not supposed to climb to the top of the tower, the picnic area around the bottom offers a magnificent bird's-eye vista of Rockwood and Watts Bar Lake. There are several shaded picnic tables and barbecue grills for the public to use. Open daily during daylight hours only. If you're driving through Rockwood during the Christmas season and see a huge star shining brightly to the west, this is where it's plugged in.

The Dream Counties

During the 1880s and 1890s, *Oliver Springs* was a central railroad town for the local coal miners. The area was booming by 1895 when the Oliver Springs Hotel opened and created a strong demand for passenger rail service to the area. As a result, the town built a new rail depot in 1896 to serve the increased needs.

That depot still stands today and is the home of a museum that highlights the area's growth to fame and fortune, although the hotel burned in 1905 and was never replaced, and the town hasn't had passenger service for decades. The town's library is located in the restored depot. A reconditioned caboose sits out back, as do several other large pieces of local memorabilia. Located on the corner of Winter's Gap Road and Walker Avenue, admission is free. You can reach the depot at (865) 435-2509.

In 1942, as World War II was raging, President Franklin D. Roosevelt approved the proposal by Albert Einstein to proceed in making a secret weapon. The Army Corps of Engineers chose an isolated 60,000-acre site here in Anderson County. Within one year, three defense plants were built and a **Secret City** for 75,000 people was cut out of the wilderness.

Throughout the war years **Oak Ridge,** the name given the community, remained under direct supervision of the government and was surrounded by a tall barbed-wire fence. Only a handful of the workers knew the true nature of the project, and all were sworn to secrecy. It was not until the dropping of the first atomic bombs in 1945 that the inhabitants behind the fence learned that they had been members of an important team of the famed **Manhattan Project. Oak Ridge National Laboratory** produced the uranium 235 and plutonium 239, the fuel necessary for the atomic bomb.

shhh!don'ttell anyone

The **World War II Secret City Festival** takes place in late June each year and features tours, diverse entertainment by national acts, a WWII reenactment, arts and crafts, and children's activities. Call (865) 425-3610, or visit their website at secretcityfestival.com.

The fences came down in 1949, and the city was incorporated. Today more than 4,000 buildings exist as a link to this era of secrecy. All three plants are still there, but the main emphasis in Oak Ridge now is energy research.

The original graphite reactor, the oldest continuously operated nuclear reactor in the world, is located in the Oak Ridge National Laboratory and open to the public. A map of the 38-mile self-guided motor tour of the entire area and other information on the area are available at the **Convention and Visitors Bureau** (102 Robertsonville Rd., Ste. C; 865-887-3429; oakridgevisitor.com). Since Sept. 11, 2001, some areas have been closed to the public.

The US Department of Energy has developed one of the world's largest energy exhibitions at 300 S. Tulane Ave. The **American Museum of Science and Energy** (865-576-3200; amse.org) includes interactive exhibits, live demonstrations, computer displays, and filmed interpretations. All forms of energy and their relationship to humanity are explained. One favorite demonstration, especially of the young, makes a person's hair stand straight up on end. Open year-round 9 a.m. to 5 p.m.; closed on Sun morning, Mon, Thanksgiving Day, Christmas Day, and New Year's Day. Closing time is extended by one hour in June, July, and Aug. The admission fee is $5 for those 18 years of age and over, $3 for those 6–17, $4 for senior citizens, and free for kids under 6.

bringhome dinner

The Clinch River has the highest trout catch rate of any stream in the eastern US.

The story behind the creation of the living areas of Oak Ridge is an amazing one. Five home designs were created and assigned to workers according to family size and job importance. Neighborhoods centered on the Town Site, which was designed to offer shopping and recreation. The high school, multifamily housing, and the hospital were also built near the Town Site. Now known as *Jackson Square,* a walking tour of that original town site is available. You can get information on the tour at the visitor center.

The **Appalachian Arts Craft Shop** (865-494-9854; appalachianarts .net) is on Highway 61 about a mile after it crosses I-75 at 2716 Andersonville Hwy. The center was started in 1970 to "enrich the souls and pocketbooks of low-income people." Today the nonprofit organization that runs the center works with local people to preserve traditional Appalachian crafts and techniques. All types of crafts are available. The center is open 10 a.m. to 6 p.m. Mon through Sat and 1 to 5 p.m. Sun. In Jan and Feb, the gallery is closed on Sun and Mon.

Less than a mile down the road from the crafts center is the **Museum of Appalachia** (865-494-7680; museumofappalachia.com) at 2819 Andersonville Hwy. Founded by John Rice Irwin in 1960, the museum is considered one of the most authentic representations of early Appalachian mountain life. Dozens of cabins and buildings have been moved here and preserved in the spaciousness of their original locations. More than 250,000 items are on display. Live music and demonstrations abound as employees go about living and working in a mountain village. *Roots* author Alex Haley said he loved the museum so much that he "built a home in sight of it." He lived across the street until his death in Feb 1992. Open daily, year-round;

admission is $18 for adults, $15 for senior citizens, $10 children ages 13–18, and $6 for children ages 5–12.

If you can, plan your visit during one of the three "authentic" annual events: *July 4th Celebration, Tennessee Fall Homecoming* in Oct, or *Christmas in Old Appalachia.*

The nearby city of *Norris* (800-524-3602; yallcome.org) is a great little community. Planned and built by the Tennessee Valley Authority (TVA) in 1934 as a demonstration of sound community development, the town features a greenbelt, a town forest that protects the city's water supply, and houses placed in a parklike atmosphere. Now an independent municipality, Norris has preserved its original look. Brochures and information are available at the police and fire departments.

The Tennessee Valley Authority Act was signed into law by President Franklin D. Roosevelt on May 18, 1933, and within a few weeks the TVA's first flood-control project, the Norris Dam, was started. As the oldest TVA facility, the dam is open to visitors on occasion, although the entire operation is now run by remote control. No tours are given, but you can drive across and get some great photos.

The dam and the lake are part of the *Norris Dam State Park,* as is the *Lenoir Family Museum* (865-494-9688). Made up primarily of Helen and Will G. Lenoir's "junk" collection, items in the state-run facility date from prehistoric times to the present. The place is filled with artifacts that visitors are encouraged to pick up and touch. As the guides walk visitors through, they tell stories that bring the items to life. Many of the stories are more fun than the items themselves. To get the full benefit here, take the tour first and listen to the stories, then go back through and look at the displays at your own pace.

The museum's most treasured artifact is a European barrel organ with tiers of hand-carved wooden figures. Research shows it was made in Germany in 1826 and probably brought to America by a traveling showman. Admission is free. Open daily during summer; Wed through Sun only for the rest of the year.

Outside, the TVA has gathered two additional buildings. The *Cosby Threshing Barn,* built in the early 1800s, was one of the first threshing barns to be built in the US. It's full of pioneer machinery, including a wooden treadmill made in 1855. Across the field from the barn is a 1798 gristmill where corn is ground during the summer months. A gift shop is on the upper level. The entire setting is very rustic and just a short distance from the dam and a picnic area.

If it's rugged wilderness and wild whitewater you're looking for, follow US 27 north to **Wartburg** and the **Obed Wild and Scenic River** (423-346-6294; nps.gov/obed). The area is managed by the National Park Service and the Tennessee Wildlife Resources Agency and consists of four streams within the same watershed. Over the years they have carved their way through the landscape and have created beautiful gorges, some as deep as 500 feet.

During the rainy season, December through April, the streams provide some of the finest, most technical whitewater in the nation. Some primitive camping is allowed. The visitor center for the area is located at 208 N. Maiden St., next to the Federal Building in Wartburg.

Frozen Head State Natural Area (423-346-3318; state.tn.us/environment/parks) was named for a 3,324-foot peak in the Cumberland Mountains, the top of which is often shrouded in ice or snow. You enter this peaceful area through a vestige of densely forested, unspoiled mountain terrain. A vintage fire tower, which is accessible only by a walking trail, offers a spectacular panorama of this majestic part of the state. The park is located off Highway 62, east of Wartburg.

capitaldujour

Four cities have served as Tennessee's state capital:

Knoxville, 1796–1817

Kingston, 1807, for one day only

Murfreesboro, 1817–1826

Nashville, 1826–present

A great way to see the Scott County area is by horseback, and the folks at the appropriately named **Tally Ho Stables** (423-569-9472) can help you get saddled up. You can rent a horse here and join in on one of the several different trail rides offered. They claim they have more than 150 miles of developed horse trails to explore. An hour ride will cost you $20; 2 hours, $30; half day, $50; and an all-day 8- or 9-hour journey will cost $80. They also have 2-day or more pack trips. Located at 6471 Grave Hill Rd., just outside of Oneida.

Of the three utopian experiments in Tennessee during the late 1800s, **Rugby**'s was the largest and has left us with the most evidence of the dreamers' struggles.

Today 20 of the 70 original buildings of **Rugby's Utopian Community** (423-628-2441 or 888-214-3400; historicrugby.org) still stand and have been preserved or restored. A few are still inhabited by descendants of the original settlers.

In 1880 English author-reformer Thomas Hughes launched this colony with the dream that it would be "a centre in which a healthy, reverent life shall grow." At its peak in 1884, the population was about 450. Today Rugby has about 85 residents.

Hughes's vision of a utopian existence in the wilderness of Tennessee brought a taste of British culture along with it. Most of the settlers were young British of good family, and today their colorful Victorian legacies line the streets, making Rugby one of the most unusual communities in the state.

A journey through town should begin at the old **Rugby Schoolhouse,** which now serves as a museum and visitor center. In addition to the school, historic buildings open to visitors include the **Christ Church, Episcopal,** with its original hanging lamps and 1849 rosewood reed organ, and the **Thomas Hughes Free Public Library** (423-628-2441) at 5511 Rugby Hwy., which still contains what is regarded as the best representative collection (7,000 volumes) of Victorian literature in America.

Two historic structures have been restored and now offer overnight accommodations with historical accuracy. The **Pioneer Cottage** and the **Newbury House Inn** are available with prior reservations.

If you're into ghosts and stories of haunting, you'll get your fill during your tour of Rugby's historic district. If your guide doesn't talk about the various sightings through the years, make sure you ask. Rugby is located on Highway 52 a few miles west of US 27. Structures are open year-round except for Thanksgiving Day, Christmas Eve, Christmas Day, and New Year's Day; during Jan, tours are by appointment. Housing, shops, and a restaurant are open year-round.

Approximately 1 mile west of Rugby on Highway 52 is the **Grey Gables Bed and Breakfast Inn** (423-628-5252; rugbytn.com). The magnificent home was built in 1990 for the purpose of setting up a classy inn that would combine the best of Victorian English and Tennessee country heritage. Decorated with country and Victorian antiques, the inn reflects the grace of the English and the cordiality of this area.

Innkeeper Linda Brooks Jones not only has a great 10-bedroom inn, but you'll have to loosen your belt a few notches after you've eaten a couple of meals here. In fact, Jones's cooking has gone over so well, and so many people were asking for her recipes, that she has written her own cookbook, called *The Table at Grey Gables*. She was born and raised in the area, and the cookbook has not only recipes but also historical narrative about Rugby and her relationship with the locals through the years.

officially speaking

The Square Dance is the official folk dance of Tennessee, and there are ample opportunities to join in the fun throughout the state. A good place to find information is through the **Tennessee State Association of Square & Round Dance Clubs Inc.** at tnsquaredance.org.

If you look around, you'll see a few photos of former president Jimmy Carter and his wife, the inn's most famous boarders to date. They stayed here on June 17, 1997, and Jones has some great, fun stories about the visit. If it's available, she may let you have the bed the famous couple slept in.

In addition to the great hospitality and the yummy cooking, the hostess offers a full array of activities and themed events. Rates include an elegant evening meal and a hearty country breakfast. Reservations are required; rates are $135 double occupancy, $85 single occupancy. Call Jones and she'll send you a calendar that highlights special themed weekends. Wheelchair accessible.

In addition to the bed-and-breakfast duties, Jones's daughter Tiffany runs the **R. M. Brooks General Store** (423-628-5252), on Highway 52 just west of Grey Gables. Linda's grandparents started the store in 1930, and it has remained in the family since. The village post office was tucked away in a corner of the store for years, and when it moved, the family made sure that the old-time postal feel of the mailboxes remained. The family wants to keep it a "typical, working country general store" where you can buy sandwiches, hoop cheddar cheese, mousetraps, soup, and just about anything else. Plus they have a selection of antiques and local crafts on sale. As in most establishments of this type, you'll find a good supply of local characters sitting around the potbellied stove just about any time you drop in. The general store is open Tues through Sun 10 a.m. to 5:30 p.m.

Forests & Cliffs

The 673-acre **Cove Lake State Park** (423-566-9701) is on the banks of Cove Lake, near **Caryville.** Established in the 1930s as a recreation demonstration area by the TVA, the National Park Service, and the Civilian Conservation Corps, the lake is home to more than 400 Canada geese each winter. Open daily year-round, the park is visited by nearly one million people each year. The **Rickard Ridge BBQ** (423-907-8202; rickardridgebbq.com) features, just as it says, barbecue chicken, pork, beef, ribs, and catfish. Located at 131 Goose Ln., the restaurant is open year-round too and features live bluegrass music on Mon and Thurs starting at 6 p.m. The park's schedule changes seasonally, so give them a call to find out more. The ranger's station and the masonry fences around it were built by the Civilian Conservation Corps.

Surrounded by the towering Cumberland Mountains, the park is perhaps more popular with visitors in the winter than the summer. **Christmas in the Park** is an annual event that county residents look forward to. The celebration features all sorts of music, lights, and decorations throughout the park. The walkways and roads are lined with candles. In the summer the park offers an Olympic-size swimming pool, tennis courts, and 4 miles of paved hiking trails.

This entire county has been described by many as one big natural museum. Ruggedness is the key word here, and one access to that ruggedness is through the **Big South Fork National River and Recreation Area** (bigsouthforkpark.com). Authorized by Congress in 1974, the park has been frequented mainly by those who have been willing to explore the wilderness on its own terms. During the last few years, more roads, overlooks, and river access sites have been built, opening up the 100,000-acre park to less adventurous visitors.

The Big South Fork River cuts a course through one of the most spectacular chasms east of the Mississippi. The gorge is rimmed by towering bluffs of weathered sandstone rising as high as 500 feet. It's considered to be one of the best whitewater rivers in the East. In all, there are more than 80 miles of prime canoeing waters within the park.

Camping is permitted just about anywhere in the park, and mountain bikes and four-wheeled off-road vehicles are permitted on designated trails and roads. There are three developed campgrounds and the ***Charit Creek Lodge*** (931-879-2276; charitcreeklodge.com), which offers dormitory-style housing with bunk beds. There is no electricity here, and no vehicular traffic is allowed. The lodge has clean restroom facilities with showers available seasonally and serves a hearty breakfast at 7 a.m. and dinner at 6 p.m. Sack lunches are available for day hikers/riders by reservation 3 days in advance.

The most comfortable way to see the rugged terrain and the river is aboard the ***Big South Fork Scenic Railway*** (800-462-5664; bsfsry.com). The 3-hour narrated trip leaves from the historic coal-mining town of Sterns, Kentucky. The 7-mile trip takes you down gently to the bottom of the gorge, through a massive tunnel, and along high rock ledges. It then hugs the banks of the river, where you might catch a glimpse of whitewater aficionados.

One of the most scenic highways in this part of the state connects Jellico with La Follette. Although it seems much longer, US 25W curves and twists for 29 very interesting miles. The road offers some spectacular views as it follows the canyons through the mountains. This route is a great alternative to interstate driving, but you'll need to adjust your speed to the road conditions, and you'll probably want to pull off a couple of times to enjoy the scenery. Several bitter skirmishes were fought around here during the Civil War.

Since 1760, treasure hunters have searched this area for the legendary Swift's Silver Mines, where John Swift and his crew mined silver, minted coins, and took it all back to the colonies. The operation ended during the Indian Wars. Several years later, Swift came back but due to his failing eyesight was unable to locate his mines, which he insisted were still full of silver. Nobody has found those mines yet.

Places to Stay in the Mountainous East

CARYVILLE
Cove Lake State Park
(camping)
US 25W
(423) 566-9701
Restaurant, hiking trails, lake, fishing

CUMBERLAND GAP
The Olde Mill Bed & Breakfast
603 Pennlyn Ave.
(423) 869-0868
oldemillbbinn.com
Country breakfast; antique/Victorian furnishings

GATLINBURG
Great Smoky Mountains National Park
(865) 436-1200
nps.gov/grsm
Camping in undeveloped areas

LeConte View Motor Lodge
929 Parkway
(865) 436-5032
leconteview.com
Fireplaces, indoor and outdoor pools

JEFFERSON CITY
EconoLodge
531 Patriot Dr.
(865) 397-9437
Pool, fireplaces, cable TV

KNOXVILLE
Volunteer Park (camping)
9514 Diggs Gap Rd.
(865) 938-6600
volparktn.com
Grocery, pools, showers, phones

LENOIR CITY
Crosseyed Cricket
Paw Paw Road
(865) 986-5435
crosseyedcricket.com
Camping (year-round)

PIGEON FORGE
Twin Mountain RV Park
(camping)
304 Day Springs Rd.
(865) 453-8181
twinmountainrvpark.com
Pool, river tubing, laundry room, bathhouses, wireless Internet, cable TV

RUGBY
Grey Gables Bed and Breakfast Inn
5809 Rugby Hwy.
(423) 628-5252
rugbytn.com
Great food, country/Victorian decor

SEVIERVILLE
Hidden Mountain Resorts
475 Apple Valley Rd.
(865) 453-9850
hiddenmountain.com
Condos, cottages, motorcoach sites, and log cabins

Oak Tree Lodge
1620 Parkway
(865) 428-7500
theoaktreelodge.com
Private balconies, fireplaces, pools

TOWNSEND
Highland Manor Inn
Highway 321
(865) 448-2211
highlandmanor.com
Tudor-style, balconies, private whirlpools available

Places to Eat in the Mountainous East

BEAN STATION

Clinch Mountain Lookout Restaurant
US 25E at the summit
(865) 767-2511
clinchmountainlookout
.com
Vinegar pie, ostrich burgers, breakfast all day
Open daily for early breakfast, lunch, and dinner

COSBY

Kyle Carver Orchards
On US 321 South, 5 miles from I-40
3462 Cosby Hwy.
(423) 487-2710
carversappleorchard.com
Country cooking with many apple dishes
Open daily year-round, 8 a.m. to 8 p.m.

CUMBERLAND GAP

The Tomato Head
12 Market Sq.
(865) 637-4067
thetomatohead.com
Award-winning gourmet pizza, salads, sandwiches
Open daily

GATLINBURG

Buckhorn Inn Restaurant
2140 Tudor Mountain Rd.
(866) 941-0460
buckhorninn.com
Four-course $35 per-person dinner served every night at 7 p.m. Southern-influenced menu. Reservations required.

Cabin Cafe
600 Glades Rd.
(865) 325-1000
visitthecabin.com
Located in Arts & Crafts Community, this cafe serves homemade salads, sandwiches, beans of the day with corn bread. Open daily.

Greenbriar Restaurant
370 Newman Rd.
(865) 436-6318
greenbriarrestaurant.com
Located in historic 1939 log cabin atop mountain, serves everything from mountain trout to lobster tail. Open daily.

The Lodge at Buckberry Creek
961 Campbell Lead Rd.
(866) 305-6343
buckberrylodge.com
Beautiful mountain views and menu that changes daily. Try the venison chop if it's on the menu.

Mountain Lodge Restaurant
913 E. Parkway
(865) 436-2547
Breakfast and lunch only at this local favorite, serves homemade biscuits and gravy

Peddler Steakhouse
1110 Parkway
(865) 436-5794
peddlergatlinburg.com
Steaks, salmon, best salad bar in town; on the river with great views
Open year-round; dinner served nightly

KNOXVILLE

Copper Cellar
1807 Cumberland
(865) 673-3411
coppercellar.com
Located just off UT campus, this is two restaurants in one. Cellar serves lunch and dinner; upstairs more casual.

Crown & Goose
123 S. Central St.
(865) 524-2100
thecrownandgoose.com
World-class food served in traditional pub setting

PIGEON FORGE

Bullfish Grill
2441 Parkway
(865) 868-1000
bullfishgrill.com
Serves aged grand
champion Angus beef,
seafood and more. Lunch
and dinner. Look for
statue of bull with a fish in
its mouth.

Dixie Stampede
Located on the parkway
(865) 453-4400
dixiestampede.com
Watch a live show while
eating a southern feast

Mel's Diner
119 Wears Valley Rd.
(865) 429-2184
meldinerspf.com
Rock 'n' roll theme
featured on menu, walls,
and jukebox

Old Mill Restaurant
164 Old Mill Ave.
(865) 429-3463
oldmillsquare.com/
restaurant
Southern cooking, fish,
chicken, steak.
Next to 1830 Old Mill
attraction at Traffic Light
#7.
Open daily for breakfast,
lunch, and dinner.

SEVIERVILLE

Applewood Farmhouse Grill
220 Apple Valley Rd.
(865) 429-8644
Offspring of Applewood
Farmhouse Restaurant
offering lighter options

Applewood Farmhouse Restaurant
240 Apple Valley Rd.
(865) 428-1222
applewood
farmhouserestaurant.com
Fresh trout, trout cake,
apple pie

SWEETWATER

Dinner Bell
I-75 and Oakland Road
(exit 62)
576 Oakland Rd.
(423) 337-5825
Home cooking, nightly
buffet, country
atmosphere
Open daily at 6 a.m. for
breakfast, lunch, and
dinner

Upper Cumberland

In a valley surrounded by the Cumberland Mountains a few miles from the Kentucky border, ***Sergeant Alvin York,*** one of America's most celebrated military heroes, was born and reared. Except for the 2 years he fought in World War I, Sergeant York spent his entire life in these mountains. But those 2 years put York in the history books and this part of the state on the map. Today the ***Alvin York State Historic Park*** (931-879-6456) commemorates his life and career. The area is about 9 miles north of Jamestown on US 127 and is open daily.

York's one-man firefight with the German army in France's Argonne Forest on Oct. 8, 1918, is now legendary. As a patrol leader, he killed 25 German soldiers and almost single-handedly captured another 132. As a result he received more than 40 Allied decorations and worldwide publicity.

His modest upbringing here in the Tennessee mountains and his refusal to cash in on his popularity by selling out to the media won the hearts of millions, and he returned to the valley as a bona fide hero.

N

0   25 mi
0   25 km

KY.
TENN.

Lafayette   Celina   *Dale Hollow Lake*   111
52   Jamestown

Cumberland R.

Livingston   127   52

UPPER CUMBERLAND

Carthage   70N   Cookeville

40

Center Hill Lake   70N

70

Smithville   70   Crossville   40

70S   70S

McMinnville   27

MIDDLE CUMBERLAND

55   75

127   Dayton   Tennessee R.

SOUTHWEST CUMBERLAND   111   11   Athens

411

127

41   OF FORESTS AND RIVERS

24   CROSSROADS OF DIXIE   Cleveland   74

Chattanooga   64

TENN.   Monteagle   TENN.
AL.   GA.

World's Longest Outdoor Sale

The 690-mile US 127 Corridor Sale now runs from 5 miles north of Addison, Michigan, to Gadsden, Alabama.

All along US 127, you'll find rural front yards loaded with items; in the cities you'll find sidewalks filled with merchandise. It's an almost endless supply of trash and treasures, and you'll find just about anything you'd ever want. Please be careful: US 127 is quite busy during the sale. Watch out for traffic and always use your turn signals if you are going to pull over. Held one weekend in Aug, Thurs through Sun. Call (800) 327-3945, or go online at 127sale.com to find out more.

York died in 1964, and 4 years later the state bought a large portion of land that included his family farm and the mill that he once operated. The exhibits are fine, but the real reason to visit this area is the park ranger, York's son, Andy York. He's often here, and he'll be more than glad to spend some time with you and tell you all sorts of stories about his famous father and the family's ties to the area. It's not too often that you get to meet a genuine hero's son whose business it is to talk about his father's life. It's a unique opportunity to put history into perspective.

Jamestown was popular with Native Americans and early travelers because of the many freshwater springs that came up through the sandy soil. In fact the original name of the community was Sand Spring. One of the early settlers here was John M. Clemens, the father of Samuel Clemens, better known as Mark Twain. On Main Street, just off the courthouse square, *Mark Twain Spring Park* is on land adjacent to the Clemens homestead and still has a small spring that was once the source of water for the early residents. Although there is no evidence that Samuel Clemens ever visited here, he was conceived here. He was born 5 months after his parents moved to Missouri.

Three miles south of Jamestown on US 127 at 2965 S. York Hwy. is the *Highland Manor Winery* (931-879-9519; highlandmanorwinery .net), which has the distinction of being the oldest licensed winery in the state and the first American winery to be awarded the International Gold Medal for Quality in Madrid, Spain. This is one of 45 commercial wineries in the state. (See Montgomery County in the Heartlands chapter for additional fruit-of-the-vine experiences.) The winery is open daily for tours and tasting.

Some huge pumpkins are grown each year in the area around James-town, and the pumpkin is king for a weekend early each Oct when the **Great Pumpkin Festival and Weigh-Off** (931-879-7125; allardtpumpkin festival.com) is held in nearby Allardt, southeast of Jamestown on Highway 52. The folks here have turned pumpkin and gourd competition into a rea-son to play. On Saturday morning the weigh-offs begin to find the year's champion. Pumpkins from all over show up on the back of pickup trucks. We were amazed at our first sight of an 800 pounder.

In addition to all the noteworthy gourds, pumpkins, watermelons, and squash, dozens of local craftspeople set up in Bruno Gernt Park to sell their unique products. There's also music, an antique tractor show, a quilt show, a street dance, beauty pageant, auto show, a bake sale and auction, a parade, and of course plenty of pumpkin-flavored goodies! Admission to all this great, rural slice of life is free.

In the heart of the Upper Cumberland region, *Livingston,* the county seat, is rapidly becoming known for its quality crafts outlets. The downtown area around the historic courthouse is known as Court Square and is home to many retail shops, antiques stores, and crafts stores.

Counted among the antiques stores in downtown is the **Antique Mar-ket** (931-823-4943), at 116 N. Court Sq. Inside you'll find more than 50 booths and two large rooms full of everything from fabulous antique jewelry

AUTHOR'S TOP TEN PICKS

Great Pumpkin Festival and Weigh-Off	Muddy Pond
	Ocoee Whitewater Center
Highland Manor Winery	Rhea County Museum
Homesteads	Russell Stover Candies Factory and Outlet Store
Horsin' Around Carving School	
International Towing & Recovery Hall of Fame and Museum	Tennessee's Badlands

to postcards to oak furniture. It's open 7 days a week. Hungry? *The Apple Dish* (931-823-3222), with a nice selection of soups, salads, and sandwiches, is located at 114 N. Court St. and offers not only great home cooking but also tremendous home-baked desserts, including Italian cream cake.

At 1825 Burkhart Rd., the *Livingston Antique Outlet* (517-548-5399; livingstonantiqueoutlet.com) features more than 200 dealers in a 32,000-square-foot red barn. Open daily.

Livingston throws a great party during July, and it is Hometown USA at its finest. The *Overton County Bluegrass Festival* (931-823-6421) fills the city square with music, food, arts and crafts, and a lot of good-neighbor howdies.

Down in the southeast corner of Overton County is *Muddy Pond,* a small Mennonite community that happens to be way off the beaten path. Entrance to the community is off Highway 164, about halfway between Crawford and Monterey, or off Highway 62, 1 mile west of Clarkrange. In either direction you'll have a nice paved road for several miles before the gravel road begins.

There are several retail shops located back here, and many of the farmers sell fresh eggs and bread out of their homes. A horse-powered mill, the *Muddy Pond Sorghum Mill,* creates the product and is where the owners also sell homemade bread and fried pies. The mill is open Tues, Thurs, and Sat 7 a.m. to 4 p.m. in Sept and Oct. The *Muddy Pond Variety Store* (931-445-3357) at 4064 Muddy Pond Rd. makes its own sorghum and carries produce and vegetables as well. The *Baken Haus* is a home-style bakery with great breads and pies; and the *Muddy Pond General Store* has sorghum, cheeses, meats, quilts, pottery, outdoor furniture, and a large variety of gift and household items. Most of the businesses are open Mon through Sat. Phone the Muddy Pond General Store at (931) 445-7829 for more information.

There are a great many houses, fences, walls, and buildings around Crossville made of the famous Crab Orchard stone—a brownish beige stone that is quarried along US 70 in the small community of Crab Orchard. The quarries are located along the north side of the highway and show years and years of mining operations.

Crab Orchard was a pioneer outpost in the 1700s, and those on a westward trek would stop here for a rest after going through the mountains

OTHER ATTRACTIONS WORTH SEEING

Creative Discovery Museum
321 Chestnut St.
Chattanooga
(423) 756-2738
cdmfun.org

Cumberland County Playhouse
221 Tennessee Ave.
Crossville
(931) 484-5000
ccplayhouse.com

IMAX 3-D Theater
1 Broad St.
Chattanooga
(800) 262-0695
tennesseeaquarium.com

Key Park Log House
Lafayette
(615) 666-5885
maconcountytn.com

Virgin Falls
Sparta
(931) 836-3552
sparta-chamber.net

and climbing onto the plateau. The crab apple trees were numerous, and the Indians caused no problems. It was a comfortable respite. In his 1985 novel, *Jubal Sackett,* Louis L'Amour wrote fondly of the area.

A few miles east on US 70 is the ***Ozone Falls Natural Area,*** where old-growth forests dominate. The highlight here is the magnificent 110-foot-high waterfall where Fall Creek cascades into the deep gorges below. How did it get its name? Local lore says that the area was named "Ozone" because of the "stimulating quality of the air" created by the mist that is generated when the water takes its long plunge. Park in the pull-out area along the highway, and you'll only have about a fifth of a mile walk to the top of the falls. Be very careful. There are no guardrails or railings. If you follow the path, you'll walk right over the edge! Also be wary of slippery stones that you might step on as you lean over to take a look. Nearby ***Cumberland Mountain State Park*** (931-484-6138) is in charge of the area.

Looking for some great cheddar cheese? ***Simonton's Cheese & Gourmet House*** (888-819-3226; simontonscheese.com), at 2280 Hwy. 127 South in Crossville, is known throughout this part of the country for its 3-pound hoop of cheddar, made from grade A milk. It's sold here along with other specialty cheeses, jams, jellies, teas, candies, and hams. They carry more than 60 domestic and imported cheeses in all! Simonton's Cheddar even has a cheer: "Red as an Apple, Yellow as Gold, I am Delicious, I am Told . . . TRY ME!" Simonton's is open Mon through Sat 9 a.m. to 5 p.m. and from Thanksgiving through Dec. 23 on Sun noon to 5 p.m.

Considered one of the South's top professional theater groups, the ***Cumberland County Playhouse*** (931-484-5000; ccplayhouse.com) is located here in Crossville. With two indoor stages and an outdoor amphitheater, the playhouse features professional theater in an unlikely rural setting and draws audiences from a great distance. Ticket prices range from $20 to $30 for adults for most shows. The theaters are located at 221 Tennessee Ave.

The ***Stonehaus Winery*** (931-484-9463; stonehauswinery.com) at 2444 Genesis Rd. offers free nitty-gritty tours daily with all aspects of the winemaking process shown. Unlike a lot of wineries, which give superficial tours, these guys take you from A to Z, from crushing to bottling—and of course they have a tasting counter. In the gift shop there is a large selection of local cheeses to choose from; in the deli they can rustle you up a great sandwich. However, if you want wine with that sandwich, you'll have to buy a bottle. They'll open it for you and give you a glass, but Tennessee

TOP ANNUAL EVENTS

JUNE

Defeated Creek Bluegrass Fest
Carthage
(615) 774-3230

Riverbend Festival
Chattanooga
180 Hamm Rd.
(423) 756-2211
riverbendfestival.com

JULY

Fiddler's Jamboree
Smithville
(615) 597-8500
smithvillejamboree.com

White Oak Mountain Bluegrass Festival
Cleveland
(423) 476-9310

AUGUST

Cherokee Days of Recognition
first weekend in Aug, Cleveland
(423) 478-0339

NOVEMBER

Christmas Parade
Last week of Nov, Cookeville
(800) 264-5541
mustseecookeville.com

law forbids them from serving it to you. Open Mon through Sat 9 a.m. to 5 p.m. and Sun noon to 5 p.m. Located at exit 320 off I-40.

The **Vanity Fair Outlet Mall** (931-484-7165; vfoutlet.com), located across I-40 from the Stonehaus Winery at 228 Interstate Dr., has enough shopping opportunities to keep you busy for hours.

South of Crossville, where Highways 127 and 68 split, is the planned community of **Homesteads.** The area, with its quaint little stone houses lining both highways, is often referred to as the "showplace of the New Deal."

In January 1934, following several years of hard times in the area, the local farm agent submitted an application to the government for one of the subsistence projects formulated by the Roosevelt administration. The application was accepted, and work began on the 10,000-acre project.

The plan was to build 250-plus homesteads, each of about 20 acres. The homesteaders were selected following a series of intense background checks and interviews of about 4,000 applicants. Cooperatives were established for the community, and family members went to these to make their families' mattresses, can their families' food, or weave at a loom house.

Today 218 of the 255 houses built are still standing. At the base of the 85-foot-tall octagonal tower that originally served as a water tower is a sandstone building that housed the administrative offices of the project. Today those offices serve as a museum depicting Roosevelt's homesteading project. If you want you can climb the 97 steps to the top of the tower.

Of the 102 New Deal projects nationwide, the **Cumberland Homesteads** (931-456-9663; cumberlandhomesteads.org) was considered one of the most successful of all. Open daily Mar through mid-Dec. A small admission is charged.

More information on Crossville, Crab Orchard, and the rest of Cumberland County can be found on the chamber of commerce's website, crossville-chamber.com, or call (877) 465-3861.

Cannon County is known throughout the state for the number of fine craftspeople it has within its borders. Just about every craft you can think of is created here by superb artists. From potters to folk artists to basket weavers to chair makers, a great many craftspeople call Cannon County home.

Unfortunately, many of the gifted craftspeople don't like you to visit their home workshops unless they know you, preferring instead to sell their crafts through various shops and at craft shows throughout the Southeast.

A directory listing more than 100 local craftspeople is available from the **Arts Center of Cannon County** (800-235-9073; artscenterofcc.com) in Woodbury.

The county's craftspeople come out in force for the local **White Oak Crafts Fair,** held in Sept. Artists from other counties are invited to participate as well, making this a wonderful place to buy items you won't find in too many other locales. The fair is held at the Arts Center of Cannon County on John Bragg Highway (US 70-S), 1 mile west of town.

Check statewide crafts show calendars, or write the Arts Center of Cannon County, 1424 John Bragg Hwy., Woodbury 37190.

soconfusing

Short Mountain in Cannon County is actually the highest point between the Ozarks and the Appalachian Mountains.

Up off Highway 96 at the very top of the county is the little community of **Auburntown,** which claims to have the "best little fish fry in the South." It is the social highlight of the area.

The local Lion's Club has been holding its fry the first Saturday of each month since 1978, when it was first put on as a way to raise money for the club. Since then it has become a tradition. They offer both deep-fried shrimp and Alaskan pollock, along with all the fixin's, for just $8 per person. Call Roger Turney for more information (615-464-5210).

The fry includes homemade hush puppies (worth the trip themselves), white beans, coleslaw, and iced tea and coffee. There's a huge repeat business from month to month from a 6-county area. It's a great place to catch up on all the gossip and to meet some great icons of rural America.

Several bed-and-breakfast facilities in the state are also bona fide tourist attractions, and **Evins Mill** (800-383-2349; evinsmill.com) in **Smithville** is one of them. James Lockhart built his mill on this spot in 1824 and had a burgeoning business through the late 19th century. Tennessee state senator Edgar Evins purchased the property in 1937, renamed it, and had a 4,600-square-foot lodge built on the bluff overlooking Fall Creek and the mill.

Today the lodge and the rustic cabins built along the bluff serve as a bed-and-breakfast. The restored mill, still with all its workings in place, is a full-service state-of-the-art conference center. The kitchen of the lodge has been turned into a modern operation with a full-time chef who provides lodging guests as well as conferencing business folks with gourmet meals. The huge stone fireplace and the original wood flooring add a neat, homey feeling to the environment. If you want someone else to do the cooking, this is a charming place to spend Thanksgiving Day! Roaring fire in the fireplace, good eating, and some great walking trails will help make the day a fun one for everyone! It's off US 70, 1.5 miles east of the junction of US 70 and Highway 56 at 1535 Evins Mill Rd.

The internationally famous *Old-Time Fiddler's Jamboree and Crafts Festival* (615-597-8500; smithvillejamboree.com) is held on the Smithville Square early each July, and for a country and Appalachian music fan, it's truly a piece of heaven. There are 28 categories of traditional music and dancing, including old-time bluegrass, clogging, buck dancing, old-time fiddle bands, five-string banjo, dulcimer, dobro, fiddling, and flat-top guitar, all for top prizes. The fiddle players have a fiddle-off to determine the grand champion fiddler. There are also seven categories for musicians under the age of 12. In 2013, a new category was added for old-time Appalachian folk singing. In addition there are more than 300 traditional crafts booths, food stands, and other great things to do and see. This is a great educational experience as well as a fun, unique event to visit. The festival is free.

Back when this part of the state was known as the New Frontier, the Wilderness Road (US 70) was the main route through the state, connecting the frontier settlements to the west and the more civilized areas to the east. The Rock House stagecoach inn and tollhouse were strategically built at the point where an early railroad connection crossed the trail. Built between 1835 and 1839 of Tennessee limestone, the inn soon became a gathering place for the *Who's Who* of the American frontier.

Preserved through the years by caring friends, this piece of Americana is now open to the public on a limited basis. The Rock House chapter of the Daughters of the American Revolution is the caretaker of the property, now known as the **Rock House Shrine** (931-836-3552) state historic area, located on US 70, 4 miles west of Sparta.

A somewhat brief but solemn and touching annual event takes place at **Edgar Evins State Park** (931-858-2446 or 800-250-8619; tnstateparks.com), 20 miles north of Smithville on Highway 96. A flag retirement ceremony is held on the Saturday before Memorial Day each year when the park rangers take down the American flag that has flown over the park's office and raise a new one. The local AMVETS and VFW posts come out and take part and provide the honor guard. It's a nice way to honor the veterans.

While you're here, check out the great southern-fried catfish at the *Galley* (931-858-5695) restaurant down at the park's marina. Located on Center Hill Reservoir, the restaurant is open daily Apr through Oct.

Cookeville, Putnam County's seat of government, had two early surges of commerce that resulted in two distinct downtown sections. The town had already established its square and business hub long before the railroads came through. When the rails came to town in 1890, they came through a residential area on the west side. That area soon became less residential and more commercial as business shifted from the established area around the courthouse to the new, prospering area around the depot. A large hotel was built, and warehouses and stores soon followed.

By 1910 a new passenger depot had been built, and the area was considered the Hub of the Upper Cumberland. Passenger service was terminated in 1955, but the locals were able to save the depot, which is now on the National Register of Historic Places and the site of the *Cookeville Depot Museum* (931-528-8570; cookevilledepot.com).

Inside is one of the best re-creations of an early depot in the state. Original fixtures, desks, time schedules, and the like have been preserved through the years. There are four rooms of exhibits, plus a caboose out back with more displays. Open Tues through Sat 10 a.m. to 4 p.m. Admission is free; its location is Broad and Cedar Streets at 116 W. Broad St.

Across the street from the museum, high atop an old dairy, you'll see a big, old-fashioned neon sign advertising Cream City Ice Cream. Atop the sign is a giant ice-cream sundae whose cherry bounces up and down (in

Fun-Filled Region

The region formed by the northern 14 counties in this area of the state is called the Upper Cumberland and is one of the most beautiful areas in the state for rolling hills, waterfalls, and foliage. A listing of sites, heritage trails, waterfalls, lakes, rivers, festivals, and accommodations can be found at uppercumberland.org. You can call the Tourism Association at (931) 537-6347.

neon) when the sign is turned on. The people who bought the location when the dairy closed chose not only to save but also restore the sign to its 1950s beauty. Now the sign is lit several times each year, much to the delight of local photographers and nostalgia buffs.

The streets are rolled back in Cookeville the first weekend after Labor Day each year. That's when the **Tennessee State Championship Barbeque Cook-off** and the **Downtown Fall Fun Fest** (931-528-4612; fallfunfest.com) run concurrently around the courthouse. The cook-off is a Kansas City Barbeque Society–sanctioned event and regularly draws 20 to 25 teams from several states. Some of the cooking teams will not only cook for competition but will also vend their products. These, of course, are the teams you cheer on and hang with.

The Fall Fun Fest runs both days and features live entertainment on two stages with a big headline act on Saturday night. One stage is reserved for the local acts that specialize in blues, jazz, and the Latin beat. Along the streets are food vendors and a top-notch crafts fair sponsored by the Tennessee Association of Craft Artists, which holds its big festival in Nashville about 2 weeks later. The local PBS television station has a big presence on Saturday with entertainment on its own stage with PBS characters and storytellers. A couple dozen activity booths are set up for the kids. Considering everything there is to offer, this is one of the most fun-filled weekend events in the state.

Attention, all candy lovers: The **Russell Stover** candy factory, located on Chocolate Drive in Cookeville, also has an outlet store. A great selection of Russell Stover candies is offered at less than retail prices. There are three levels of prices: The first quality level is the exact candy you'd buy at a retail store, but for a little less. The intermediate level is for overstocked items that exceed the company's strict peak of freshness standard but are still of top quality. The seconds are imperfectly shaped or are lacking the standards necessary for them to be included in regular packaging. (Yes, they do give out free samples.) The **Russell Stover Candies Factory and Outlet Store** (931-526-8424; russellstover.com) is open daily 9 a.m. to 6 p.m. Take the Cookeville/Algood exit off Highway 111, 3 miles north of I-40, and turn toward Cookeville. Almost immediately take a right onto Chocolate Drive. The store is on your left about 0.5 mile down the road.

Looking for some truly off-the-beaten-path, funky, laid-back outdoor fun? Cookeville's **Hidden Hollow** (931-526-4038; hiddenhollowpark.com) fills that bill. The place is hard to explain and is certainly something you don't see every day. Back in 1972 Arda Lee retired in order to live out his childhood dream and transformed an old, 86-acre discarded farm into a fun place to picnic. Among its offerings now are a small petting zoo with rabbits, goats, chickens, ducks, and other birds; a dandy beach complete with kiddie swimming pool; and cane-pole fishing in the pond.

Lee died in 2004 at the age of 88. With his death, the future of the park was in question and the property went up for auction a few years later. Vince and Amanda Taylor stopped by the auction, although they had no intention of buying anything. However, when the bidding started, something got into the couple. Some say it was fate. For whatever reason, the Taylors raised their bid paddle and suddenly the property was theirs.

The couple, along with their two sons, Skylar and Dalton, work hard to maintain Lee's tradition and vision. When October rolls around, Vince begins the tedious task of stringing lights around the property for the holidays. The Taylors are at the park every night from Thanksgiving through New Year's Day, replacing bulbs and making sure all is bright. In a move to save money on electricity, Vince is in the process of changing the old incandescent-style bulbs to LEDs.

Hidden Hollow also has a gingerbread house for the kids to play in, a covered bridge, a waterwheel, a wedding chapel, rock gardens, and fountains. Located at 1901 Mount Pleasant Rd., Hidden Hollow is open daily year-round. Admission is $4 adults, children and seniors $3; swimming and cane-pole fishing are each $1 extra.

There's definitely artistic magic in a remote hollow in the beautiful hills of northern Jackson County. About 3.3 miles west of Whitleyville, along Highway 56, you'll find North Fork Lane. If you follow that gravel road for about a mile, you'll discover the hideaways of two nationally known potters: Tom and Sally Freestone of Freestone Pottery.

Tom and Sally moved here from New England in 1986 and established **Freestone Pottery** (401-647-1939; freestonepottery.com) at 707 N. Fork Ln. They had met in early 1985, got married, and decided to start a new life and lifestyle in Tennessee. Tom, an Englishman, was a well-known gristmiller and had earned a reputation for restoring old mills throughout England. Sally was a potter and an art teacher. They both are now full-time potters and can barely keep up with their orders.

They specialize in functional pottery, and what makes their stuff so unique is that each piece has a short Bible verse on it. "They are all happy love and faith verses. None of this doom, gloom, and damnation for us," Sally says with a smile, adding that this work combines her three loves: clay, comforting and inspiring words, and God. Their property, which houses their showroom, home, and studio, has a waterfall and a lot of room to "come on out and have a picnic," Tom adds.

Gainesboro is the seat of Jackson County and has several antiques stores on the main square in the downtown area. It also has two drugstores, **Anderson & Haile Drugs** (931-268-2183) at 101 E. Gore Ave. and **Gainesboro Drugs** (931-268-9919) at 100 E. Hull Ave., which still have the old-fashioned soda fountains in operation.

If you think marbles are just for kids, then you haven't met the gang of marble players in **Celina.** For the group of dedicated players around here, the simple ring marble game is unheard of. What they play in "these here" parts is called Rolley Hole.

The game is a team sport, played on a 40-by-20-foot field called a marble yard. There are three holes evenly spaced down the middle. The object of the game is for each team of two to get their marbles into each hole in succession, down the court, back and down again, three times.

The top players make their own marbles or buy them from other local players. The best of the best was Dumas Walker, who died in 1991. He was the world champion Rolley Hole player, and people would come from miles to watch him play. If that name sounds familiar, the old marble player was saluted in a popular 1990 song by The Kentucky Headhunters.

In his memory the **National Rolley Hole Marble Tournament** (931-823-6347) is held each Sept in conjunction with the county's Homecoming Day celebration. Players from other Rolley Hole hotbeds, namely, Kansas City and parts of New Jersey and Kentucky, come to Celina to compete in that tourney. The national championships are held at the nearby Standing Stone State Park. Several English players usually show up for that one as well.

The **Dale Hollow National Fish Hatchery** (931-243-2443), just north of Celina on Highway 53, produces yearly about 300,000 pounds of 9-inch rainbow trout, which are used to restock public waterways. They also hatch and ship about 500,000 fingerlings each year.

Most of the public waterways in the Southeast are too warm for trout to breed, hence the need for this facility. Trout fishing is allowed and encouraged on most dam and river sites owned by the government, so periodic restocking is necessary.

The hatchery offers self-guided tours, but there are plenty of workers around to answer any questions. The long greenhouse-type building is where the eggs are hatched, and then the small trout are taken outside to spend the rest of their time here in one of the more than 100, 8-by-100-foot concrete raceways.

Feeding times, early morning and late afternoon, are probably the best times to visit. The larger fish are fed food pellets from a truck. A certain amount of food drops down onto a base and then is blown across the water by a current of air. The smaller fish are fed by hand. Open every day year-round; admission is free.

During the first half of the 20th century, **_Red Boiling Springs_** was a bustling health and vacation resort known for its medicinal waters. The resort enjoyed its heyday in the years between the world wars, when as many as six large hotels and 10 boardinghouses were in business. Today the spa resort feeling hasn't totally vanished. The springs are still here, as are three of the hotels, and you can still get a mineral-water bath. A major flood

What the Heck Is Poke Sallet?

There are only three **poke sallet** festivals in the US, and downtown Gainesboro is home to one of them. That distinction is something to be proud of, even though this is basically a festival to celebrate a weed. Poke sallet grows wild in the South and is cooked the same as (and tastes something like) turnip and mustard greens. Events that you won't want to miss include the poke sallet–eating contest, continuous country music, and the outhouse races. (No, not a race to the outhouse, but rather a race of outhouses.) The terrapin (turtle) races are also a highlight. Found locally in the countryside, the terrapins are placed in a circle by up to 60 contestants, and the first turtle to cross the outer line of the circle wins. There are also crosscut saw contests, a hay bale roll, and the Miss Poke Sallet Festival contest. It has been held during early May each year for about 25 years; proceeds from the festival fund the Rescue Squad. Their number is (931) 268-0971, or you can visit pokesalletfest.com.

in the 1960s wiped out much of the old-time charm, but the community has rebuilt and has restored much of that ambience.

Brenda Thomas realized back in the early 1990s that Red Boiling Springs still had a life to it and that some of the charm and history of the area could be brought back. She and her husband, Bobby, both born and raised in the area, bought and renovated *Armour's Red Boiling Springs Hotel* (615-699-2180; armourshotel.com), built in 1924 at 321 E. Main St. In the fall of 1999, Reba and Laban Hilton visited the inn and decided they wanted to own it. Then in 2008 Dennis and Debra Emery became the owners of this charming piece of Americana. They were quick to assure us that nothing has changed and all the atmosphere that Brenda Thomas created is still there—along with a total renovation to make the hotel even more lovely. There are 16 rooms, including 2 suites, all with private baths. Rates are $49 single, $69 double, and $115 for suites (2 persons). Rates also are available for a full country breakfast; dinner is available for an additional $14 per person, plus tax. A treatment consisting of a steam bath, mineral bath, and 30-minute massage is $79; $99 with a 60-minute massage; $79 for a 60-minute massage only; and $35 for steam room and mineral bath only.

Just down the street at 520 E. Main St. is a 2-story brick hotel, the *Thomas House* (615-699-3006; thomashousehotel.com). Owned by Evelyn Thomas Cole, who was born and raised in the area, the hotel differs in style from the others in that it has a courtyard and a European feel to it.

This historic hotel was ravaged by fire in 2001 and was closed during much of the renovation. Now there are 14 rooms back in operation, as are the kitchen and dining room. The Thomas House has the only swimming pool in town, and Sun from 11 a.m. to 2 p.m., the dining room is open to the public for an all-you-can-eat buffet—with no reservations required. Lunch and dinner are served family style, Mon through Sat, reservations required.

This town was famous for four types of water: black, red, double and twist, and free stone. Each is quite different in its mineral analysis, and each was considered a "cure" for different ailments. A self-guided tour brochure of the area is available at the small log cabin visitor center on E. Main Street.

Over in *Lafayette,* the county seat, you don't have to have a map to find the biggest loafers in the county. On any fair-weather day, be it in January or June, you'll find a group of men of indeterminate age sitting under an old oak tree on the southeast side of the Macon County Public Square.

With knives in hand, these whittlers have become part of small-town life around here. The chamber of commerce likes them because of their almost unlimited knowledge of the area. But you don't have to have kin in the area to ask after; just walk right up and start talking with them. Of course you'll always walk away wondering whether the directions they gave you will really take you where you want to go or whether these good ole boys have played another trick on a city slicker.

Al Gore is from the small town of **Carthage,** the county seat of historic Smith County. A good way to start your visit in this area is to stop by the **Smith County Welcome Center** (615-683-6410), located in a log cabin at mile marker 267 on I-40, in a rest area just east of the Carthage exit. It's 60 miles east of Nashville and is accessible from both east- and westbound traffic. Inside, you'll find plenty of printed information, plus people who not only know the area but knew Al Gore as a young boy who loved showing his cattle at the county fair. If the weather's cold, sit a spell in the rocking chairs in front of the fireplace; if the weather's nice, take a short walk down to Caney Fork River. It's a pleasant setting.

In downtown Carthage, the circa 1879 courthouse is a must-see. Built in the Second Empire architectural style, the building has undergone extensive renovation and is now listed on the National Register of Historic Places. A lot more history is alive and well in Carthage, including the old city cemetery and the circa 1889 Carthage United Methodist Church. The church has amazing stained-glass windows, with several dating back to when the church was built.

In 1936 the **Cordell Hull Bridge** replaced an old toll bridge. Named for the former secretary of state of the US, who served under President Franklin D. Roosevelt, the bridge's unique steel grid work makes it not only an interesting sight but also a great place from which to view the river valley.

Upriver about 5 miles from Carthage, the 12,000-acre **Cordell Hull Lake** (615-735-1023) was built by the US Army Corps of Engineers primarily for navigation, hydropower generation, and recreation. Construction began in 1963, and the lake was fully functional in 1973. The power plant visitor center is open every day Memorial Day through Labor Day. It's located on Highway 263 north of Carthage. There are 11 access areas to the lake with boat ramps, and there are eight different recreation areas, some with camping.

On Highway 25, about halfway to Hartsville, is **Dixon Springs.** It was founded by Revolutionary War major Tilman Dixon on a military land grant. There are many of the area's original homes still standing, including Dixonia, the home of Major Dixon, now a private residence. The **Smith County Chamber of Commerce** (615-735-2093) can provide more information on the area.

If Civil War history fascinates you, here's an unusual chance to find out quite a bit about General John Hunt Morgan and the Battle of Hartsville. A 17-stop self-guided tour of Hartsville starts at the site where General Morgan, known as the **Thunderbolt of the Confederacy,** crossed the Cumberland River with his troops the night of Dec. 6, 1862, and ends at the Hartsville Cemetery, where more than 50 Confederate soldiers are buried.

The general and his men seized the *Hartsville Vidette* newspaper while raiding the town, and they ended up publishing it themselves when they could find the opportunity and paper. The newspaper still publishes and still bears that historic name. The tour brochure is available from the **Hartsville** chamber of commerce (615-374-9243; hartsvilletrousdale.com), 200 E. Main St., Ste. 111.

Middle Cumberland

It's hard to believe that **Dayton,** a small city 40 miles north of Chattanooga, was probably a household word from coast to coast during the long, hot summer of 1925. That's when the silver-tongued orators William Jennings Bryan and Clarence Darrow engaged in a legal battle in the Rhea County Courthouse. The Scopes "Monkey Trial" let the world know that a Dayton outside of Ohio actually did exist. Although John Scopes, a schoolteacher, didn't reach the heights that the Wright brothers of the other Dayton did, he earned himself a place in history.

The Romanesque Revival, Italian Villa-style courthouse was built in 1891 and has been restored to its 1925 vintage. The Scopes trial courtroom is on the second floor and contains the original judge's bench, four tables, railing, jury chairs, and spectator seats.

The **Rhea County Museum** (423-775-7801; rheacounty.com) is housed in the courthouse and contains exhibits, photos, and actual newsreel footage of what many still call the first major trial treated as a media event.

Scopes was accused of teaching the Darwinian theory of evolution to a high school biology class in violation of a recently passed Tennessee statute making it unlawful "to teach any theory that denies the story of the divine creation of man as taught in the Bible."

Scopes wasn't even the school's regular biology teacher, but a math teacher filling in. He was fined $100, a fee he never paid. The museum is open Mon through Fri 9 a.m. to 5 p.m. admission is free.

The **Scopes Trial Play and Festival** (423-775-9847; scopesfestival.org) take place each summer in mid-July when a special drama is acted out in the courtroom where the trial took place. A crafts fair, an antique car show, and traditional music are all a part of the festival. Of course there's plenty of great southern cooking available as well.

Like strawberries? If so, plan your visit to the Dayton area during the first or second week of May. That's when the annual **Strawberry Festival** (423-570-0105; tnstrawberryfestival.com) takes place, featuring the "World's Longest (line of people eating) Strawberry Shortcake" and 3 days of eclectic fun.

Other events include a carnival midway full of rides, various sports tournaments, an arts and crafts show, and a music festival.

An unlikely resident of the wonderfully named Soddy Daisy, Tennessee, is the **Horsin' Around Carving School** (423-332-1111; horsin-around.net) at 8361A Dayton Pike. Owner and chief carver Bud Ellis teaches classes, does historic carousel restoration, and enjoys talking about his art. He'll give you a free tour of the place—and for only $1,250 to $1,650, you can sign up, take a course in carving, and bring home your own carousel horse. The brass ring is extra.

Ellis is responsible for the restoration and the horse carving on the Coolidge Park Carousel, next to the Walnut Street Bridge in Chattanooga. The carving school is located behind the Wal-Mart at the Soddy Daisy exit off US 27 North, 14 miles north of the Tennessee River.

Out on Highway 30 is the small community of **Meigs,** the county seat of Decatur, where a historic town square will attract your attention. Unlike many of the older courthouse squares, this one is a bit barren and free of large trees.

But in the shadow of the courthouse, you'll find the area's version of the **Spit and Whittle Gang,** a bunch of old-timers who gather each day to—well, you guessed it.

When you've worked up an appetite, stop at **Uncle Gus's Mountain Pit Bar B Q** (423-334-2487) at 810 Peakland Rd., open Tues through Sat. Uncle Gus's features pulled pork, brisket, fried pickles, homemade potato salad, and peach cobbler. Breakfast also is served.

In **Athens,** just off Highway 30, rests **Tennessee Wesleyan College** (423-745-7504; twcnet.edu), a liberal arts school established in 1857. The first building on campus, appropriately called the "Old College" building, is still standing and up until 1989 housed the county's heritage museum.

The structure, built in 1854 and also used as a hospital during the Civil War, faces the quad grounds of the school. Behind Old College on Dwain Farmer Drive, you'll find a marker explaining one of the most poignant legends in Tennessee history.

A wounded English officer from nearby Fort Loudoun was befriended by an Indian chief and nursed back to health by Nocatula, daughter of the chief. The soldier, given the name of Connestoga (the oak), was accepted into the tribe and married Nocatula. A jealous suitor attacked Connestoga with a knife. As he lay dying, Nocatula confessed her eternal love for him and plunged a knife into her breast.

The pair were buried together, and the chief placed an acorn in Connestoga's hand and a hackberry in Nocatula's hand, symbolizing undying love. From these there developed two trees that grew intertwined on this spot for more than 150 years.

After these two original trees died in 1957, two others were planted. Those have since died, and today the stumps are all that remain.

The **McMinn County Living Heritage Museum** (423-745-0329; livingheritagemuseum.com) is located in Athens's old high school building, about a half mile from downtown at 522 W. Madison Ave. The museum's collection of 19th- and 20th-century quilts is one of the finest in the state. In addition to the permanent display of quilts, a nationally known quilt show is hosted by the museum each year. Check to see when it will be held, as it varies from year to year.

There is also a great children's collection that includes china and bisque-head dolls, toys, and clothing, along with school desks, books, and maps dating from 1850. Admission is charged; open daily except Sun.

The **Mayfield Dairy** (423-745-2151 or 800-362-9546; mayfielddairy.com) at 4 Mayfield Ln. has been serving the folks in this part of the state for more than a century with fresh milk products and some of the best ice cream you've ever wrapped your tongue around. The dairy now offers fun tours, which conclude at a gift shop and dairy bar where you can sample (for a price) some of the products you saw being made.

The **Swift Museum Foundation** (423-745-9547; swiftmuseumfoundation.org) at 217 CR 552 is housed here at the McMinn County Airport, which is also the Swift Aircraft international headquarters. The small planes with the home-built feel to them were first built in Texas in the mid-1940s and today have quite a fanatic following. You can learn the history and see a few of the planes at the airport, but if you really want to get a big dose of them, drop by in June each year. That's when the annual **Swift Fly-In** takes place, usually attracting more than 100 aircraft.

Out on CR 52, 8 miles west of I-75 at 198 CR 52, Dave and Vicki Rhyne make "fruitcakes for people who don't like fruitcakes." Really, that's their slogan. Dave told me his pecan fruitcakes don't have the raisins or citrus peel that the others do and that his contain 25 percent pecans by weight. Their **Sunshine Hollow Bakery and Exhibition Gardens** (423-745-4289 or 800-669-2005; sunshinehollow.com) pumps out about 10,000 pounds of the holiday treat each year.

When they aren't making fruitcakes, they are out in their greenhouse hybridizing daylilies and hostas. The farm is also home to National Daylily and Hosta exhibition gardens. Right now they grow and sell about 800 varieties of daylilies and 200 varieties of hostas. They sell them at the farm as well as by mail order. They have a 2.5-acre shade garden and a 7-acre daylily garden, displaying many of their varieties. For 5 weekends in June and July, visitors can enjoy the Daylily Bloom Festival and receive a free daylily. The store sells other items as well, including pecan pralines, chocolate-covered pecans, jams, and jellies. Admission is free.

At the turn of the 20th century, the site of present-day Etowah on US 411 was muddy farmland. Then news came that the Louisville and Nashville Railroad (known as the L&N) was to build a new line between Cincinnati and Atlanta. The land was purchased to build a rail center. A boomtown named Etowah soon sprang up, and the **L&N Depot** was built in 1906. It became the community's central point from which social, economic, and cultural activities evolved for many years.

By 1974, passenger travel had declined to the point that the depot was abandoned and sat empty until the town purchased it in 1978. It was restored and placed on the National Register of Historic Places. It now houses a railroad museum that examines what it meant to be a railroad town in the "New South."

You've never seen a railroad depot like this one! As you drive up, the elegant Victorian structure looks more like a hotel or an elegant private home than a railroad depot. It's made of yellow pine and has 15 rooms. The depot is also home to the Depot Gift Shop, but the building itself is the star here.

The grounds around the depot remain a community gathering spot and are the site of several fairs, festivals, and weddings during the year, including a popular old-time July Fourth celebration. The train yard is still active and can provide rail buffs a fun time watching all the switching and maneuvering. You'll find it on US 411 in downtown **Etowah** (423-263-2228; etowahcoc.org).

The city fathers of Etowah have also purchased the circa 1918 **Gem Theater** (423-263-3270; gemplayers.com) and are restoring it to its cultural splendor. At one time the Gem was considered the largest privately owned theater in East Tennessee. Today it has a full schedule of live stage presentations at its 700 Tennessee Ave. location.

There aren't too many museums around that spotlight women in industry, but in the little village of Englewood you'll find such a place. This area of the state is unusual in that it was built on textile manufacturing, the one Appalachian industry that employed large numbers of women. The **Englewood Textile Museum** (423-887-5455) traces the area's textile industry from 1850. Exhibits present examples of different textiles and machinery from 1890 and emphasize the role of working-class women in the mills, their home life, and their role in the development of the community. Located at 17 Niota St., the museum is open Mon through Sat noon to 5 p.m. There is free admission, but help them out by throwing a couple bucks in their donation bucket.

Adjacent to the Textile Museum is **The Company Store,** an antiques and "attic treasures" store. Local crafts and gift items are also available.

Southwest Cumberland

In *Tracy City* US 41, you'll find *Henry Flury and Sons* (931-592-5661) general store, which has had "staple and fancy groceries" for sale since 1905. The proprietors like to call their little establishment the "living museum of mountain life and the gathering place for friends."

Henry Flury and his three sons are all gone now, but Paul Flury, Henry's grandson, runs the store. "I guess you could say I'm the last of the Mohicans," he laughs.

Along with the groceries the store offers fresh meats, hoop cheese, produce, deli sandwiches, deli trays, and hand-dipped ice cream. Call ahead and they'll pack a picnic for you. The old wooden floors and the high ceilings are just what you would think you'd find in a store like this. Feed bags hang from the ceiling, baskets line the top shelves, and old-time items are sitting around the shop. The local folk use the store as a handicraft outlet for their homemade products.

Stay on US 41 and head to *Monteagle,* where, just across I-24 on US 64/41A at 850 W. Main St. you'll find one of the best places for pit barbecue and hickory-smoked meats in the state. *Jim Oliver's Smokehouse* (800-489-2091; thesmokehouse.com) complex offers a great country store, meeting rooms, a lodge, a motel, cabins, a wedding chapel, and his famous restaurant. In all, he has 20 acres full of all sorts of things to do. The motel's swimming pool is a sight in itself; it's in the shape of a ham.

letmomvote

Women today can thank the state of Tennessee for helping them get their right to vote. It was the state's ratification in 1920 that added the 19th Amendment to the Constitution, giving women the vote.

If you're heading toward Monteagle, make plans to stay at the *Edgeworth Inn* (931-924-4000; edgeworthinn.com), located on the grounds of the historic Monteagle Assembly at 19 Wilkins Ave. The inn, owned and operated by Jeanine Clements, is a first-class, 10-bedroom bed-and-breakfast. Built as a boardinghouse in 1896, the structure has been completely renovated to its Victorian splendor and offers guests a respite from the real world. The owner accepts pets and children. Rooms start at $125.

Grundy County is gaining a national reputation as a mountain crafts center thanks to several artisans whose works are known and in demand from coast to coast. Many of these craftspeople have settled in the center of the county and have established homes and local ties.

On the other side of Beersheba Springs, Phil and Terri Mayhew live and work in an 1850s log cabin. Phil's work with high-fired, functional porcelain pottery is represented by 10 galleries in 12 states. Terri creates porcelain and hand-wrought silver jewelry. Phil, a former arts professor, has developed a porcelain that will fuse at a higher temperature, thus making it more durable and giving it a unique color range.

Although they do some shows and are still represented by some of the country's finest galleries, Phil and Terri do about half of their business out of their home. **Beersheba Porcelain** (931-692-2280; beershebaporcelain.com) has no showroom, no fancy gallery, just a lot of great art. In the warmer months they'll have stuff on the front porch; the rest of the year, "we kinda sleep and eat around our business" in the house, Phil said.

The Mayhew cabin is in the historic district, just off Highway 56. They have a small sign out front, so you'll have to look hard or you might miss it. If you do, drop by the **Beersheba Springs Market** at 19564 TN 56 (931-692-3314), the only store in town, and the friendly folk there will direct you to the Mayhews.

Beersheba Springs was a bustling resort area during the last half of the 1800s, and its grand hotel, which was built in 1850, is still standing. Down the road a couple of blocks from the Mayhews, the building is now owned by the United Methodist Church and used as a summer meeting facility. The view from the front of the hotel is nothing less than breathtaking.

When the hotel was active, stagecoaches would stop at the foot of the mountain and sound a horn once for each guest they had aboard for the hotel. By the time they reached the top, the hotel's band was ready to greet them. Dinner and a clean room had also been prepared.

The **Beersheba Springs Arts & Crafts Fair** (931-692-3691) takes place on the hotel grounds each Aug and is considered one of the best shows in this part of the state. The setting alone sets this show apart from most of the rest.

Cumberland Caverns (931-668-4396; cumberlandcaverns.com), located about 7 miles southeast of McMinnville just off Highway 8 at 1437

Howdy, Y'all Welcome

There's plenty of mountain hospitality at the annual **Mountaineer Folk Festival** at Fall Creek Falls State Park. Handmade mountain crafts, traditional mountain music, country cooking, bluegrass music, and pioneer skills demonstrations are plentiful. The festival is held in early Sept, so it's a great time to stock up on genuine Tennessee mountain-made Christmas gifts. At Highways 111 and 30, west of Pikeville. Call (423) 881-5708.

Cumberland Caverns Rd., is the second largest cavern system in the US, after Kentucky's Mammoth Cave, and is a US National Landmark. Unless you happen to be an expert in this sort of thing, most of the tour through the cave reminds you of just about any other cave journey.

One room here, however, is impressive no matter what your interests are. The Underground Ballroom is 600 feet long, 150 feet wide, and 140 feet high. It is the largest cave room east of the Mississippi River. The room's man-made amenities are built alongside the natural formations. Of these constructed features, the most amazing is the dining room, which will seat 500 for a banquet. High above the tables is a 15-foot, 1,500-pound chandelier from a theater in Brooklyn, New York. And all this is more than 300 feet below the hustle and bustle of the real world!

Falcon Rest (931-668-4444; falconrest.travel.com), in McMinnville, is both an elegant bed-and-breakfast and a tourist attraction. In fact, owners Charlien and George McGlothin had so many requests for tours of the house that they now offer daily ones from 9 a.m. to 5 p.m. for $12 for adults and $6 for children. The hour-long tour, peppered with local color and anecdotes, is a great way to learn the history of this magnificent Queen Anne–Victorian mansion, built in 1897 by entrepreneur Clay Faulkner for his wife, Mary.

Faulkner promised Mary that he would build her the finest house in Warren County if she would move next to their woolen mill, then 2.5 miles from town. She agreed, and a year later the couple moved in with their five children. In 1946 the 10,000-square-foot mansion was converted into a hospital and nursing home. By the mid-1950s the building had been added onto and named the Faulkner Springs Hospital. Today bloodstains can still be seen on the floor in a couple of spots, and the nursing station now houses some of the modern kitchen equipment.

In his tour of the house, George proudly points out that this was the first house built with central heat and air-conditioning in the county and that its foundation goes 17 feet below ground to solid bedrock. George was born and raised locally, and his sister was born in this house when it was a hospital. As a bed-and-breakfast, the mansion offers 4 guest rooms on the grounds of the mansion. Rooms are lavishly furnished with period antiques and private baths. No guest rooms are inside the mansion. Rates start at $105 per room, per night, with a full breakfast. A honeymoon suite, complete with brass bed, has been built in the old kitchen. The house next door has been added to the complex and now serves as a visitor center with a large Victorian gift shop, a tearoom, a Jacuzzi suite, and a wedding chapel. Falcon Rest is off the US 70 bypass at 2645 Faulkner Springs Rd.

Warren County, for which McMinnville serves as county seat, is known as the ***Nursery Capital of the World.*** More than 500 commercial nurseries throughout the county produce trees, shrubs, and plants, many of which are located along the major highways and provide miles of flowering beauty for you to observe as you drive along. Several of the nurseries are open for tours; some have small retail outlets. For a listing of those open to the public, contact the chamber of commerce at (931) 473-6611 or warrentn.com.

Of Forests & Rivers

If you happen to be in this part of the state and are tired of beautiful, lush mountains and forests, trek on over to the ***Ducktown*** area, a portion of the state often referred to as ***Tennessee's Badlands.*** Here you won't be surrounded by lush, green vegetation. In fact, you'll be surrounded by a 56-square-mile area of barren red hills, stunted pine trees, and washed-out gullies. This area of raw landscape is similar in looks to the famed badlands area of the Dakotas.

The story about this area, known officially as the ***Copper Basin*** area of Tennessee, Georgia, and North Carolina, is a fascinating tale of hard work and inadvertent destruction of the environment. The area is steeped in the history of copper mining. Copper was first discovered in 1843 near Potato Creek, between Ducktown and Copperhill, and by 1860 copper mining was in full swing and dominated and dictated the lifestyle of the basin for generations until the last mine closed in 1987.

By the time the industry called it quits, there was a 56-square-mile area of denuded red hills shimmering with glowing colors ranging from soft pastels to dark copper hues. The area stood out because of the otherwise lush green of the Cherokee National Forest. From space, NASA photos show the area looking like a moonscape.

Through vigorous reforestation programs, most of the area now has some vegetation growing, and it will only be a matter of years before the Copper Basin blends in with the rest of the area. However, some historians are hoping to keep a part of the area barren as an example of their active copper mining heritage.

The copper mining story is told through numerous methods at the **Ducktown Basin Museum** (423-496-5778; ducktownbasinmuseum.com) on the Burra Burra Mine site at 212 Burra Burra St., now on the National Register of Historic Places. Founded in 1978, the museum sits on 17 acres that include the buildings, mining structures, and mechanical operations of the mine site just as they were when it went out of business. The state purchased the museum in 1988, making it the first state-owned historic industrial site.

This is a fascinating part of the state that few residents even know exists. It's also an industry that isn't much talked about in the state. Your visit here should begin at the museum. You'll learn about the industry, why the area looks as it does, why the social life was affected so drastically by the industry, and what part Native Americans played. You'll also get a chance to tour the mine site, but you are not permitted to go underground.

Hoist House held the equipment used to pull men and ore from the mines. This structure and the steam boiler building were two of the first edifices built at the turn of the 20th century by the Tennessee Copper Company. The museum is open Mon through Sat, year-round. Adults are charged $5; seniors, $4; children (ages 13–17) $2, and $1 for younger children (ages 12 and under).

In the quaint little village of Ducktown, around the corner from the museum at 318 Main St., is the **Company House Bed & Breakfast** (423-496-5634 or 800-343-2409; companyhousebandb.com). Built in 1850 by the mine company's doctor, the building has had a colorful past. After standing empty for nearly a decade, it was purchased by Margie Tonkin and Mike Fabian, who dove in and undertook 90 percent of the massive renovation project by themselves. That was 1994. "It took us 2 weeks just to figure out where to start and we did it one room at a time," Mike said. Now the structure is listed on the National Register of Historic Places.

Ask Tonkin and Fabian about the renovation and they'll pull out a volume of "before" and "after" photos that will astonish you. They'll also show you photos of the Italian Olympic whitewater team that stayed here during the Olympic trials that took place on the nearby *Ocoee River.*

The seven bedrooms, all with private baths, are named for area mines and are quite nice, as is the marvelous hearty breakfast the couple puts out every morning for their guests. All rooms are nonsmoking; well-behaved children over 12 years of age are welcome, Margie notes. Rates are from $89 to $99 per room for 2 adults.

A great many residential and industrial structures within the Copper Basin are listed on the National Register of Historic Places. More than 200 are listed as part of the *Copper Basin Historic District.* Along with Ocoee, *Copperhill,* across the Ocoee River from Georgia, was another major town during the copper days. It was the corporate headquarters for the Tennessee Copper Company in 1904 and still resembles the company town that it was.

The storefronts along Ocoee Street and the stone steps that lead to the houses on various levels of the hill above the town offer a glimpse of early life there. As in any company town, the workers lived at street level, closest to the factory or mine. Other employees lived farther up the hill in order of importance, most often with the president at the top so that he could

Rugged & Cool Counties

The *Tennessee Overhill Heritage Association* promotes the counties of McMinn, Monroe, and Polk, and there's plenty of cool stuff to promote in this southeast area of the state! This is where the best whitewater rafting and outdoor adventures take place. Plus, some of the most spectacular scenic drives in the state are here. The association has a great website at tennesseeoverhill.com where you can order all sorts of specialty brochures, or call (423) 263-7232.

overlook the entire operation. Many of those houses are still in use today and are a part of a walking tour of Copperhill's residential area. Maps are available throughout the town.

In 1911 the Grand Avenue Bridge was built across the Ocoee and connected the mining town of McCaysville, Georgia, with Copperhill. Take a walk across the bridge and look for the spot where you can stand with one foot in Tennessee and one in Georgia. Farther down US 64, between Ducktown and Cleveland, you'll find yourself driving along the Ocoee River, one of the top 10 whitewater rivers in the country. You'll also find numerous business establishments that will be more than happy to rent you a raft, canoe, or kayak so that you, too, can experience an adventure of a lifetime. The river is such a good area for whitewater events that it was chosen as the site of the whitewater competition in the 1996 Summer Olympics, held in nearby Atlanta.

The *Ocoee Whitewater Center* (423-476-9700; r8web.com/ocoee), a few miles northwest from Ducktown along US 64, was the site of the 1996 Olympic Slalom Canoe/Kayak events and following the games became a visitor center and a hub for both land- and water-based recreation activities in the Cherokee Forest and Ocoee River areas.

Now open to the public, the center houses a gift shop, the Olympic Legacy exhibit, and a conference center. Open daily 9 a.m. to 5 p.m. during spring, summer, and fall; Fri through Sun in Nov through Apr.

Outside, a native flower garden and a magnificent pond have been created. A path has been built along the whitewater channel where the races took place, and you can hike or bike the Old Copper Road, a section of which has been restored adjacent to the center.

A walk along the 2.4-mile-long section of the *Old Copper Road* takes you across four footbridges from the 1850s era. Built in 1851, the 33-mile-long road was used to haul copper ore from the mines in Ducktown to the railhead in Cleveland. Most of the original section was destroyed when the adjacent US 64 was built in the 1930s, and this is the only original section still intact. Along the road you'll find an abundance of flora and fauna. Take time to go out on the deck overlooking a beaver pond. Neat place!

If you're not of the adventurous variety or don't have the time, there are several pull-offs where you can experience the danger and the excitement of the whitewater vicariously. The mostly 2-lane road is very busy here, so be careful to exit the road completely before you take in the beauty.

If you do choose to be adventurous (and you really should), a good place to stop is the **Ocoee Adventure Center** (888-723-8622; ocoeeadventure center.com), at 4651 Hwy. 64, 3 miles east of the Ocoee Whitewater Center. The proprietor of this outpost worked the river for decades for other people. When he decided to go off on his own, he brought along some of the best river guides in the area.

You'll get a lesson on how to best combat the whitewater adventure awaiting you, then you'll be told how you must respect the river itself. "It's a wild, unpredictable ride, and you must be ready to handle everything. This is not an amusement park ride," our guide told us.

With life jackets and helmets in place, you'll climb aboard a school bus for a 4-mile trip down to the river's entry point. There you'll be launched for one great ride through areas of the river with such ominous names as Grumpy's Ledge, Hell's Hole, Tablesaw, and Double Trouble. The cost here and at most outfitters along the river usually depends on the day of the week you choose for your trip, with Sat during peak season costing approximately $49 for a half-day journey. It's $45 per person Sun through Fri. No one under 12 years of age is permitted.

Look closely through the trees on the other side of the river and you'll see the largest wooden flume known to exist in the US. The **Ocoee Flume** is 5 miles long, 11 feet wide, and 14 feet tall. Originally built in 1912 by the Tennessee Valley Authority (TVA), it was closed for a few years in the late 1970s and then rebuilt.

Its major function is to divert water from the river to help produce hydroelectric power, but it has also been a savior of the river for the whitewater aficionados. With the diversion the flume creates, the TVA can produce their power and the river can still run to the point of whiteness.

The **Webb Bros. Float Service** in Reliance, along the Hiwassee Scenic River at 3708 TN 30, is not only a professional outfitter, but the **Webb Brothers Store** (423-338-2373 or 877-932-7238), in which it is located, is a fun and funky general store to visit.

If it's a peaceful, easy journey down a scenic river you're looking for, this is your place. They rent 1- or 2-passenger rubber "duckies" that are self-bailing and hard to flip over. Resembling a kayak, they rent for $27 per person, including the 5-mile trip up the river where you're dropped off. You then paddle and float the current back downriver and get out at the store, where you began your journey.

The trip can be direct, or you can stop and swim, rest, or just sit and watch the other boats go by. If you like, pack your lunch and take it along. This is a great first river adventure for smaller children and the weak at heart, and it's a beautiful journey as well.

In addition to its river services, the store sells groceries, prepared foods, snacks, gasoline, and just about anything else you'll need while you're in the area. The store, built in 1955, also serves as the town museum and has photos and memorabilia of early *Reliance.* Entry is free.

The Webbs is a good starting place for your tour of the *Reliance Historic District,* listed on the National Register of Historic Places. You can pick up information and quite a few stories about the area that will make your visit a lot more fun. The district, off Highway 30 along the river, has five principal buildings, including a hotel and the first house to have indoor plumbing. None of the restored structures are open to the public on a regular basis, but they are beautiful to look at. The area is still quite under-developed, so a drive through can give you a good idea of what life was like along the river at the turn of the 20th century.

For a spectacular view of the Hiwassee River, you'll want to walk all or part of the *John Muir Trail,* a 20-mile-long path that meanders along the river. Not only are the views of the river fantastic, but you'll also see a tremendous amount of wildlife and native plants. Watch for the beaver activity all along the trail. In addition you'll have the opportunity to view ruby-throated hummingbirds, mink, raccoons, and great blue herons. What are those things sunning themselves on the flat rocks in the river? Chances are they are North America's largest salamander, the hellbender.

The trail begins at Childers Creek, near Reliance (follow the signs), and ends near Highway 68 at Farner. If you have your entire family to watch out for, you might want to stick to the first 3-mile section of the trek; it has been designated as an easy walk but still covers some beautiful terrain.

Mention mountain forests and fantastic views, and most people think of the Smoky Mountains. That's why the 620,000-acre *Cherokee National Forest* (423-338-3300) here in the southeast portion of the state remains virtually untouched by crowds. Admission is $3 per vehicle.

More than 1,100 miles of roads have been cut through the dense forest, opening up all sorts of opportunities for outdoor enthusiasts or for those who simply enjoy driving and looking. Take your time; there's a real good chance that no one will be honking and trying to get around you. The Forest Service maintains 29 camping areas, horse trails (bring your own horse), and 105 hiking trails. This area is every bit as beautiful as the Smokies, making it a great alternative that most locals are hesitant to tell too many people about. The supervisor's office can give you more specifics; call (423) 476-9700.

When you're in *Cleveland* you're deep in Cherokee country, and history abounds. This was the geographic center for Native American culture in the Southeast, and there are reminders of that fact throughout the city and county.

The historical area of Cleveland is known as the Downtown Historic Greenway. Johnson Park, in the heart of downtown, is a great place to start a walking tour of the city. There are 20 different historic sites on the tour, including restored churches and buildings. While in Johnson Park, stop by and marvel at the *Cherokee Chieftain,* a wonderful sculpture of an Indian chief carved from a tree by internationally known Native American artist Peter Toth.

To get a better idea of the role the county played in the everyday life of the Cherokee, two self-guided tours have been developed. Maps and additional information are available at the *Cleveland Convention and Visitors Bureau* (800-472-6588; visitclevelandtn.com), at 225 Keith St. The Cherokee Heritage Wildlife Tour points out the best locations in the area to view wildlife and allows you to get a good feel for the Cherokee heritage. The Cherokee Scenic Loop Tour begins and ends in Cleveland and takes you throughout the county, where you'll visit many of the areas mentioned in this chapter, including Red Clay and the Ocoee River. Both maps offer a well-organized way to see the best the county and the region have to offer.

One of the state's most forward-looking historical museums is located in the 5ive Points area of downtown Cleveland. Opened in late 1999, the *Museum Center at 5ive Points* (423-339-5745; museumcenter.org) incorporates the *Cleveland Bradley Regional Museum* and the *Amanda T. Gray Cultural Center.*

Unlike most historical museums included on our off-the-beaten-path journey through Tennessee, this one merits a few words because of its

Celebrating Agriculture

The one-of-a-kind *Polk County Ramp Tramp Festival* takes place each year during the fourth week of April at Camp McCroy 4-H Camp in Greasy Creek, on Highway 30 south of Reliance. The day begins with a trip to Big Frog Mountain to dig, and then you come back to camp and cook and eat the ramps. A popular annual event since 1958, the festival features local bluegrass music along with your ramps. Call (423) 338-4503, or visit ramptrampfestival.com.

community-minded, contemporary mission. It's really much more about today than it is about yesterday, and it's way beyond your father's typical stuffy local museum. Hats off to you folks in Cleveland!

The museum center was created to fill four distinct community needs: Create a place to preserve heritage in order to give residents, children, and visitors a sense of the area's rich history; create a showcase for the entrepreneurial spirit that continues to fuel the community; create a cultural center to showcase the talents of residents; and create an anchor for the 5ive Points revitalization project.

Located at 200 Inman St. East, the center opens Tues through Sat at 10 a.m. Admission is $5 for adults, $4 for seniors and students; children under 5 are free.

If you're looking for some great food and want to have a little fun at the same time, head out to the *Apple Valley Orchard* (423-472-3044 or 877-472-3044; applevalleyorchard.com), 351 Weese Rd., 10 miles southeast of Cleveland. There you'll visit a farmers' market and bakery that offers a variety of foods. Fresh-baked apple goods don't get any better than this!

Apple Valley Orchard also has a lovely story about how it all began. During the early 1960s, Charles McSpadden planted two apple trees in the backyard. He was so pleased that the family added about 40 more trees. When Fay McSpadden saw how much her husband loved his new hobby, she suggested that he plant a few more trees. She had in mind about 40 more. But Charles brought home 10 times that amount. Then even more—and more. Today, the orchard has about 8,000 trees.

The McSpaddens sold their first apples in 1974. At the time, that was the only product they sold. But, as the business grew, the family started adding other items. They installed a cider mill in 1978. In 1987, they built a new apple house complete with bakery. In 1996, a new strain of the Gala apple was discovered in the orchard. In honor of their daughter, the family named the new strain the "Caitlin Gala." In 2001 they enlarged the sales floor of the apple house. Today, son Chuck is in charge of the family business. Open daily; no admission charge. Wagon rides and tours are available Aug through Oct on Sat and Sun at 2 and 4 p.m. Closed mid-Apr through June 30.

About 12 miles south of Cleveland, off a series of back roads, you'll find the **Red Clay State Park** (423-478-0339). Red Clay was the site of the last council ground of the Cherokee nation before their forced removal in 1838. It was the site of 11 general councils, national affairs attended by up to 5,000 Native Americans each.

The US government wanted the Cherokees to surrender their eastern lands and move the entire tribe to lands in Oklahoma. The Cherokees fought it for quite a while, but controversial treaties resulted in their losing the land. The journey to Oklahoma, known today as the Trail of Tears, actually began here at Red Clay.

The march, often referred to as the Great Removal, was a wintertime cross-country journey that covered more than 1,000 miles. Reportedly, 4,000 of the 18,000 who were forced to leave perished during the trek. That was almost one-fourth of the entire Cherokee nation.

Today people can drive that same path across the state on the **Trail of Tears State Historic Route.** It's marked quite well, and maps that explain the various historical activities along the way are available at Red Clay. About 80 percent of the original trail is now covered by modern highways.

Here where it all began, a 275-acre state historic area has been developed. The only original part left is the council spring, locally known as the "blue hole." It was this pure running spring that probably attracted the Cherokees to this site in the first place.

Also on the grounds are various reproductions of early Native American homesteads and an interpretive center with displays and historical exhibits.

It's not an easy place to find. Take Highway 60 south out of Cleveland and follow the signs. They are good signs, but often understated in size and can be easily overlooked if you happen to be looking at the cows and horses along the way. If you see a sign that reads WELCOME TO GEORGIA, you've gone about a half mile too far. Open daily; admission is free.

For more information on the Cherokee Mountains, the Ocoee River, Cleveland, and the entire Bradley County area, call (800) 472-6587 or visit the chamber of commerce website at clevelandchamber.com.

Crossroads of Dixie

Chattanooga, the state's fourth-largest city, with a population of fewer than 160,000, is located along a 7-mile bend in the Tennessee River. The deep ravine along the river is often referred to as the *Grand Canyon of the South.*

Lookout Mountain is probably the best known of the three major "ledges" that loom over the city. As in any major tourist destination, the beaten path and the unbeaten path catch up with each other here, with the same attraction often offering different things to different people.

A lot of states have large public aquariums, but none can beat the *Tennessee Aquarium* (800-262-0695; tnaqua.org) here in Chattanooga at 1 Broad St. next to the Tennessee River. The location is quite appropriate for the theme of this beautiful facility, which opened in 1992.

Billed as the "world's largest major freshwater life center," the aquarium salutes the state that has more species of freshwater fish than any other. Few of us will ever have the chance to personally explore the entire length of the magnificent Tennessee River, but here's your chance, and it will take less than 2 hours. During that time you'll have the opportunity to see more than 9,000 creatures that swim, fly, and crawl—all in their natural habitats.

Through exhibits of live and luxuriant flora and fauna, you can take a journey from the river's source in the Appalachian High Country through its midstream and finally to the Mississippi Delta. A visit to the aquarium is an enjoyable experience for the entire family. Open every day except Christmas and Thanksgiving. Admission is charged.

The *Chattanooga Visitor Center* (800-322-3344; chattanoogafun.com) is a great place to start your visit here. The center is temporarily located at 1398 Market St. while its main site adjacent to the aquarium is being renovated. Open 7 days a week 8:30 a.m. to 5:30 p.m., the center offers a wide assortment of brochures on the area's attractions, accommodations, and restaurants. Information specialists are on hand and will be glad to point you in the right direction. Among the bright and shiny brochures is a set of four historical and architectural tour brochures. Pick them up, as they offer a vast amount of information on various areas and neighborhoods of the city, places you might otherwise overlook. Inside the center are public restrooms, vending machines, a gift shop, and an ATM.

The city is obviously quite proud of its river heritage. To prove that point, the city founders have created the **Tennessee Riverpark** along the mighty Tennessee River, adjacent to the aquarium. Beware; there are some steep grades and a lot of steps, but it does appear to be wheelchair accessible via a series of ramps. The area includes parks, fishing piers, a riverside amphitheater carved out of the bluff under a highway overpass, and playgrounds.

whatadeal forabuck!

The first franchised Coca-Cola bottling plant in the world was built in Chattanooga in 1899 by two local attorneys, who bought the franchise bottling rights for $1 each.

Along the Riverwalk, which runs through the Riverpark, you'll come upon the 2,370-foot-long **Walnut Street Bridge** spanning the river. The circa 1891 bridge is considered the longest pedestrian walkway in the world. Once the only way across the river within the city, the structure underwent a $4 million renovation in 1993 and is now a fun place to walk, jog, or sit upon one of the benches and enjoy a fantastic view of the river far below and the Ross's Landing area of the city.

A fun event takes place on the Walnut Street Bridge in late Sept each year. The **Wine Over Water Festival** (423-265-2825; wineoverwater.org) is a wine-tasting event that offers a fine selection of wines, entertainment, and activities.

While tasting the fruit of the vine on the bridge, make sure you walk over to the north shore and visit Coolidge Park, located on the waterfront between the Walnut Street and Market Street Bridges. You'll find a historic carousel that operates most of the year, offering rides for $1.

A stroll farther up the Riverwalk takes you to the **Bluff View Art District** (800-725-8338 or 423-265-5033; bluffviewartdistrict.com), where you'll uncover a classy little conclave of arts and dining. The area, on E. Second Avenue, high on a bluff overlooking the Tennessee River, is definitely the hippest area in the city.

There among the tall shade trees, you'll find the **Hunter Museum of American Art** (423-267-0968; huntermuseum.org), housed in a restored classic revival mansion at 10 Bluff View Ave. It offers the most complete collection of American art in the Southeast. Nearby, the **Houston Museum of Decorative Arts** (423-267-7176; thehoustonmuseum.org) at 201 High St. houses the renowned decorative arts collection of Anna Safley Houston.

The **River Gallery** (423-265-5033; river-gallery.com) is housed in a turn-of-the-20th-century home at 400 E. Second St. and showcases an extensive collection of regional, national, and international fine art and crafts, including paintings, sculptures, and studio art glass. Across the street is the **River Gallery Glass Studio,** where you can watch resident glass artists demonstrate a variety of glassblowing styles and techniques.

The 2-acre **River Gallery Sculpture Garden** overlooks the Tennessee River and features 30 pieces of original art placed around a beautifully landscaped garden. All the art is for sale through the River Gallery.

The **Bluff View Inn** (423-265-5033 or 800-725-8338) at 411 E. Second St. consists of three turn-of-the-20th-century restored homes, all offering spectacular bird's-eye views of the river. Rates start at $105, including breakfast.

Once you've settled into a classy room, get out and walk around the area. It's amazing up here, with everything only a couple of steps away from everything else.

There are several restaurants to choose from. **Tony's Pasta Shop and Trattoria** at 212 High St. serves up a classic Italian menu specializing in fresh house-made pastas, sauces, and European-style breads. Open daily year-round for lunch and dinner. **The Back Inn Cafe** at 412 E. Second St. offers upscale cuisine and desserts to die for and has extensive wine and beer lists. Open daily for lunch and dinner, it has terrace dining overlooking the river, weather permitting.

If it's good coffee and a fresh pastry or overstuffed sandwich you're looking for, **Rembrandt's Coffee House** at 204 High St. is open all day, every day.

The newest addition to the Bluff View family is the **Bluff View Bakery** at 411 E. Second St. The vision of Bluff View head baker Rob Alexander, the establishment is located in the renovated Powers & Condon building across from the River Gallery Sculpture Garden. Here you'll find the famous Bluff

View Art District's signature breads, including the ciabatta and the country loaf, and of course a bunch of other really cool baked goods.

The popular **Riverbend Festival** (423-756-2211; riverbendfestival.com) takes place along the river each June and usually attracts about a half million people during its 9-day run. It's so spread out, however, you don't usually feel crowded. More than 100 musical artists perform on five different stages, offering up everything from rock, country, and blues to jazz and folk. Of course, there are all kinds of food and drink and other festival-style activities as well.

Selected as one of the top 20 children's museums in the nation by *Child* magazine, the **Creative Discovery Museum** (423-756-2738; cdmfun.org) in downtown Chattanooga is all about child's play. Located at 321 Chestnut St., the museum is an awesome place to spend time playing and learning. Kids can climb up to a crow's nest, dig for dinosaur bones, see how bees make honey, spray jets of water to spin whirligigs, build robots, make a sculpture, and make music with all types of musical instruments.

The museum's Rooftop Fun Factory is designed to provide hours of fun and education—and it's only one of the choices at the Creative Discovery Museum. The Rooftop Fun Factory takes play outside and opens it up under a big sky. Explore the world of simple machines with sound, movement, and fun galore. Blow soap bubbles and watch as they gently sail through the sky. Turn a wheel to play a pretty tune. Use pulleys to lift yourself off the roof. Work a hand pump up and down to launch balls into the air and make them bounce through a cage. Crank a huge ball into the air and watch as it shakes the roof on its way back down.

In 1916, while steering a Tin Lizzie over a bumpy road, a Chattanooga motorist took a sharp right when he shouldn't have and helped create a major invention. When the dust cleared, John Wiley and his son found themselves unhurt. Their car, however, was submerged in the Chickamauga Creek. Only one wheel peeked above the water. When he got to the closest phone, Wiley called Ernest Holmes, a former student from his business college who now operated a garage and automobile repair shop. Holmes feared it was a hopeless cause, but the ingenious scheme he came up with worked. Using three poles, a pulley, and a chain hooked to the frame of a 1913 Cadillac, Holmes pulled the vehicle back up on the road. From that, the Wrecker King was born. With more and more horseless carriages chugging along the nation's roads, Holmes foresaw a need for handling wrecked and disabled vehicles. In the fall of 1917, the Chattanooga man created the first wrecker in the US. That tale is recounted at the ***International Towing & Recovery Hall of Fame and Museum*** (423-267-3132; internationaltowing-museum.org) at 3315 Broad St. in Chattanooga.

At the museum, visitors can see all kinds of spiffy wreckers and towing equipment. A green 1929 Chrysler with a Weaver 3-ton auto crane sparkles everywhere, from its protruding headlights to its glistening black tow hook. Its gold-rimmed tires look as though they have never seen a spot of dirt. Then there's the 1936 Chevy truck emblazoned with the notice IT'S A DIRTY JOB BUT SOMEONE HAS TO DO IT. The wrecker is waxed to the max. Opened in September 1995, the museum was built by the Friends of Towing, an organization boasting over 350 members throughout 21 counties. A Hall of Fame portion of the museum honors people who have in various ways significantly advanced the industry.

Children of all ages love a trip to the zoo and the ***Chattanooga Zoo at Warner Park*** (423-697-1322; chattzoo.org) is a great place for walking around and animal watching. Located at 301 N. Holtzclaw Ave., the small 7-acre zoo is ideal for a day's visit. One of its most popular exhibits is the Himalayan Passage, which houses the world's largest indoor red panda habitat. In 2006, the Himalayan Passage was expanded to include habitats for snow leopards and Hanuman langurs (Asian primates).

Children never seem to tire of visiting the Ranch Exhibit, where each day is a new adventure. Visitors are welcome to interact with "ranch" animals at a petting zoo. Animals making their home here include goats, sheep, Vietnamese potbellied pigs, miniature horses, Sicilian donkeys, dromedary camels, and man's best friend—dogs. The ranch also features tools used by ranchers and farmhands—saddles, bridles, saws, shovels, pitchforks, and more. Children will learn that before tractors and other farm machines were invented, farmers and ranchers used animals to prepare fields for planting, as well as for herding livestock and for transportation.

The zoo's Walkin' the Tracks showcases animals found in the US. The Gombe Forest features two waterfalls, a vine-draped indoor viewing area, and an outside play yard where critters can be seen at play. The Corcovado Jungle highlights the rainforest of Latin America.

Chattanooga is one of those cities where there is an abundance of off-the-beaten-path things to see and do. Everywhere you look there are unique and fun experiences. Unfortunately we don't have room to cover them all here. Call the visitor bureau at (800) 322-3344 for a bevy of additional activities, or visit chattanoogafun.com. But we'll come back to the city after a brief detour up Lookout Mountain.

Up on **Lookout Mountain**, one of the Civil War's most famous battles was fought. Known today as the "Battle above the Clouds," the fight at Chickamauga Creek and the Battle of Chattanooga are immortalized in the nation's first and largest national military park. The huge **Chickamauga-Chattanooga National Park,** established in 1890, contains more than 400 markers on the battlefield that outline the series of events that claimed 34,000 casualties. The park also contains 666 monuments honoring the men who fought on the grounds.

Just when you think you've seen all the ways that Civil War history can be taught, you walk through the front doors of the **Battles for Chattanooga Electric Map** (423-821-2812; battlesforchattanooga.com), and get a huge surprise! This spectacular electronic 3-D battle map of the area's Civil War history features hundreds of lights, 5,000 miniature soldiers, and a computerized sound system and soundtrack. The presentation provides exceptional details of the battles fought here in November 1863. You'll also see a relic and weapons collection, and there's a well-stocked bookstore on hand for further reading about the Civil War. Located across from Point Park, at 1110 E. Brow Rd., the center is open daily year-round 10 a.m. to 5 p.m., with extended hours during the summer. Admission is $8 for adults, $6 for children (ages 5–12).

The visitor center is a good place to start your education on the area's Civil War history. It's located at the top of the mountain across from the entrance to Point Park, the site of the Battle above the Clouds. Call (423) 821-7786.

As you continue to climb Lookout Mountain, you'll pass several other well-known attractions, including the incredible **Ruby Falls** (423-821-2544; rubyfalls.com). They are very much on the beaten path but shouldn't be overlooked just because you don't like crowds or don't want to visit a place where everyone else in the world has been first. Open every day but Christmas; admission is charged.

The ***Mountain Memories*** (423-821-6575) gift shop is located on the Scenic Highway, less than a mile up the mountain from Ruby Falls, and if you're looking for some funky stuff, this is the place to stop. The outside of the building is covered with advertising signs, and the porches are overflowing with rustic crafts. They offer the best price around on ***"See Rock City"*** birdhouses and bird feeders, and they have one entire area dedicated to beautiful handmade quilts. Located next to the incline tracks, the store is open daily year-round.

safecave

Stocked with water and dehydrated food, Ruby Falls was a designated fallout shelter during the Cuban Missile Crisis in 1962. It could hold 720 people.

Many Tennessee natives don't realize that one of the most popular attractions on Lookout Mountain, ***Rock City*** (706-820-2531 or 800-854-0675; seerockcity.com), is actually across the state line in Georgia.

"See Rock City" birdhouses and painted barn roofs throughout the Southeast have made this attraction a genuine piece of Americana. There's nothing like it anywhere else. Ten acres of natural rock gardens, some with formations looming 20 stories high, and a barren spot called ***Lover's Leap,*** from which seven states can be seen, are the highlights of the attraction. Twisting paths take you through wonderfully landscaped gardens and narrow crevices. One such crack is thoughtfully named "Fat Man's Squeeze."

The founder, Garnet Carter, first built a hotel on the property and in early 1928 developed a recreational outlet that changed leisure-time activities from coast to coast. Using the natural hills, rocks, hollow logs, and pools of water as hazards, he created a miniature golf course for his guests who didn't want to take the time to play a complete round of regulation golf.

Within a short time various other hotels in the country asked him to design courses for them, and ***Tom Thumb Golf*** took the country by storm. By 1930 about 25,000 miniature golf courses were operating in the US, many of which were Carter's courses.

The original course and the hotel are now gone, but several of the small characters that were placed around the course are a part of the Fairyland portion of Rock City. Admission is $19.95 for adults and $11.95 for children (ages 3–12).

See Rock City

That's a phrase you've seen painted on the roofs and the sides of barns throughout America. Have you ever wondered who painted most of those barns? Clark Byers can be given that credit. As the Depression drew to a close in the 1930s and more and more tourists began hitting the nation's highways once again, Rock City Garden's owner, Garnet Carter, enlisted Byers to paint the barns as unique billboards. Legend has it that when Byers asked what he was supposed to paint, Carter gave him a slip of paper with three words: See Rock City.

Farmers welcomed the new paint jobs on their barns, and Carter enjoyed the increased business the signs brought to him. Being a creative person, Byers often added mileage and the best route to the attraction on his own. The barns can still be seen as far north as Michigan and as far west as Texas. The barns became legendary, and today birdhouses can be purchased with "See Rock City" on their roofs, and modern billboards for the attraction are in the shape of a barn (or birdhouse) with the famous words on top. There are also several new books that feature the barn art. For more information visit seerockcity.com.

Less than a mile from Rock City, at the very top of the mountain, the *Castle in the Clouds Resort Hotel* was built in 1928. Today the old hotel, since restored, is the main building for *Covenant College* (706-820-1560; covenant.edu), a small liberal arts school. Other buildings on the campus also have historical as well as nostalgic appeal. Call ahead of time and school officials or students will be glad to give you a tour.

If you're a little leery about driving up the mountain, there's a solution. Built in 1895, the *Lookout Mountain Incline Railway* (423-821-9056; ridetheincline.com) is now a part of the city's transit system. Billed as the "World's Steepest and Safest Incline Railway," it has a 72.7 percent grade near the top. At the top of the mile-long ride, the upper station has been developed into a small retail village, which happens to have some of the best ice cream in the Chattanooga area. A round-trip costs $15.

At the foot of the "other side" of the mountain, the west side, at 400 Garden Rd. in Lookout Valley, the *Chattanooga Arboretum and Nature Center* (423-821-1160; chattanooganaturecenter.org) is an environmental education facility. This is a great place for your family to learn about the wonders of nature through interpretive activities. It features passive solar-design buildings that house a wildlife diorama, a touch-and-feel discovery room, and interactive exhibits. There's a 1,200-foot boardwalk out over the wetlands, with interpretive signs along the way.

Next to the nature center, **Reflection Riding** (423-821-1160; reflectionriding.org) is a 300-acre nature preserve and botanical garden that are absolutely beautiful during the spring. That's when all the wildflowers are in bloom. A 3-mile loop meanders through the area, and you can drive, walk, or ride a bike along the path. You might spot some deer or wild turkeys as you enjoy the flora of the park. Both facilities are open year-round. Admission to both the Chattanooga Nature Center and Reflection Riding is $10 for adults and $7 for seniors and children (ages 4–11).

Pardon me, boy, is that the **Chattanooga Choo Choo**? Down in the city, the **Choo Choo** (800-872-2529; choochoo.com) is one of the most unusual shopping areas in the state. Located at the old Terminal Station, 1400 Market St., the complex features 48 guest rooms aboard passenger cars plus standard rooms in three hotel buildings. The complex also has landscaped gardens, and myriad Victorian-era shops and restaurants. It's a train, it's a song, and, yes, it's a hotel! All play on the train theme.

If sleeping in a vintage railroad car sounds romantic to you, here's an opportunity to give it a shot. The 48 sleeper cars offer a nice nostalgic touch to the journey of an off-the-beaten-path road warrior. Several of the cars overlook a formal garden area, which offers a nice selection of plants and shrubs. In early summer the roses are wonderful. A bandstand in the garden features free live entertainment several nights of the week during the summer months. This is a huge complex. In addition to the sleeper cars, the hotel consists of three buildings of hotel rooms, plus one indoor and two outdoor swimming pools.

The hotel's lobby, the original railroad terminal, was built in 1909 and is considered an architectural wonder. The 85-foot-tall freestanding brick dome is the largest of its type in the world.

The city was one of the country's earliest and largest railroad centers, and this station was the hub of that activity. On the top floor of one of the terminal buildings, one of the world's largest model railroad layouts showing the area as it was during its heyday has been created by a local model railroad club. During the week it can be seen running under automated control, but on weekends members of the club come out and "play" with their creation.

The entire display is 174 feet long and contains more than 3,000 square feet of space. The HO-gauge layout has about 100 locomotives and several hundred passenger and freight cars on about 100 miles of track. Admission is $4 for adults and $2 for children (ages 3–12), but is usually included in the various hotel packages.

Several stores sell copies of Glenn Miller's version of the "Chattanooga Choo Choo" song. The phrase itself was coined in 1880 when a reporter took the first train ride out of Cincinnati on the new Cincinnati-Southern Line. Since the tracks went only as far as this city, he called the train the "Chattanooga Choo Choo." The original recording is framed and hanging in the old terminal, now the hotel lobby.

Climb aboard a train at the **Tennessee Valley Railroad Museum** (423-894-8028; tvrail.com) and see what all the choo-choo excitement is about. Located at 4119 Cromwell Rd., the museum helps relive the golden age of railroading. The museum offers a wide variety of trips, such as the 55-minute Missionary Ride Local. It's quick, but it packs in all sorts of entertainment, from a ride through a Civil War-era tunnel to a guided tour of the restoration shop, as well as a chance to witness how a locomotive is turned around using a turntable. Looking for something a little longer? Try the Chickamauga Turn, a 5.5-hour round-trip journey to historic Chickamauga. For true rail enthusiasts, multiple Dixie Land Excursions are offered throughout the year. Among the most popular is the North Pole Limited with refreshments, storytelling, and sing-alongs. As the train gently rolls down the rails, a number of lighted holiday displays can be seen outside. Once the train pulls into the "North Pole," a special guest boards for a visit. During the return ride, Santa makes his way through the train cars to greet every child and present a keepsake item to each one.

In downtown Chattanooga at the corner of Martin Luther King Boulevard and Broad Street, the historic **Sheraton Read House Hotel** (423-266-4121) has undergone a $2 million renovation and now has much of the same charm it possessed through the years when five US presidents, Winston Churchill, and Eleanor Roosevelt were numbered among its guests. The building is listed on the National Register of Historic Places.

Bessie Smith, the First Lady of Blues, was born in Chattanooga in 1894 and is today immortalized in the city's **African American Museum** (423-266-8658; caamhistory.com). There the **Bessie Smith Performance Hall** features concerts, lectures, and seminars. There are several exhibits about her life and plenty of samples of her music. Her death certificate and piano are on display and among the museum's permanent collection. Elsewhere in the museum, there's a fun, interactive wall map of Africa before there was an America and several exhibits of local African-American history. There's a nice display of African art as well. Located at 200 E. Martin Luther King Blvd., the museum is open Mon through Fri 10 a.m. to 5 p.m. and Sat noon to 4 p.m. Admission is $7 for adults, $5 for students and seniors, and $3 for children (ages 6–12).

Do any of your kids have a passion for dragons? Well Barbara Newton turned her special love for the critters into a dragon museum called **Dragon Dreams** (423-892-2384; dragonvet.com). Her collection of more than 2,000 dragons spans eight rooms. The dragons are awake and ready to greet you Wed through Sun except for major holidays. "Even the dragons need a day now and then to visit their friends and family," Newton told us. At 6724-A E. Brainerd Rd., admission for adults and children ages 14 and up is $10, for children 13 and under $4.50; no charge to enter the dragon-filled gift shop.

Leave Chattanooga via US 41/64/72, also known as Will Cummings Highway, and you'll be in the Raccoon Mountain area, on the "other" side of the city. Follow the signs to the **Raccoon Mountain Caverns & Campground** (800-823-2267; raccoonmountain.com), quite a fun complex tucked away in the mountains.

Outside the entrance to the Raccoon Mountain Caverns, you can pan for your own gemstones just like the old-timers did. Entrance to the caves is through the gift shop. During the 45-minute guided tour, you'll meander past many beautiful formations and squeeze and duck through many small passages.

Don't miss the unique shield formation toward the end of the tour. There are only 20 such formations known to exist throughout the world, our guide told us. A map of Tennessee can also be seen outlined by formations on the ceiling in one of the rooms. On a hot day, the wonderfully cool cave can be a fun treat. Admission is charged; open daily. The campground has a full-service RV camp as well as tent camping sites. The complex is located 1.25 miles north from I-24 at exit 174.

Pickers and singers have been gathering together each Friday night since 1979 in the old schoolhouse at the top of Signal Mountain, just north of Chattanooga at 2501 Fairmount Pike. "We call it the **Mountain Opry**

(423-886-3252), and we play from 8 to 11 p.m.," said Ken Holloway. He won't take credit for starting the weekly event but will say he was with the group that did get it going. "We were looking for a reason to get together and play some music," he told us.

Specializing in acoustic Appalachian-style bluegrass and country music, the Opry features a half dozen or so different groups each Friday night. "Whoever shows up usually gets to play," he said. It's free to get in, but the 325 seats usually fill up, so get there a bit early if you can. The schoolhouse is located just off US 127 on Fairmount Parkway, at the top of the mountain in the little village of Walden. They'd appreciate a donation to help pay the rent and utilities, but pay as you please.

In **Dunlap** there's a developing historic site that most overlook mainly because it was the illegal town dump for decades. Through the dedication of volunteers, headed up by Carson Camp, history is being uncovered on the 62-acre **Coke Ovens Historic Site** (423-949-2156 or 423-949-3483; cokeovens.com).

A huge coal industry was present in this area at the turn of the 20th century, and in this Dunlap industrial complex, coal was turned into coke for use in the iron and steel foundries in nearby Chattanooga.

When the company went out of business in 1917, there were 268 beehive-shaped coke ovens in operation. Through the years, the ovens were forgotten, covered up, and neglected. During the past few years, Camp and members of the Sequatchie Valley Historical Association have uncovered a lot of the area's heritage that had almost been forgotten.

During 2001, Camp discovered that the land upon which the ovens were built was the site of an overnight encampment of the Cherokee Indians during their Trail of Tears trek to Oklahoma. Camp figures the Indians stayed here for the same reason the ovens were built: flat land and closeness to a spring.

The 77-acre park has been listed on the National Register of Historic Places, and a replica of the original coal company store commissary has been built on the original foundation of the old structure. That building now serves as a museum, which houses the largest collection of regional historic coal mining photographs in the state. Hundreds of donated mining artifacts are on display in the museum, and one room has been set aside as a local history museum for Sequatchie County and Dunlap.

Outside, the excavation by Camp and historical association volunteers is continuing. The museum is open Sun through Wed year-round. During peak summer months, it's also open on Sat. Dunlap is 50 miles north of Chattanooga on US 127, and the Coke Ovens Historic Site is 0.75 mile west of downtown, just off US 127 on Walnut Street. A *Bluegrass Festival* takes place on the grounds the first Fri and Sat in June, and a *Fall Fest* is held on the first Sat in Oct.

Farther up US 41, just across the county line, you'll see the sign for the TVA's *Raccoon Mountain Pumped Storage Facility* (423-825-3100) on your right. It is the most unusual of all the Tennessee Valley Authority's operations. This hydroelectric plant uses more power than it generates. The safety officers on duty will usually agree with that arguable fact, but they will quickly tell you that the plant is very cost-effective.

The visitor center is located at the top of the mountain, about 9 miles from the front entrance, and what a view of the Tennessee River Valley it offers. Also at the top is a 528-acre lake. Deep inside the mountain is the mammoth power plant, totally protected from the elements and enemy attack.

At night, during off-peak hours, the extra energy produced at TVA coal-burning plants is used here to pump water from the Tennessee River up a 1,100-foot pipeline to fill the reservoir above. This is cheaper than shutting down and restarting those plants, and the electricity that would have been wasted is now used to stockpile water that will, in turn, create more power.

During the day, when the demand for electricity is greatest, the water is released from the reservoir and tumbles down the 35-foot-diameter intake tunnels to turn the four large generators, thereby producing electricity.

There are fewer than two dozen pumped storage facilities in the US, and this is the only one that is completely underground. There are several scenic pull-offs on the drive to the top and quite a few picnic areas. At the foot of the mountain, there are fishing areas along the river, all courtesy of the federal government. Admission is free.

When it comes to southern cooking, few meals can be complete without fresh corn bread, dripping with real butter! The folks in South Pittsburg loved their corn bread so much that they created another reason to eat more of it. The annual *National Cornbread Festival & World Championship Cornbread Cook-off* (423-837-0022; nationalcornbread.com) is held in late Apr, with a 2-day party to remember.

Main Street is closed off and lined with food vendors and exhibits, a carnival comes to town, and a juried show for artisans and crafters takes place. Usually there will be 50 or so crafters working, showing, and selling their wares. *South Pittsburg* is located a few miles west of I-24. Take exit 152 to US 72 West. Don't miss this festive event. The website also has winning corn bread recipes from past years that you can make yourself. Yummy!

Places to Stay in Plateaus & Valleys

ATHENS

Majestic Mansion B&B
202 E. Washington Ave.
(423) 746-9041
themansionbnb.com
Roomy B&B with unusual choices of decor, from Japanese to country

CELINA

Horse Creek Resort
1150 Horse Creek Rd.
(931) 243-2125 or (800) 545-2595
horsecreek-resort.com
4 miles from Celina on Dale Hollow Lake
Cabins, houseboats, motel

CHATTANOOGA

Bluff View Inn
412 E. Second St.
(423) 265-5033 or (800) 725-8338
bluffviewartdistrict.com
Spectacular view of river from restored homes

Sheraton Read House Hotel
At corner of Martin Luther King Boulevard and Broad Street
(423) 266-4121
sheratonreedhouse.com

Sky Harbor Bavarian Inn
2159 Old Wauhatchie Pike
(423) 821-8619
skyharborbavarianinn.com
Great views of Tennessee River from private balconies; whirlpool tubs, kitchens, cable TV, hardwood floors

StoneFort Inn
120 E. 10th St.
(888) 945-7866
stonefortinn.com
Brick and limestone structure built in 1909

CLEVELAND

Clarion Inn
185 James Asbury Dr.
(423) 559-1001
clarioninn.com
Close to Ocoee whitewater rafting; continental breakfast buffet

Mountain View Inn
2400 Executive Park Dr.
I-75, exit 25
(423) 472-1500
Exercise room, valet, laundry, outdoor pool

DUCKTOWN

Company House Bed & Breakfast
318 Main St.
(423) 496-5634
companyhousebandb.com
On National Register of Historic Places

MCMINNVILLE

Falcon Rest Mansion & Gardens
2645 Faulkner Springs Rd.
(931) 668-4444
falconrest.com
Bed-and-breakfast in Queen Anne–Victorian mansion

MONTEAGLE

Edgeworth Inn
On Assembly grounds
(931) 924-4000
edgeworthinn.com
Victorian bed-and-breakfast

Jim Oliver's Smokehouse
US 64/41A
(800) 489-2091
thesmokehouse.com
Motel with swimming pool in shape of a ham

MONTEREY

The Garden Inn
1400 Bee Rock Rd.
(888) 293-1444
thegardeninnbb.com
An atmosphere of relaxed elegance; mountain and garden views

RACCOON MOUNTAIN

Raccoon Mountain Caverns & Campground
1.25 miles north from I-24 at exit 174
319 W. Hills Rd.
(800) 823-2267
raccoonmountain.com
Full-service RV camp and tent camping sites

RED BOILING SPRINGS

Armour's Red Boiling Springs Hotel
321 E. Main St.
(615) 699-2180
armourshotel.com
Mineral baths, steam baths, and massages available

SMITHVILLE

The Inn at Evins Mill
1535 Evins Mill Rd.
(800) 383-2349
evinsmill.com
Lodge and rustic cabins serve as a bed-and-breakfast

WATERTOWN

Watertown Bed & Breakfast
116 Depot Ave.
(615) 237-9999
watertownbandb.com
Restored 19th-century railroad hotel; private baths, nonsmoking, breakfast

Places to Eat in Plateaus & Valleys

CHATTANOOGA

Big River Grille & Brewing Works
222 Broad St.
(423) 267-2739
bigrivergrille.com
Microbrewery, sandwiches, snacks
Open daily at 11 a.m.

The Blue Plate
191 Chestnut St.
(423) 648-6767
theblueplate.info
Where every dish is a blue plate special

Hennen's
193 Chestnut St.
(423) 634-5160
hennens.net
Great seafood, steaks, across from the aquarium

Rib & Loin
5946 Brainerd Rd.
(423) 499-6465
ribandloin.com
Considered the city's best rib restaurant
Open daily at 10:30 a.m.

TerraMae
120 E. 10th St.
(423) 710-2925
terramae.org
Progressive American
cuisine, name means
"Mother Earth" in
Portuguese

212 Market Restaurant
212 Market St.
(423) 265-1212
212market.com
Grilled salmon, chicken,
steaks

CLEVELAND

The Gondolier
3300 N. Keith St.
(423) 472-4998
Greek and Italian cuisine
Open daily for lunch and
dinner

DECATUR

Shoreline Cafe
18194 State Hwy. 58
North
(423) 334-2361
Good home cooking and
fried fish

LIVINGSTON

The Apple Dish
114 N. Court Sq.
(931) 823-3222
Great home cooking and
desserts
Hours vary, call first

MCMINNVILLE

Prater's BBQ
9576 Manchester Hwy.
(931) 635-2259
Good barbecue and more

MONTEAGLE

**Jim Oliver's
Smokehouse**
850 W. Main St.
(800) 489-2091
thesmokehouse.com
Pit barbecue and hickory-
smoked meats

MONTEREY

**Cup & Saucer
Restaurant**
118 E. Commercial Ave.
(931) 839-6149
Home-style cooking

THE HEARTLAND

→

Heart of the Heartland

Nashville. It very well could be the smallest city with the biggest reputation in the world. Anyone who has ever listened to a radio knows that Nashville is the country music capital of the world.

What a lot of people don't realize, however, is that the city's nickname is Music City, not Country Music City. It has some of the best recording studios in the world and absolutely the best studio musicians in the business. Everyone from Paul McCartney to Pearl Jam to Garth Brooks has recorded in Nashville. They come for the quality of the city as much as for the state-of-the-art studios.

There is an active jazz and blues culture, as well as rock and rap cultures. Clubs all over town offer a wide variety of music. The Tennessee Performing Arts Center in downtown Nashville has a Broadway Series that's second to none, and the Gaylord Entertainment Center, home of the Nashville Predators NHL club, hosts some of the world's biggest stars, from Luciano Pavarotti to Shania Twain to the Rolling Stones.

The National Football League's Tennessee Titans play in the Coliseum across the Cumberland River from downtown, and on Football Sundays the action is definitely in the various downtown districts. Nashville is far from a mainstream city. It's one of those unique areas where the unbeaten path crosses the well-traveled path and merges for a few miles and dozens of experiences. The city's maternal relationship to country music has created quite a few one-of-a-kind attractions and events.

Music City is not only a place where musicians record, it's also the place they call home. While you won't find Vince Gill or Brad Paisley listed in the phone book, it's not hard to find their homes. It's also not unusual to see the stars at the local supermarket, or at a gas station or musical event.

With all that Nashville has going for it, the majority of the visitors to the city still come to see the music-associated attractions—and that's good news for those who don't visit those attractions. The crowds are smaller (and sometimes nonexistent) at the doors of many of the city's other fun experiences.

The city of Nashville and the county of Davidson are one and the same, with a metropolitan government running the place. The 2010 census showed the area with a population of 609,644, a growth of nearly 10 percent over 2000.

There's plenty to do in downtown Nashville, but let's start our journey in the northwest quadrant of the city, where you'll find the mammoth Gaylord Opryland Resort & Convention Center approximately 13 miles from downtown.

Across from the Opryland complex and the world-famous WSM-AM radio station, the broadcast station of the Grand Ole Opry for more than 60 years, is the Music Valley Area and its complex of shops and activities. That's where you'll find the *Nashville Palace* (615-889-1540; nashvillepalace.net) at 2611 McGavock Pike. The Palace is where country superstar Randy Travis was discovered while working as a dishwasher. Live music nightly and a delicious menu that includes "the best catfish in town" are featured.

The *Ernest Tubb Midnight Jamboree* (615-889-2474; etrecordshop .com), the second-oldest live country music radio show in America, is broadcast each Saturday night from the Texas Troubadour Theater, 2416 Music Valley Dr., a few blocks behind the Nashville Palace. The show is broadcast

AUTHOR'S TOP TEN PICKS

Bell Witch Cave	Jack Daniel Distillery
Cannonsburgh Pioneer Village	Mule Day Festival & Parade
Elephant Sanctuary	Nash Trash Tour
Ernest Tubb Record Shop	Nashville Cowboy Church
Hatch Show Print	Schermerhorn Symphony Center

on WSM-AM 650 and features top-name country talent, many of whom may have played the Grand Ole Opry earlier that night across the street at the Opryland complex. Be there by 11:30 to get a good seat. Admission is free. Check the website late in the week to see who's booked for the Saturday show. If you're looking for vintage country music, the ***Ernest Tubb Record Shop*** next door is the place to search.

The Texas Troubadour Theater is also the site of the famous ***Nashville Cowboy Church*** (615-889-2474). It's a unique Nashville experience. Where else can you hear top-shelf southern gospel music while a genuine Stetson hat is passed for the offering? Services are held each Sun at 10 a.m.

The ***Gaylord Opryland Resort & Convention Center*** (615-889-1000; marriott.com) at 2800 Gaylord Dr., formerly known as Opryland Hotel, is a huge, amazing place. With 2,884 guest rooms, 177 suites, 776 atrium garden-view rooms, 12 restaurants, 10 lounges, and 30 retail stores, all inside, you can start to realize why this place is so amazing. Add to that 5 ballrooms, 152 meeting rooms, and nearly one million square feet of exhibit space, and you have quite a unique hotel. It's worth a visit, but make sure you wear your tennies; you'll be doing a lot of walking.

The fun thing to see and do here is to visit the three different atrium areas, which are under nearly 9 acres of skylights. The Conservatory and the Cascades are each 2-acre atriums featuring tropical gardens, running streams, and multilevel viewing areas. The newest area, the Delta, is a 4.5-acre interiorscape with a flowing river and 25-passenger flatboats that take guests on a voyage through the area. Gaylord became part of Marriott International in October 2012.

Christmas at the hotel is especially fun. Nearly two million lights decorate the exterior of the hotel, and inside there are holiday-themed dinner shows, an arts and antiques show, and other seasonal activities.

The new concept of "shopper-tainment" has come to Nashville via the 1.2-million-square-foot *Opry Mills* (615-514-1100; simon.com) next to the resort at 433 Opry Mills Dr. The 200-plus retailers offer up a bevy of fun experiences, shopping opportunities, and dining facilities. Among the tenants: Bass Pro Shop, Rainforest Cafe, and an IMAX Theater.

Outside Opry Mills, in the plaza of the nearby Grand Ole Opry House, the *Grand Ole Opry Museum* (615-871-OPRY) at 2804 Opryland Dr. offers an extensive salute to the stars who have walked the Opry stage. Interactive exhibits, artifacts and costumes, photos, and plenty of music provide tribute

OTHER ATTRACTIONS WORTH SEEING

Adventure Science Center
Sudekum Planetarium
800 Fort Negley Blvd., Nashville
(615) 862-5160
adventuresci.com

Cheekwood Gardens & Art Museum
1200 Forrest Park Dr., Nashville
(615) 356-8000
cheekwood.org

Elliston Place Soda Shop
2111 Elliston Place, Nashville
(615) 327-1090
Original soda shop dating back to
1939

Frist Center for the Visual Arts
919 Broadway, Nashville
(615) 244-3340
fristcenter.org

The Hermitage
4580 Rachel's Ln., Hermitage
(615) 889-2941
thehermitage.com
Home of Andrew Jackson

Ryman Auditorium
116 Fifth Ave. North, Nashville
(615) 889-3060
ryman.com
Home to the Grand Ole Opry for 31
years

Smith-Trahern Mansion
101 McClure St., Clarksville
(931) 648-9998
Restored 1851 mansion

Tootsie's Orchid Lounge
422 Broadway, Nashville
(615) 726-0463
tootsies.net
Famed country music honky-tonk next
to Ryman Auditorium

to the likes of Minnie Pearl, Marty Robbins, and Roy Acuff. The gift shop has some fun and funky country music souvenirs. Admission is free.

The **Grand Ole Opry** is the show that started it all. And this is the place the Opry has called home since moving from the Ryman Auditorium in 1974. Located at 2804 Opryland Dr., the Grand Ole Opry is known for its mix of music and stars. A typical Opry performance might feature traditional country, bluegrass, comedy, Cajun, new country, gospel, and more. Performers include country legends as well as up-and-coming artists. The lineup is released a couple of days before showtime, but you never know who might turn up. It's not unusual for a special guest to drop by for a duet or surprise appearance during these unrehearsed performances. Tickets start at $25.

For a better understanding of the show, take a backstage tour of the **Grand Ole Opry House** (615-871-OPRY; opry.com) to get an authentic look behind the scenes. Tour guides have a wealth of fascinating stories about the Opry and about country music greats past and present. Video host Blake Shelton will share what it's like for him backstage on show night.

Tours include a visit to the Opry House artist entrance as well as a stop in Studio A, a live television studio and former home of *Hee Haw*. Also showcased during the tour are artist dressing rooms, newly refurbished following the Nashville flood of 2010, and the world-famous Opry stage. Look for a circle of wood in a prime spot on the floor. It was cut from the original Ryman Auditorium as a reminder of the greats who once stood there.

Daytime tours are available 7 days a week Feb through Oct. On evenings in which there is only one Opry performance, tours are also available immediately after the show. Opry House Backstage Pass Tours can be booked up to two weeks in advance. Tour schedules and times vary based on Opry House availability. Tours cost about $20 per person.

About 15 minutes from downtown Nashville is a massive structure that is said to be the world's largest log cabin home. Built by Barbara Mandrell and her husband Ken Dudney in 1987, **Fontanel Mansion and Farm** (877-357-8094; fontanelmansion.com) is now open for tours. After Mandrell sold the mansion and moved in 2002, the place was opened to the public in June 2010. Because the artist left behind so many of her personal possessions, it seems as though visitors are walking through her private home and might come upon the famous singer around the next corner. On display are her stage costumes, awards, furniture, and much more. The home has 3 stories,

TOP ANNUAL EVENTS

APRIL

Main Street Festival
Franklin
(615) 591-8500
historicfranklin.com
Crafts, food, entertainment

MAY

Old Timer's Day
Dickson
dicksoncountyoldtimersday.com
Crafts, flea market, quilt show, first
weekend in May

JULY

Annual Irish Picnic
St. Patrick's Church
McEwen
(931) 582- 3493

SEPTEMBER

African Street Festival
American Cultural Alliance
Nashville
(866) 721-0007

Polly Crockett Arts & Crafts Show
Winchester
(931) 967-6788

DECEMBER

Yulefest: A 1780s Christmas
at Mansker's Station Frontier Life
Center
Goodlettsville
(615) 859- 3678

more than 20 rooms, 13 bathrooms, 5 fireplaces, 2 kitchens, an indoor pool, and even an indoor shooting range. Guests are invited to touch, see, photograph, and relax in the magnificent home. Mandrell's daughter Jaime was leading a tour once when I was there, and it was interesting to hear her reminisce about growing up in the huge house with her two brothers. And if you wonder where the mansion got its unusual name, Jaime explained that "fontanel" refers to the soft spot on a baby's head. "My mother just liked the way it sounded," she said.

After touring the mansion and hiking the trails, guests can dine at Cafe Fontanella and shop at the Silo Gift Shop and Farm House art studio. Concerts also are scheduled at the outdoor amphitheater. The mansion is located at 4225 Whites Creek Pike. In downtown Nashville, an area called **The District** is centered on Second Avenue, running north off Broadway to the county courthouse. It's where you'll find the typical tourist traps, but it's also where you'll find some great restaurants and drinking emporiums.

All the businesses are in restored turn-of-the-20th-century buildings and warehouses.

Country music wasn't always as slick as it is today, and that wonderful old-time sound is still alive and well and being played daily in the honky-tonks of Lower Broadway, just around the corner from The District.

There's a big difference between a honky-tonk and a country music club. First of all, honky-tonks are real beer joints with small, crowded dance floors and live music from great musicians you've probably never heard of—and if you order a glass of wine or a fancy drink, you'll probably be laughed right out the back door!

Lower Broadway's honky-tonk neighbors are the genuine articles, left virtually untouched through the years. Most keep their doors open so that you can hear the music from the sidewalk, and most have the bands up front so that you can watch the performers through the large windows.

Hillbilly heaven is anchored by the grandmother of all Nashville honky-tonks, **Tootsie's Orchid Lounge** (615-726-0463; tootsies.net), at 422 Broadway. The back door of Tootsie's is across the alley from the back door of the Ryman Auditorium, where the Grand Ole Opry took place for years. Hattie Louise "Tootsie" Bess ran the joint from 1960 to 1978 and during that time welcomed some of the greatest Opry performers through the

The Performing Arts Are Alive!

The **Tennessee Performing Arts Center** (TPAC) is an oasis of the arts in downtown Nashville. Its three separate theaters are home to the Nashville Ballet, Tennessee Repertory Theatre, Nashville Opera, and the Nashville Symphony. The building also houses the Tennessee State Museum. In addition to the resident groups' activities, the management of TPAC promotes a quality Broadway series each year, as well as other special shows and attractions. They're at 505 Deaderick St.; call (615) 782-4000, or go to tpac.org. Most tickets are available through Ticketmaster, (615) 255-ARTS.

Other performing arts venues in Middle Tennessee include Darkhorse Theatre, 4610 Charlotte Ave., Nashville (615-297-7113); Austin Peay State University, Clarksville (931-221-7011; apsu.edu); Roxy Regional Theatre, 100 Franklin St., Clarksville (931-645-7699; roxyregionaltheatre.org); and Chaffin's Barn Theatre, 8204 Hwy. 100, Nashville (615-646-9977; dinnertheatre.com).

back door while they waited for their turn to perform on the stage. When Tootsie bought the club, she hired a painter who mistakenly painted the exterior purple. She kept the color, and today the purple facade stands out from the rest.

While Tootsie's has the history, it also attracts more of a tourist crowd; it's the place many locals take visitors from out of town. Try a few of the others that will probably be less crowded: **Roberts Western World,** at 416 Broadway (615-244-9552; robertswesternworld.com); **Layla's Bluegrass Inn,** at 418 Broadway (615-726-2799; laylasbluegrassinn.com); and the **Second Fiddle,** at 420 Broadway (615- 251-6812; thesecondfiddle.com).

Across Broadway from these honky-tonks at 417 Broadway is the funkiest of the three **Ernest Tubb Record Shops** (615-255-7503; etrecordshop .com) we have in town. This one was opened by the country star himself in 1950 and was the location of the Midnite Jamboree, now held at the Music Valley location, every Saturday night for many years. During those years, Tubb featured many of the top Opry stars on his stage. Today the shop's walls are lined with autographed pictures and album covers. The shop is a good place to find a huge selection of bluegrass and country music. They specialize in the older, harder-to-find artists on CDs.

If it's vinyl records (remember those?) you are looking for, visit **Lawrence Record Shop** (615-256-9240; lawrencerecordshop.com), at 409 Broadway, a few doors down from Tubb's establishment. You'll find a huge selection of country and bluegrass and some early rock 'n' roll on LP vinyl, and it's all factory sealed and in original condition. In business since 1954, the owners have amassed a great selection. Open Tues through Sat 10 a.m. to 6 p.m.

Situated among the honky-tonks and shops is **Hatch Show Print** (615-256-2805; countrymusichalloffame.org) at 316 Broadway. Open to the public, this is one of America's oldest surviving show poster printers. Founded in 1879 by two brothers, the business printed posters for the circus, sporting events, and vaudeville shows. It won the Grand Ole Opry account and printed not only the Opry's posters but also the show posters for most of country music's greatest legends. Thousands of posters printed from the original cuts are available for purchase. Admission is free.

The **Country Music Hall of Fame and Museum** (615-416-2001 or 800-852-6437; countrymusichalloffame.org) opened in 2001 to much ballyhoo in

Nashville and the world's country music circles. The place is a classy celebration of the musical genre that made Nashville famous worldwide.

The building takes up an entire block at the corner of Fifth and Demonbreun Avenues and houses an extensive collection of memorabilia, gold records, the Hall of Fame, and Elvis's 1960 solid gold Cadillac. Even if you're not into country music, this is a fun and quite educational place to visit. In the rotunda there's a plaque depicting country great Kitty Wells. You might notice that her nose is smudged on the plaque. It's now a ritual that if you rub her nose as you walk by, you'll have good luck. Don't know who started it or if it's true, but it's probably worth a rub, just in case.

The **SoBro Grill and SoBro2Go** are located in the conservatory and do not require an admission to visit. Live performances are a part of the museum experience, and Country Music Television broadcasts a live daily show from the conservatory. Everyone is invited to be a part of the live audience.

The design of the building sets this place apart from all other buildings in Nashville. The symbolism is amazing. Here is a short narrative, direct from the building's architects, Tuck-Hinton: "Note the dark windows on the face of the building meant to resemble piano keys. Can you see the hint of a '50s Cadillac fin in the sweeping arch of the structure? And yes, that's a radio tower rising

abitofnashville trivia

The world's first nighttime airplane flight took off from Cumberland Park on June 22, 1910.

President Theodore Roosevelt coined the phrase "good to the last drop" while drinking coffee at the old Maxwell House Hotel.

The Grand Ole Opry House is the world's largest broadcast studio.

Iroquois, a Nashville horse, was the first American horse to win the English Derby. The Iroquois Steeplechase race held here each May is named for him.

While visiting the Belle Meade Plantation, President William Howard Taft got stuck in the bathtub. The owners then installed a stand-up shower for his next visit.

With more than 800 churches, synagogues, and temples, the city is known as the "buckle of the Bible belt."

The driveway at the Hermitage, home of President Andrew Jackson, is shaped like a guitar.

Elvis Presley recorded more than 200 songs at RCA's Studio B.

from the silo-like rotunda honoring the WSM tower, so instrumental in the rise of country music."

Look for the suggestion of a drum kit in the rotunda's exterior, while the four disc tiers of its room trace the evolution of recording, from 78 to 45, the vinyl LP, and the CD of today (all in proportion). The stones that ring the top of the rotunda wall are more than an ornamental arrangement; they're also a musical arrangement. Each stone represents a note in the classic Carter Family song, "Will the Circle Be Unbroken." Great stuff!

The museum opens daily at 9 a.m. and closes at 5 p.m. Admission is charged.

One beautiful Nashville landmark, comparable to the greatest music halls in the world, is the $120-million **Schermerhorn Symphony Center** (615-687-6400; nashvillesymphony.org or schermerhorncenter.com), opened in 2006 and designed to be an acoustic masterpiece. Located at One Symphony Place, the center is home to the **Nashville Symphony Orchestra.** Designed by architect David M. Schwarz, the 197,000-square-foot center has 30 sound-proof windows above the hall, making it one of the only major concert halls in North America with natural light. Named in honor of the late orchestra conductor Kenneth Schermerhorn, the center is a sophisticated modern building that is neoclassically inspired, with a classic limestone exterior and columns. A garden is open to the public throughout the day and during concerts.

In May 2010, severe flooding caused significant damage in and around Nashville, including about $40 million in damages to Schermerhorn Symphony Center. At the height of the flood, the lower reaches of the building were filled with 24 feet of water. Among the losses were electrical and mechanical equipment, a large kitchen, and numerous instruments. Significant instrument losses included two Steinway & Sons pianos and the blower and console units of the Schoenstein pipe organ. Repairs to the center began almost immediately, and it reopened less than 8 months later with a concert featuring Itzhak Perlman on New Year's Eve 2010. The organ restoration was completed in time for a May 2011 concert by organist Cameron Carpenter.

Nashville welcomed a big new kid in town in May 2013. The **Music City Center** (nashvillemusiccitycenter.com) is an impressive $585 million facility that totals 2.1 million square feet. That includes 1.2 million square feet of public spaces and a 900,000-square-foot garage with 1,800 parking spaces.

Major features include a public art collection comprised of more than 80 pieces. The center is so massive that Sixth Avenue runs through the building. It has a 57,500-square-foot Grand Ballroom that seats 6,000 people. Green features include solar panels and a green roof. The building is on track to receive LEED Silver certification.

The new center is designed to serve as the city's "front porch," located in the heart of downtown Nashville, just steps from the Ryman Auditorium and the Broadway honky-tonks. It also is able to host 75 percent of the conventions in the country, compared to the 25 percent that could be accommodated at the old Nashville Convention Center.

Along with being a place to host visitors, the Music City Center also serves as a central meeting point for Nashville residents. A wide green pavilion circles the building on all sides, designed to serve as public space for art, music, and just sitting a spell and visiting.

The Music City Center sits just south of Broadway on a 16-acre site that runs from Fifth Avenue to Eighth Avenue, west to east, and from Demonbreun Street to Franklin Street, or the future Korean Veterans Boulevard, north to south. It is adjacent to both the Bridgestone Arena and the Country Music Hall of Fame.

The building features a 350,000-square-foot exhibit hall. It also offers 90,000 square feet of meeting room space—approximately 60 meeting rooms—and 32 loading docks that provide ultimate flexibility and ease of loading for convention planners.

The center was designed by Atlanta-based Thompson, Ventulett, Stainback & Associates and Nashville-based Tuck Hinton Architects and Moody-Nolan Architects. Have a favorite song or two? Know who wrote those lovely words and music? Stop by the new *Nashville Songwriters Hall of Fame* to see some famous songwriters and their creations. Located in the lobby of the new Music City Center, the Hall of Fame features songwriting artifacts as well as three 55-inch touch screens. The screens allow visitors to access sound, video, and other digital information about the history of Nashville-connected songwriting and all 184 members of the Hall of Fame.

From every genre of music, the names of Hall of Fame members are engraved in a special outdoor Songwriters Square at the corner of Fifth Avenue and Demonbreun, as well as on the stone steps leading from Fifth Avenue up to the interior display.

"The music industry is a vital part of Nashville's unique culture, and songwriters are often the 'unsung heroes' of the business," Nashville Mayor Karl Dean said at a dedication service. "This location at the Music City Center is a fitting space to honor songwriters and their creativity, and it gives both local residents and visitors from out of town yet another reason to stop by our new convention center."

Songwriting is a revered occupation in Nashville. No other city pays attention to its writers the way **Music City** does, and radio announcers are just as apt to say who wrote a song as who performed it. Writers' nights are held in various locations on a regular basis and are great places to get right down to the basics of country music. Hearing a popular writer singing his or her list of hits that others made into million-sellers is like listening to an oldies jukebox.

Perhaps the best-known cafe in the city, the **Bluebird Cafe** (615-383-1461; bluebirdcafe.com), is also one of the best places to attend a writers' night. The food is good, the talent is excellent, and chances are that you might be sitting next to a country superstar. They hang out here a lot, especially during writers' shows. Several of today's superstars were regulars here on their way up the ladder, including Garth Brooks and Kathy Mattea. If you want to talk, dance, or be rowdy, the Bluebird is not the place to go, however. Music lovers will politely tell you to "Shush!" so they can hear what they came to hear. The Bluebird is located in the Green Hills area of the city, about 15 minutes from downtown at 4104 Hillsboro Pike.

Remember when coffee was just another cuppa joe? Those days are now gone forever. On 21st Avenue, down in Hillsboro Village, the **Bongo Java Roasting Co.** shares the old Jones Pet Shop with **Fido,** a cafe named for the dog who discovered coffee (615-777-3436; bongojava.com). The cafe opened when the pet shop closed in 1996, after 50 years in business. The funky neon pet shop sign has been restored and sits upon the roof.

Fido features a breakfast menu served all day, with such items as the McFido eggs and cheese on a bagel. During the rest of the day for lunch and dinner, there's a full menu of sandwiches, soups, snacks, bagels, and full meals, including grilled salmon, fish tacos, steak and hash, and the popular green chile mac and cheese.

There are plenty of specialty coffee drinks, and the desserts are great. Every year around its birthday on Oct. 11, Fido hosts a Stuffed Animal

Immaculate Confection

The Bongo Java Coffeehouse was birthplace of the world-famous NunBun. Baker Ryan Finney decided to eat one of the rolls he was baking one morning, and he caught a divine image just before taking a bite. The roll possessed an uncanny likeness to Mother Teresa. It was indeed the immaculate confection, Finney said. "I was horrified because I almost ate this religious piece of dough," he was heard to say. It was stored in a freezer for a week and then became the center of a 9-minute video documentary titled *A Music City Miracle: The Story of the Nun-Bun.* Local papers and television stations ran stories, and before long it appeared on David Letterman, Paul Harvey, *Hard Copy,* in the *Calcutta Times,* on the BBC, and other media worldwide.

Properly preserved, the NunBun was on display at the coffeehouse so the masses could take a look for themselves. On Christmas Day 2005, the unthinkable happened. The NunBun was stolen and has never been seen since. Go online to read the saga for yourself at bongojava.com. Located at 2007 Belmont Blvd., across from Belmont University; call them at (615) 385-5282.

P.S. Don't forget to eat while you're there; they have some great nontraditional food items. But take a look before you bite and you may discover something cool. Open daily for all three meals.

Hospital where kids of all ages bring in their stuffed friends for checkups, minor surgery, and physical therapy. They open Mon through Fri at 7 a.m. and on Sat and Sun at 8 a.m., and they stay that way until 11 p.m. daily. Their address is 1812 21st Ave. South.

When a country music record company executive or a group of songwriters want to meet for a "power breakfast," there is usually no discussion of where that meeting will take place.

The **Pancake Pantry** (615-383-9333; pancakepantry.com) has served the Music Row area for more than 4 decades now, and it's a great place for breakfast at any time of the day, even if you aren't into the music business. The wild blueberry pancakes, sweet potato cakes, buttermilk stacks, and myriad other choices are all quickly served by waitresses who have been here so long, they probably have seen it all. But they don't usually have time to tell it all because they are busy taking care of the constant crowds that frequent the pancake fixture at 1796 21st Ave. South in Hillsboro Village, a few doors down from Fido's. Open daily for breakfast and lunch.

The state of Tennessee turned 200 years old in 1996, and as a present to itself, officials created the ***Bicentennial Capitol Mall State Park*** (615-741-5280; tennessee.gov/environment/parks/bicentennial) at 600 James Robertson Pkwy., down the steps and across the parkway from the state capitol. In addition to being a nicely appointed park and gathering place, the mall has permanent state historical exhibits and a great view of Capitol Hill.

The 19-acre state park and outdoor history museum feature an amphitheater, a 200-foot-long granite map depicting every city in the state, 31 fountains representing each of the state's rivers, a botanical garden, and a 1,400-foot wall engraved with images of Tennessee's historic events. Free; open 6 a.m. to 10 p.m. daily.

The more than 360,000 Tennesseans who served their country in World War II are honored here in the ***World War II Memorial,*** located on the west side of the mall. We've all seen war memorials before, but we think this one is quite impressive and well worth a visit. There are 10 granite pylons, which feature interesting information about the major events that took place during the war.

The prominent single landmark of the memorial is an 8-ton solid granite globe, the largest of its type ever made. The 1940s-world globe pinpoints major battle sites to illustrate how far Tennesseans traveled during the conflict. The sphere rotates on a thin cushion of water and can be turned by hand. Take time to study, learn, and appreciate. A free park tour is conducted every Wed at 2 p.m. Additional times are at 10 a.m., 1 p.m., and 3 p.m. on the first Mon of each month. The tour meets under the train trestle

More than a Candy Cane

Howell Campbell, a Nashville candy maker, invented the King Leo peppermint stick in 1901 for the Standard Candy Company, the makers of the popular Goo Goo Cluster. King Leo differs from the traditional candy cane in that it is lighter and crunchier, and as it dissolves in your mouth, it releases its flavor. It's also porous to use as a straw, which in turn adds flavor to your glass of milk as you sip it! Once strictly a southern treat, King Leo, now owned by the Quality Candy Company, is available nationally and has been featured in high-level shops such as Restoration Hardware. It also now comes in several other flavors, such as Key lime and chocolate.

outside the Visitor Center. The tour lasts about an hour and discusses the significance of the park and the history of Tennessee. No sign-up necessary, except for groups of 25 people or more. The mall is open daily, year-round. Adjacent to the Bicentennial Mall at 900 Rosa L. Parks Blvd. is the **Farmers' Market** (615-880-2001) covering 16 acres of urban land. Here, you'll find fresh Tennessee-grown produce, from apples to zucchini, plants, flowers, and trees. On the inside are two restaurants, an international market, a hot sauce vendor, and fresh fish and meat peddlers. Early-morning crowds consist mostly of buyers from local restaurants coming in for their fresh-picked produce. Open year-round, with peak operating hours during the summer growing season from 5 a.m. to 9 p.m., but with shorter hours during the winter months. A flea and crafts market takes place here each weekend, year-round, and there are various festivals on the grounds every second Sat of the month, May through Nov. The **Grow Local Kitchen** opened in 2012 and offers a dynamic culinary class and event schedule.

Also in the heart of downtown Nashville lies the **Tennessee State Capitol** (615-741-2001; tnmuseum.org). Finished in 1859, it was designed by William Strickland, who also helped design the US Capitol. The beautiful building at 600 Charlotte Ave. was recently renovated and should not be undervalued by tourists. Strickland loved the place so much that he requested to be interred in its walls. President James K. Polk is also buried there. Admission is free.

The city has its own **Arcade** (615-244-8060; onepaper.com/nashville arcade), and it has been restored to its finest. It was built in 1903 as a two-tiered shopping mall, an identical copy of the Galleria Vittorio Emmanuele II arcade in Milan, Italy. Today it is occupied by specialty shops, including several restaurants and the mandatory roasted-nut store, whose aroma pervades the entire complex. The arcade runs 350 feet long to connect Fourth and Fifth Avenues, between Church and Union Streets. Check out their great website for a history of the Arcade as well as a listing of its current tenants.

Across the street and down a few storefronts from the Arcade's Fifth Avenue entrance is Nashville's funkiest art gallery, the **Arts Company** (615-254-2040; theartscompany.com). Headed up by one of the city's great arts cheerleaders, Anne Brown, the full-service art gallery represents regional, national, and international artists in photography, painting, sculpture, and

Wackiest Tour in Town

The Jugg Sisters, Sheri Lynn and Brenda Kay, wear boots and tight pants and have some of the biggest hair around. They also promise to take you on a country music tour of Nashville you'll never forget. In fact, you probably won't even pay attention to what the girls are talking about outside the bright pink bus you'll be riding on because there's so much going on inside the bus.

The **Nash Trash Tour** is the wackiest tour in the state, no doubt. It's truly tacky and tasteless, and if you're into political correctness, stay off their bus! A journey with the Juggs is comedy kitsch at its best. They point out the underbelly of the city's music industry. They dig up the dirt on countless notables. Bubba, or Bubbette, depending on who's available to drive the bus, takes you past the county jail, and the girls roll off a roster of famous names who have slept there. The sisters sing original songs about the seamier side of Music City, and they even have a bit of choreography to go with it. They point out the pool where Elvis went skinny-dipping and the bar where Tanya Tucker took off her shirt for a national reporter.

Other highlights of the tour include celebrity sightings. You might see Garth Brooks, Burt Reynolds, Dolly Parton, or Willie Nelson. "Of course the stars all look different without their hair and makeup on," the girls are quick to point out.

The Juggs offer makeup and styling tips, casserole recipes, and fancy cracker-and-cheese hors d'oeuvres. They make sure all their passengers are aware that the major tour operators in the city don't have snacks aboard. "No cheese, no crackers," they sing.

This is a fun and very, very entertaining 90 minutes, and it's cheaper than a ticket to a comedy club. The bus loads at the north end of the Farmers' Market, next to the Bicentennial Mall, downtown. Get there at least 30 minutes early, because the fun and jokes begin as soon as you arrive. And if you aren't there at least 15 minutes before the tour's starting time, you will be considered a "no-show." Guests are encouraged to bring coolers with drinks but not food inside. Tours leave at 10:30 a.m. on Thurs and Fri and at 11 a.m. and 2 p.m. on Sat and Sun. Rates are $35 for adults under 55, $32 for guests 55 and up; there's a tip bucket if you are so inclined. Find out more by calling (615) 226-7300 or (800) 342-2132 or go online at nashtrash.com.

contemporary folk art. The latter category is what sets this fun place apart from the rest of the great galleries in the city. If you're looking for eclectic art, from fine Parisian art to rusted tin monkeys, this is the place! Located at 215 Fifth Ave. North. Open Tues through Sat 11 a.m. to 5 p.m. The gallery's website offers links and calendars for other cultural events in Nashville as well as a photographic inventory of their own offerings.

Look! Up in the sky! At 632 feet, the Bell South Building, fondly known locally as the **Batman Building** because of its uncanny resemblance to the caped crusader, is the tallest building in the state. It has 27 floors of office space and above that several other storage, mechanical, and open floors. At the very top, two spirals go heavenward from either side, hinting of Batman's pointed ears. The behemoth makes quite a statement.

"That's what the architect wanted to do," said a Bell South official. "The design philosophy was to be unique, be distinctive in the Nashville skyline, and avoid being another boxy skyscraper." He noted that while not planning to make it look like Batman, the design "does evoke that image, and others as well. Many people think it looks like a phone receiver

civilwarfacts

More battles were fought in Tennessee than in any other state except Virginia.

Tennessee was the last state to secede from the Union and the first state to be readmitted after the war.

East Tennesseans were primarily on the side of the Confederacy.

The free booklet *A Path Divided: Tennessee's Civil War Years* provides a thumbnail history of the war and a list of related events and attractions throughout the state.

and handset at the top," he said, adding that he has been told the 9-level underground parking garage was the largest building construction excavation ever in the state.

When the **Frist Center for the Visual Arts** (615-244-3340; fristcenter .org) opened its doors in 2001, the fine art museum set the stage for a new city cultural landscape. The Frist is located in Nashville's historic downtown post office, which was built in 1933–34. The beautiful art deco structure is listed on the National Register of Historic Places. The Frist has no permanent collection but showcases changing exhibits, always a new reason to return. Since opening, the Frist has brought world-class exhibits to the city, contributing to a vibrant arts scene. The Frist has a 250-seat auditorium, gift shop, and the Frist Center Cafe. Be sure to visit the gift shop. I have bought some lovely jewelry, scarves, and gifts there every time I visit. The Frist Center is located at 919 Broadway. Open Mon through Wed 10 a.m. to 5:30 p.m.,

Thurs and Fri 10 a.m. to 9 p.m., Sat 10 a.m. to 5:30 p.m., and Sun 1 to 5:30 p.m. Admission is $10 for adults, $7 for senior citizens and college students, free for under 18.

When the ***Hermitage Hotel*** (615-244-3121; hermitagehotel.com) was built in 1910, it was the city's first million-dollar hotel, and it became a symbol of Nashville's emergence as a major southern city. It flourished for more than 50 years, only to start deteriorating with the rest of the downtown area in the 1960s. Now, as the downtown area has gained a new life, so has the Hermitage Hotel. From its Beaux Arts design—the only commercial example

The Plant That's Eatin' Tennessee

That's **kudzu** (pronounced cud-zoo) you see growing all over the roadsides throughout Tennessee. The large hairy-leafed, bright green invasive vine is also known as the mile-a-minute vine and the vine that ate the South. It grows as much as a foot a day or 60 feet a summer in good weather and can take up to a decade to kill. It is said that southerners keep their windows shut at night to keep out the kudzu.

Kudzu was introduced to the US in 1876 at the Centennial Exposition in Philadelphia by the Japanese. During the Great Depression of the 1930s, the Soil Conservation Service promoted kudzu for erosion control, and hundreds of men planted it on roadsides throughout the south. Farmers were paid by the government to plant fields of the vines in the 1940s.

It does control erosion, but it also runs rampant and kills virtually everything in its path and climbs anything it contacts, including telephone poles and trees. Where it grows, kudzu has the ability to out-compete and eliminate native plant species and upset the natural diversity of plant and animal communities.

The vine has been known to kill entire forests by preventing the trees from getting light. During warm weather, the plant, classified a weed by the government in 1970, bears 6- to 10-inch spikes of small, fragrant purple flowers. The state has been having some success eradicating the vine by using various tools available. Methods include mechanical treatment (usually brush-hogs and shredder mulchers), prescribed burning, herbicides, and biological control. The emphasis is on persistent and consistent attempts to eradicate kudzu.

Don't be tempted to dig up any of the plants to take home with you. They will soon become a nuisance, and you'll spend the rest of your life trying to get rid of them.

of it in Tennessee—to its magnificently ornate lobby, the hotel is once again a symbol of pride for downtown Nashville. Make sure you check out the men's room, next to the Capitol Grille on the lower level. It is the coolest restroom in the city. A bronze plaque mounted next to the door reads "Once the site of many business transactions, this unique art deco bathroom has been the selected location of several interviews, music videos, and fashion photography. It has been said that more women have toured this men's room than any other in the country." Ladies, make sure you announce yourself before entering.

The Hermitage, owned by Historic Hotels, received a $15 million renovation in late 2002 and early 2003, and within a short time of reopening on Valentine's Day 2003, it received a five-diamond ranking, followed by a five-star listing as well. It is now the only five-diamond, five-star hotel within a 9-state area.

Located across from the Tennessee Performing Arts Center and the State Capitol, at 231 Sixth Ave. North, the hotel is a comfortable, classy place to call home while exploring Music City.

Several decades before the city was known for its music, it had a reputation as a regional center of culture and education. Numerous colleges advanced the learning of the classics, and it wasn't long before the city was known as the *Athens of the South.* In 1896 it was only natural for planners of the state's centennial celebrations to elaborate on this classic theme.

An exact replica of the *Greek Parthenon* (615-862-8431; nashville .gov), with a tolerance of less than one-tenth of an inch, was built for the huge exposition, held in what is now known as Centennial Park, just a few miles out West End Avenue from downtown at 2600 West End Ave. Now fully restored and still the world's only full-size replica, the Parthenon houses art exhibits and serves as a backdrop for various cultural events in the park. A 42-foot replica of Athena Parthenos has been sculpted and is on display in the main hall. Open Tues through Sat 9 a.m. to 4:30 p.m. Admission is $6 for adults and $4 for senior citizens and children (ages 4–17).

Next to the Parthenon, the neatest structure in the park is the concrete ship's prow, near the 25th Avenue North entrance. Now more than 100 years old, the reinforced concrete replica of the front end of a ship has an ornate metal figurehead, the original cast that was used to make the one on the *Tennessee,* a US cruiser that plied the waters during the 1898

Spanish-American War. The decorative metalwork was exhibited at the 1909 Seattle Exposition, and when that event was over, the metalwork was shipped here by request of Nashville-raised Navy admiral Albert Gleaves. The concrete prow was built and the metalwork mounted, making the structure look like "a ship that had been driven ashore in the shrubbery," as one Nashville journalist described it at the time.

Centennial Park is the site of many events during the year, including three quality arts and crafts fairs. In May the *Tennessee Association of Craft Artists (TACA)* (615-736-7600; tennesseecrafts.org) produces a juried crafts festival that is one of the largest marketplaces for quality crafts anywhere in the state. Nearly 200 Tennessee craftspeople show up to peddle their wares.

In June the *American Artisan Festival* takes place over Father's Day weekend. More than 150 craftspeople from 35 states show up for the weekend. The food at this particular festival could be considered the best of any food at any festival in the state. It's eclectic, with an emphasis on the unusual and the healthy. This show is sponsored by the American Artisan Crafts Gallery, just down the road from Centennial Park.

Held in late September the *TACA Fall Crafts Fair* is a juried show for all craftspeople, not just those from Tennessee (as is the May festival). Again, quality crafts are abundant, and the show comes at a perfect time to start Christmas shopping.

There are notables buried in just about every cemetery in the world, and Nashville is no exception—except that we have more than our share of country crooners interred.

At the huge *Woodlawn Memorial Park* (615-383-4754), between I-65 and Nolensville Road just south of downtown at 660 Thompson Ln., several country and music legends are buried, including Roy Orbison, Webb Pierce, Marty Robbins, Red Sovine, Eddy Arnold, Webb Pierce, Porter Wagoner, and Tammy Wynette. To find exact locations, go to the office; someone there will provide you with a map.

Roy Acuff, Floyd Cramer, John Hartford, Kitty Wells, Keith Whitley, and Hank Snow are among the country notables buried at the *Spring Hill Cemetery* (615-865-1101), 5110 Gallatin Rd. Also there is Beth Slater Whitson, who wrote the lyrics to "Let Me Call You Sweetheart."

Nashville City Cemetery (615-862-7970; nashvillecitycemetery.org) is the oldest public cemetery in the city, and with 23,000 graves dating back to 1822, you can imagine the scope of the historical figures buried here, including three Civil War generals—Bushrod Johnson, Richard Ewell, and Felix Zollicoffer; William Carroll, who served as Tennessee governor from 1788 to 1844; and James Robertson, the founder of Nashville. Also here is Captain William Driver, who first called the American flag "Old Glory."

The cemetery is run by the Metro Historical Commission and is listed on the National Register of Historic Places. Historical markers are placed throughout with specific information. Located at 1001 Fourth Ave. South, at Oak Street, this historic site is open daily until dusk.

Over at the **Tennessee State Fairgrounds** (615-862-5016; tnstatefair .org) at 500 Wedgewood Ave., the state's largest flea market takes place the fourth weekend of each month. There are nearly 2,200 vendors on any particular weekend, with 600 of them located indoors. They are open 6 a.m. to 6 p.m. Sat and 7 a.m. to 4 p.m. on Sun. *Hint:* Vendors can set up anytime after 3 p.m. on Fri, and most will sell to you if you drop by while they are at it. That's when they all wheel and deal with one another, and it's when you'll definitely get the best choice. Admission is free.

The **Tennessee State Fair** (615-862-8980; tnstatefair.org) is held on these same grounds the second week of Sept. Lots of carnival rides, great-tasting (albeit fatty) foods, and plenty of farm animals are on hand for the entertainment and education of guests. There's usually a circus and a major country concert held during the event. A village with log cabins and working craftspeople provides a glimpse into the early days of the state.

Two close-by, fun, and delicious places to eat can be found on Elliston Place. **Rotier's** (615-327-9892; rotiersrestaurant.com) is located just east of Centennial Park, behind Eckerd's Drugs at 2413 Elliston Place. Year in and year out, "Mama" Rotier's comes in at the top, or very close to the top, in the best hamburger in town competition. Served on French bread, the burgers and all the fixings are held together with a toothpick when they reach you. It seems like everyone comes here, and at times it also seems like all the waitresses know everyone! I've seen some of country music's top stars here enjoying a burger and a chocolate milk shake. The popular spot also has daily luncheon specials, including some very good meat loaf, and a big variety of bottled beers.

Continue east on Elliston to find the **Elliston Place Soda Shop** (615-327-1090) on your right at 2111 Elliston Place, just before you get to the

Krispy Kreme, the doughnut den of heaven. Virtually unchanged from when it opened in the 1940s, the shop has turned into much more than a funky soda shop. The milk shakes are the best in town, and it's fun sitting there sipping your shake in your own booth, choosing music on your personal jukebox. Country ham, fresh biscuits, a bevy of vegetables including black-eyed peas, and plenty of other "meat-and-three" offerings can be found on the menu. Breakfast is served daily.

Another classic blast from the past is **Bobbie's Dairy Dip** (615-463-8088) at 5301 Charlotte, at the corner of 53rd Street. It's an old-fashioned, walk-up ice-cream stand, which also serves a great burger and fries. They sell soft serve and real, premium ice cream and are great at piling it together to create some wonderful concoctions.

On Charlotte, between Bobbie's and 49th Street, there are a bunch of other notable places to spend a bit of your time. The **Southern Thrift Store** (615-292-1807; southernthriftstore.com), at 5010 Charlotte, is the best-stocked thrift shop in Nashville. It is constantly getting new (old) stuff, and it has some of the best deals. If you're looking for a country star T-shirt, you'll find a huge selection here, hung neatly on hangers, for as little as 99 cents. There is also plenty of furniture and other thrift-shop couture. The store has branched out to three other locations: 2701 Gallatin Pike (615-228-1368), 412 Metroplex (615-833-1319), and 2710 Old Lebanon Pike (615-872-0499).

For a truly amazing site visit the **Upper Room Chapel and Museum** (877-899-2780; upperroom.org) at 1908 Grand Ave. The stars of this estab-lishment are an 8-by-17-foot wood carving of da Vinci's *The Last Supper* and an 8-by-20-foot stained-glass window with a Pentecost theme. Beautiful!

The museum features religious paintings and art objects dating back to the 1300s as well as religious artifacts from throughout the world. At Christ-mastime the museum displays its collection of Ukrainian eggs and more than 100 nativity scenes. Open Mon through Fri 8 a.m. to 4:30 p.m.; free, but donations are graciously accepted.

Opened in 2013, **Music City Marketplace** (615-259-4747) is in the heart of downtown Nashville in the iconic glass tower of the Bridgestone Arena at Fifth Avenue South and Broadway. The Visitor Information Center is a great place to get brochures, tickets, souvenirs, friendly assistance, and hear live music. Musicians share their talents here for free. If the stage is not being used, visitors are invited to step up and snap a souvenir photo from Music City.

The Marketplace shop offers items with a musical touch. Works from local artists adorn the walls and items are displayed in vintage instrument cases. The center is open Mon through Sat 8 a.m. to 5:30 p.m. and Sun 10 a.m. to 5 p.m.

For sports fans, the *Tennessee Sports Hall of Fame* (615-242-4750; tshf.net) is a must stop. Located inside the Bridgestone Arena at 501 Broadway, the interactive facility chronicles the history of sports in Tennessee from early 1800s to today. The Tennessee Sports Hall of Fame is open Tues through Sat 10 a.m. to 5 p.m. and later on days of Bridgestone Area events. Admission is $3 for adults and $2 for children.

For assistance in planning a trip to Nashville, the *Nashville Convention and Visitors Bureau* (800-657-6910; visitmusiccity.com) features streaming headlines on their website and plenty of quick links to more than 50 area attractions, upcoming events, tours, and shopping.

Next to the Loveless Cafe, the Natchez Trace Shell gas station about 15 miles from downtown out West End Avenue (which becomes Highway 100), could really be called Last Chance Gas & Food. It's located at the entrance to the *Natchez Trace Parkway* at 8456 Hwy. 100, after which you won't find any food, gas, or lodging for your entire 450-mile trip to Natchez, Mississippi.

If you're going to travel the wonderful Natchez Trace for more than a couple of days, you'll probably want to stay overnight close to the trace, and a bed-and-breakfast inn is definitely your best choice. The trace itself is very noncommercial, with no buildings and no billboard or lodging signs, so it's a good idea to plan ahead and have reservations. The *Natchez Trace Bed & Breakfast Reservation Service* (800-377-2770; natcheztracetravel .com) is a good way to get access to and information on the nearly 40 inns close to the trace.

Just west of the entrance to the Natchez Trace at 8750 Hwy. 100, you'll find some of the best fresh produce in middle Tennessee. *McNeil's Fresh Produce Stand* (615-673-1016) is open Apr through Oct, and the open-air stand is known widely for carrying the best of whatever is in season. The corn is the best I've found in this area, and the locally grown vine-ripened tomatoes are huge and plump. It's a good place to load up on some healthy snacks before you hit the trace.

The Loveless Cafe

The "new" Loveless Cafe has the same food and the same ambience but new owners. Nashville's own Tom Morales, owner of the noted movie-location catering business, TomKats, purchased the business and closed it for 3 months to make major renovations, including expanded seating, new restrooms, and a new kitchen. In addition to work on the restaurant itself, he created a retail deli and store in one of the old motel rooms.

More than 60 years of serving thousands of people the best country ham breakfasts in the South had put quite a stress on the little house in the country. The house needed repairs, and its dining room needed to be extended to keep up with the demand. The old kitchen had trouble staying on top of the orders. Donna McCabe, one of the owners, was ready to retire, and her son George, the other owner, decided to sell—but not to just anyone. Both the McCabes were very selective about whom they allowed to buy the business. They were looking for someone who would keep the name, the menu, and the ambience while investing in the business to guarantee that it would be around for many more years.

Through the years, anyone who is (or was) anyone has eaten here. Country stars, national TV celebrities, and politicians from all over are spotted here almost on a daily basis. ABC–TV called the Loveless "the best country restaurant in America," and Martha Stewart told her audience once that the best breakfast she ever had was served at the Loveless Cafe. Breakfast is served all day. Bottled beer, house wine, and moonshine also are served.

Located on the grounds of the Loveless Cafe, the Loveless Barn was built to host celebrations and concerts. Since opening in 2009, the Loveless Barn has done just that. With two large lawns, covered porches, and walls that roll open to the outside, the Loveless Barn can handle large or small groups. Every Wednesday night, guests descend on the barn for *Music City Roots, Live from the Loveless Cafe*. This weekly live radio show is Music City's salute to the city's wide diversity of music. The trademark neon sign still marks the spot on Highway 100 in the little community of Pasquo where the Loveless Cafe is located. Open 7 a.m. to 9 p.m. 7 days a week. Check it out at (615) 646-9700 or lovelesscafe.com. The website also features great Loveless recipes including the famous Bacon Apple Pie. That's right—this pie features a crispy bacon lattice top instead of the traditional pie dough lattice. And it is *g-o-o-o-d*!

About 30 miles east of Nashville, the downtown square of ***Lebanon*** is antiques heaven. Within a 2-block area there are more than a dozen antiques stores and antiques malls. Most are open daily. The largest, and probably the most packed with the biggest selection, is ***Cuz's Antiques*** (615-444-8070; cuzantiques.com), in the corner on the square. There's plenty of parking, and there's always plenty of action in the downtown area.

The award-winning ***Wilson County Fair*** (615-443-2626; wilsoncounty fair.net), voted the state's best county fair several times, is held each Aug at 945 E. Baddour Pkwy., and it truly is small-town Americana at its finest. Former vice president Al Gore showed animals here as a child, and thousands of kids before and after him prepare for the fair all year long. The carnival is colorful and fun, the exhibits are great, and the entertainment is top-notch.

The fair takes place at the James E. Ward Agricultural Center, where picturesque ***Fiddlers Grove*** is also located. The grove consists of more than 30 original and replicated log cabins moved to the fairgrounds, creating a compound of what a Wilson County community would have looked like in the 1800s.

There are such frontier staples as a jail, post office, blacksmith shop, and general store, and it's still growing year by year. Here is a low-key, out-of-the-way community where the early life of Tennessee is preserved and presented. It's a lot of fun, and the workers here are well versed in this particular era of the state's history. It's open during the fair and 10 a.m. to 3 p.m. Tues through Sat May through mid-Oct. Admission is free.

If you like wildflowers, make sure you visit the ***Cedar Glade Wild-flower Festival*** (615-443-2769) each year in mid-Apr at the Cedars of Lebanon State Park, just outside Lebanon. The 2-day event is structured to dazzle the experts and to create an interest in those just learning to appreciate one of nature's best gifts.

The country stars and the top bankers and businesspeople of the state might make their millions in Nashville, but when it comes to investing in their lifestyles and families, many come south to ***Williamson County*** (Williamson County Convention and Visitors Bureau: 615-791-7554; visitwilliamson.com). It consistently has the state's highest per capita income and the lowest unemployment rate.

Lee Greenwood, Kenny Chesney, Tim McGraw, Brad Paisley, Faith Hill, Vince Gill, Amy Grant, Ted Danson, Mary Steenburgen, the Judds, and Tom T. Hall are among the inhabitants of the area. If you want to see them, though, you probably have a better chance hanging out at the local Kroger store than in front of their houses.

Franklin, the county seat, is 17 miles and "100 years" south of Nashville and is associated with old, restored homes and businesses, antiques shopping, and the Civil War. The entire downtown section is on the National Register of Historic Places.

It's got a funky name, and it's located in a surprising place. But the *Frothy Monkey* (615-465-6279; frothymonkey.com) in Franklin serves some very good coffee as its dedicated patrons can attest. Housed in an old parsonage in downtown Franklin at 125 Fifth Ave. South, the shop opened in late 2012 to serve breakfast, lunch, and dinner (along with beer and wine) with late risers able to enjoy breakfast until 5 p.m. Open Mon through Sat 7 a.m. to 9 p.m., Sun 8 a.m. to 9 p.m.

As locals themselves, the owners try to honor other local businesses. For example, all the milk used at the Frothy Monkey comes from the Hatcher Family Dairy. The sausage burger contains Allan Benton's meat. The trout comes from Bob White Springs from the small town of Only, Tennessee. The pasta is locally made from Al Fresco Pasta. Take time to read the menu. It's a joy and a difficult decision. The cider-glazed Viola Farms pork pot roast, sweet potato-pear gratin, mustard greens, and green tomato chow chow makes a good choice, as is the Bear Creek Farms Rada brisket, sweet potato herbed bread pudding, fried farm eggs, and buttered asparagus. Look for some familiar faces in the Frothy Monkey. Country music stars like Brad Paisley and other performers who live in Franklin have already discovered the charming critter.

The *Carter House* (615-791-1861; battleoffranklintrust.org), south of downtown on Columbia Avenue, was caught in the middle of the fight aptly known as the *Battle of Franklin* on November 30, 1864. Bullet holes are still evident in the main structure and various outbuildings. One of the outbuildings has 203 bullet holes in it, making it the most battle-damaged building from the Civil War still standing anywhere.

The property is one of the 11 historic sites in the state owned and operated by the Association for the Preservation of Tennessee Antiquities. Open daily; admission is charged.

About 5 miles away, the *Carnton Mansion* (615-794-0903; battleoffranklintrust.org) also played an important role in the Battle of Franklin. On the rear lines of the Confederate forces, the elegant estate witnessed a steady stream of dying and wounded during the battle. At one time the bodies of five slain Confederate generals were laid out on the back porch. Within view of that historic porch rests the only privately owned Confederate cemetery in the US. Open daily; admission is charged to the house; the cemetery is free.

A few blocks east of Franklin's town square, where the Confederate monument (circa 1899) rests, is the *Hiram Masonic Lodge.* When the 3-story building was built in 1823, it was said to be the tallest structure in Tennessee. It was constructed to house the first Masonic Lodge in the state, which was chartered in 1803; later, in 1827, the first Protestant Episcopal Church in Tennessee was founded here.

The historic downtown area of Franklin is quickly becoming known as the newest "antiques capital of Tennessee." There are nearly three dozen antiques and craft stores within the downtown area, all within walking distance of one another. *Franklin Antique Mall* (615-790-8593) is the city's oldest and largest antiques mall. Used as a flour mill in the 1800s, the handmade-brick structure was the county's icehouse at the turn of the 20th century. Today it houses the goods of more than 60 different antiques dealers spread out over 12,000 square feet of space. At Second Avenue South and S. Margin Street at 2512 Second Ave. South; open daily.

With all the pickers in town, you should expect the Nashville area to have some excellent guitar shops. The one in Franklin—*Artisan Guitars* (866-265-5993; artisanguitars.com)—is a player's paradise. Heck, even the website could fascinate a musician or wannabe musician for hours. Artisan Guitars proudly represents some of the world's finest acoustic guitar builders of this century. Known as luthiers, these talented builders are true artists. Owners Bill and Ellie Warmoth share a wealth of guitar information and can help a seasoned pro or a beginner find the perfect instrument for them. In today's world, it is surprising to find a store that still offers layaway. Artisan Guitars does. As the Warmouths explain, it is difficult to find the guitar of your dreams. And when you do, you might not have the money in your pocket to buy your treasure at that particular time. Artisan Guitars offers a 90-day layaway plan so that a special guitar doesn't get away. If all that doesn't tempt you to visit the shop, be aware that many well-known musicians like to frequent Artisan Guitars. In fact, the owners guarantee that they won't publicly mention any of those star customers. But I know that Brad Paisley likes to drop by the 230 Franklin Rd. location and play around with the inventory.

On US 31 is the **Rippavilla Plantation** (931-486-9037; rippavilla.org). Built in 1852, the home has been restored and is the headquarters for the Tennessee Antebellum Trail organization and houses the **Armies of Tennessee Civil War Museum,** which chronicles the effects of the war on the family, the plantation, and the community.

The Confederate army spent the night on the property before they moved north to join the Battle of Franklin, one of the last major battles of the Civil War. Legend has it that all five of the Confederate generals who were killed in that battle had slept at Rippavilla and had breakfast together before heading off to battle.

Today the beautifully restored home features many of the original family's heirlooms and furnishings and is open to the public Tues through Sat. There is an admission fee to enter the home, but you can walk the grounds and visit the welcome center for no charge.

Columbia is the center of commerce for Maury County. In addition to its reputation as the Antebellum Homes Capital of Tennessee, Columbia claims James K. Polk, one of the three presidents from the state, as a former resident. **Polk's ancestral home** (931-388-2354; jameskpolk.com) is open to the public at 301 W. Seventh Ave. Built by his parents in 1816, this is the house where Polk began his legal and political career. There is plenty of one-of-a-kind memorabilia housed here, and the gift shop has more books written about Polk than you could have ever imagined.

A unique structure among Tennessee's antebellum homes is the **Athenaeum Rectory** (931-381-4822; athenaeumrectory.com), built in 1837 in a Moorish-Gothic architectural design. In 1852 it became the home to the Columbia Athenaeum School for Young Ladies. Today the building is owned by the Association for the Preservation of Tennessee Antiquities and is operated as a historic house museum.

Among things to look for as you tour the house is the chandelier in the reception room. It is made of seven metals and is original to the house. The front door side panels are flashed glass containing gold leaf from Europe, and the walnut and oak floors throughout are in a design known as wood carpeting.

Open for guided tours Tues through Sat 10 a.m. to 4 p.m., the house is located at 808 Athenaeum St. Call (931) 381-4822 or go to athenaeum rectory.com.

Oh, to Be a 19th-Century Lady Again

Columbia's Athenaeum Rectory was a well-respected girls' school for more than 50 years, teaching a wide range of quality courses, including mathematics, physics, science, and business—studies that were normally reserved only for young men. The school flourished from 1852 to 1904.

Today the Association for the Preservation of Tennessee Antiquities, owners and operators of the restored structure, conducts the 1861 Athenaeum Girls' School each summer. For 1 full week each July, young ladies ages 14 to 18 from all over the country dress in authentic 19th-century costumes and study the same courses in etiquette, penmanship, art, music, dance, and social graces as did the young ladies of 150 years ago. The week is highlighted on Friday evening with graduation ceremonies, followed by a formal ball.

All is not lost for you older ladies, age 19 and over. A condensed 2-day version of the school is offered each May just for you. And you get to dress up, too! For more information call (931) 381-4822.

The Polks were quite the building family here in Columbia. In addition to the James K. Polk Home and and the Athenaeum Rectory, the family built three other historic structures—the Hamilton Place, St. John's Episcopal Church, and **Rattle and Snap Plantation** (931-388-2354; rattleandsnap plantation.com). All five were built within a 30-year period and only a few miles from one another. Special tours have been developed to visit all Polk structures.

The James K. Polk Home and Rattle and Snap Plantation are two of the 60-plus homes along the **Tennessee Antebellum Trail.** Within a 30-mile radius of Nashville lies the highest concentration of antebellum homes in the South today. Eight of the houses are open to the public. A splendid tour map that lists and describes each house is available at area attractions or by contacting the **Maury County Convention and Visitors Bureau** (888-852-1860; antebellum.com).

If you think you have stubborn friends, they are probably nothing compared with the critters that gather here each year during the first week of April! That's when the **Mule Day Festival & Parade** (931-381-9557; mule-day.com) take place to celebrate Columbia's proud heritage as the mule-raising capital of the state. The parade features mules pulling just about everything down the highway, and the festival is loaded with arts and crafts booths, all kinds of food (no mule meat, they assure us), a liar's contest, square dancing, and a mule show.

On Highway 50W about 8 miles from downtown Columbia, you'll find a good example of how industry and nature can live together. From 1937 to 1986, the *Monsanto* company had a plant here that produced elemental phosphorus. Through the years, as the company finished up strip mining an area of 5,345 acres, it planted trees and created lakes. Wildlife began moving in, and when the plant closed in 1986, the company worked with the Tennessee Wildlife Resources Agency to turn the entire area into a wildlife enhancement zone.

Out US 43 from Columbia is *Mount Pleasant,* a small community that calls itself the Best-Kept Secret in Middle Tennessee. Their other slogan, which might be a bit more appropriate for this sleepy little burg, is Stop, Shop, Eat, and Tour.

The town witnessed a great deal of troop movement during the Civil War, and after discovery of high-grade phosphate in 1896, the village of 400 residents became a boomtown of more than 2,000 when workers from 25 states and 10 countries came to toil in the local phosphate mines. By the early 1900s there were more than a dozen companies operating here, and it was known as the "phosphate capital of the world."

Today the phosphate heritage and hundreds of other historical artifacts are preserved in the *Mt. Pleasant-Maury Phosphate Museum* (931-379-9511), downtown at 108 Public Sq. Open most weekdays and Sat 9:30 a.m. to 4:30 p.m. Closed Wed and Sun. Admission is $1 per adult or $3 for the entire family.

One mile from downtown Murfreesboro is an obelisk marking the geographic center of the state. The *Dimple of the Universe,* as it is called locally, is on Old Lascassas Pike. Turn left off Greenland Drive opposite the football fields at Middle Tennessee State University.

In the early days *Murfreesboro* was a little village known as *Cannonsburgh.* Today *Cannonsburgh Pioneer Village* is a living museum depicting 125 years of southern life amid the hustle and bustle of the metropolitan area the city has become. Among its collections are a log house, blacksmith shop, general store, gristmill, one-room schoolhouse, and museum.

But the real star here is the **World's Largest Red Cedar Bucket,** manufactured locally by a bucket factory that toured the oddity as an advertising gimmick. It was built in 1887, is 6 feet tall and 24 feet around the top, and holds nearly 2,000 gallons of water. The museum here also holds what officials feel is the World's Largest Spinning Wheel. It stands 8 feet tall and was made by a local mortician.

Cannonsburgh is the site of the popular **Uncle Dave Macon Days** (800-716-7560; uncledavemaconday.com) early every July. There's plenty of music, food, games, and activities for the kids. There is a juried arts and crafts show and a special gospel music celebration on Sun morning. Cannonsburgh is open May through Oct, Tues through Sun, at 312 S. Front St. Grounds open year-round; admission is free.

More information on Murfreesboro, Smyrna, and the rest of Rutherford County can be found online at rutherfordchamber.org, or call the Tourism Council at (800) 716-7560.

One of the most interesting factory tours in the state is located north of Murfreesboro, just off US 41. The **Nissan Motor Manufacturing Corporation Truck/Auto Plant** offers tours on Tues and Thurs at 10 a.m. and 1 p.m. During the hour-long tram ride through the modern plant, you'll see men and women working side by side with hundreds of robots to produce more than 1,000 vehicles a day.

The complex covers about 800 acres and employs more than 6,000 local workers. Reservations are required (615-459-1444). Admission is free, and, of course, they don't give samples. No children under 5 are permitted on this tour.

Mr. Miller ran Christiana's only grocery store at 7011 Main St. for 75 years, and in that funky old building today is **Miller's Grocery and Country Cafe** (615-893-1878; millersgrocery.com). It's a "meat and three" during the week, a bluegrass music and catfish eatery on Fri night, and fine dining and jazz room on Sat night. It's also the tiny town's only restaurant.

Two meats and an array of veggies are available as a blue-plate lunch Tues through Sat 11 a.m. to 2 p.m., and the dinners are served Fri and Sat nights 5 to 9 p.m. A Sun buffet is served 11 a.m. to 2 p.m. There's a lot of old-time flavor in this old building: oilcloth-covered tables, wood floors, and all kinds of antiques and memorabilia that line the walls. Live bluegrass music is performed every Fri night, and live music of other genres is performed on Sat night. Located about 8 miles from Murfreesboro and 7 miles south of I-24 off US 231. Head south, and when you see the Christiana signs, turn left onto Highway 269. Cross the railroad tracks, make an immediate left, and you're in the neighborhood.

The little crossroads community of *Triune,* 25 miles south of Nashville at the corner of Highway 96 and US 31A/41A, has two claims to fame—the weekly *Triune Flea Market* and the annual Tennessee Renaissance Festival at Castle Gwynn.

The flea market is of the small-town, let's-dig-deep-for-a-bargain type of event. Cars pull up, open their trunks, throw out a few blankets full of stuff, and start selling. If it rains, you'll get wet and plenty muddy. As in any type of flea market, there's a lot of junk out there; but if you are patient, you'll probably find some good things. Prices seem a bit high on the true antiques and popular collectibles, but the dealers will usually come down, especially on Sunday afternoon. It's open every Sat and Sun 7 a.m. to 5 p.m. at 7960 Nolensville Rd.

The 16th century is celebrated at the *Tennessee Renaissance Festival* (615-395-9950; tnrenfest.com), held every weekend in May each year at Castle Gwynn, a wonderfully eclectic 20th-century castle at 2124 New Castle Rd. in Arrington. This is the time of King Henry VIII, and he's joined in the festivities by plenty of court jesters, street entertainers, musicians, Shakespearean actors, period games, combat chess, and full-armor jousts. Hundreds of craftspeople are open for business in the medieval marketplace, and there's a whole lot of great, unusual food and beverages. Located 25 miles south of Nashville on Highway 96, about halfway between I-24 and I-65 in Triune.

Southeastern Heartland

If you happen to be in *Manchester* during late Oct, be sure to visit the *Old Timer's Day celebration* (931-728-7635). The city fathers shut down the streets around the square for a Saturday and fill it with fun things to do, including a bluegrass music concert, arts and crafts, kiddie rides and games, and a whole lot of food.

Foothills Crafts (865-470-0669; foothillscraftbuild.org) in Manchester at 418 Woodbury Hwy. may be the ultimate quality crafts store. Run entirely by volunteer members of the Coffee County Crafts Association, the shop has an amazing array of handcrafted items for sale. It's a hard process to get your crafts represented here, but that process ensures that only the highest-quality items will be on display. Currently more than 200 different artisans are selling their work out of this old-time grocery store; it's open daily year-round.

On Highway 55, just before you reach Tullahoma, be on the lookout for the **Coca-Cola Bottling Company** plant. Next to it is the **Company Store** (931-454-1030), a retail outlet open to the public. You'll be amazed at how many things are made with the Coke and Dr Pepper logos on them. It's a virtual plethora of red-and-white merchandise, from clothes to antique reproductions to glasses. Open Mon through Sat 10 a.m. to 5 p.m.; closed Sun.

The **Tullahoma Fine Arts Center** and the **Regional Museum of Art** (931-455-1234; tullahomafinearts.wordpress.com) share space in the city's oldest brick house, at 401 Jackson St. The arts center features work of local and regional artists, including crafts as well as the fine arts. All items on display may be purchased. The Regional Museum of Art features traveling exhibits and the museum's private collection. Open Mon through Fri; admission is free.

When George Dickel first discovered tranquil Cascade Hollow outside Tullahoma, he knew he had found a gold mine. It was the water from a nearby spring that Dickel considered so valuable. The ancient limestone shelf of the plateau provided water that ran fresh and clear, without mineral deposits. That iron-free water was the perfect ingredient for smooth sippin' whisky. Dickel also made another important discovery—the batch of whisky he had made in the winter with that water was far smoother than the whisky he had produced in the summer. Dickel used the traditional Scottish spelling of "whisky" (as opposed to "whiskey") because he believed his product to be as high in quality as the best Scotch whiskies.

First produced in 1877, George Dickel whisky is still handcrafted. After a 4-year shutdown, the **George Dickel Distillery** (931-857-3124; dickel .com) at 1950 Cascade Hollow Rd. reopened in October 2003 and is now going stronger than ever. The distillery offers tours of this isolated spot surrounded by true hill beauty. Visitors also can watch a George Dickel video in the visitor center, which is filled with antiques and photos. The **George Dickel General Store** is a nice place to shop and look. On-site is a US Post Office—the only working post office at any distillery in the US. Visitors can also see Oscar, a 1910 replica of the George Dickel Whisky delivery truck with the old-fashioned Dickel sign painted on the side.

If your taste in bed-and-breakfasts is more rustic and rural than froufrou and finery, here's a place for you! *Ledford Mill Bed & Breakfast* (931-455-2546) is located inside an 1884 gristmill and is on the National Register of Historic Places. John Spear purchased the inn during June 2002. The previous owners, who had turned the mill into a bed-and-breakfast, decided not to remove the equipment but instead created a bed-and-breakfast around all the milling apparatus.

In the Loft Room, the corn-cleaning machine separates the sleeping and sitting areas. The Creek Room has an entire wall of stone, an old-time tub, and a large private deck with a view of the falls and wooded hillside. The Falls Room, with a wall of Chattanooga shale, is the closest to the falls and has a large bathroom that showcases the main wheel—the "heart" of the mill. Plank flooring is used throughout.

Located in a "holler" at the spring-fed headwaters of Shipman's Creek, the mill sits over the water; that same spring water is what comes through the taps to drink.

Rooms run from $95 to $125, and the facilities are pretty well booked up in advance, so you'll probably need to do some planning if you want to stay here. Turn onto Ledford Mill Road at the Lowe's Superstore on US 41A, and go 3 miles to the mill at 1195 Shipman Creek Rd.

Shelbyville, the Bedford County seat, is also the center of Tennessee's horse country. It plays host each year to the *Tennessee Walking Horse National Celebration* (931-684-5915; twhnc.com), an event during which the World Grand Champion is named. The Celebration Grounds are located on Madison Avenue, which is US 41A, east of downtown Shelbyville.

This special breed of horse, developed during 150 years of selective breeding, is promoted today as the world's greatest show and pleasure horse. The horse has an unusual rhythmic, gliding gait in which each hoof strikes the ground separately in an odd one-two-three-four beat.

The breed emerged from the plantations around here during the later part of the 19th century but today can be found across the country. The area around Shelbyville is still known for its farms, and most of the owners are happy to show off their facilities. Many have signs out welcoming you.

Nobody seems to know exactly how *Rover* got its name, but the most accepted story is that a bunch of bickering regulars at a local drinking establishment decided to name their community. After hours of arguing over a name, one of them piped out, "Why don't we just call it Rover—we all fight like dogs anyway." So be it.

Along Highway 269 in the northern corner of the county lies the quaint little village of *Bell Buckle.* The little downtown area, located along Railroad Square facing the active railroad, is a trip back in time. A covered wooden sidewalk leads you from one store to another. All the benches, rocking chairs, flowers, and store displays have a tendency to slow down pedestrian traffic a bit, but it gives you more time to look in the window or watch a train go by.

Ten little antiques and craft shops make up the downtown lineup. Margaret Britton Vaughn (friends call her Maggi), the state's official poet laureate, runs the *Bell Buckle Press* (931-389-6878) at 105 Webb Rd. Take time to drop in and chat with her for a few minutes; she's a true southern lady.

Featured prominently a few shops down is *J. Gregry's Bell Buckle Cafe and Music Parlour* (931-389-9693; bellbucklecafe.com). In addition to some great hickory-smoked barbecue and the world's greatest hand-squeezed lemonade, the cafe features live music three nights a week and is the site of a Sat afternoon live broadcast on WLIJ Radio 1580 AM from 1 to 3 p.m. You'll hear a lot of new and old country and bluegrass coming from the back room here. There are at least a couple shows each Friday and Saturday night. Food is served 7 days a week.

Phillips General Store (931-389-6547) has an amazing assortment of cool things. Of course beauty is in the eye of the beholder, but this shop at 4 Railroad Sq. has it all. From architectural items to folk art to garden art, the place is heaven. Open daily.

The roads to Bell Buckle are lined with daffodils, and the city founders felt those flowers were a good reason for a party. *Daffodil Day* is held on a Sat in mid-Mar each year, and the town celebrates with a bake sale, Easter egg hunt, old-fashioned menu at the Bell Buckle Cafe, and people dressed up like it's the 1800s all over again.

For a bit of the true South, be here during June to help celebrate the *Moon Pie Festival.* That's when you'll get to join in the celebration of one of the area's finest traditions, Moon Pies and RC Cola. Yum yum! Contact the **Bell Buckle Chamber of Commerce** (931-389-9663; bellbucklechamber .com) for more information.

The village is also the home of **Webb School** (931-389-9322; thewebb school.com), a preparatory school that has produced 10 Rhodes Scholars and the governors of three states. The Junior Room, the original wood-shingled one-room schoolhouse built in 1870, has been preserved as it was then, complete with potbellied stove and teaching paraphernalia. It's open for visitors daily and is free. The school hosts a well-respected arts and crafts festival the third weekend of each Oct.

The area west of Shelbyville on Highway 64 is loaded with horse stables and horse farms. A drive along this corridor into the city of **Lewisburg** definitely reminds you that you're smack-dab in the middle of Tennessee Horse Country. If you see training sessions taking place, chances are the owners won't mind if you stop and watch, but of course it's always polite to ask first.

If you'd like to learn a little history while you're in the Lewisburg area, drive south on US 31A from downtown and you'll run into the **Abner Houston home,** across from the Lone Oak Cemetery. The log cabin was the site of the first court of Marshall County in October 1836. It was moved to this site in 1957.

Deep in dry Moore County at 182 Lynchburg Hwy., you'll find a famous distillery known for its Tennessee sour mash whiskey. **Jack Daniel Distillery** (931-759-6357; jackdaniels.com) put Lynchburg, a community of 360

Claim to Fame for Miss Mary

Miss Mary Bobo, a close personal friend of Jack Daniel's and the proprietress of Miss Mary Bobo's Boarding House in Lynchburg for many years, holds the distinction of being the oldest woman to ever appear in the pages of *Playboy* magazine.

A Jack Daniel Distillery advertisement ran in the magazine in June 1980, congratulating Miss Mary on her 99th birthday. The ad ran a photo of her and encouraged everyone to send her a card. As a result of that ad, she received thousands of cards, 36 cakes, and numerous gifts.

Miss Mary ran her boarding business for another 3 years, dying in 1983—just shy of her 102nd birthday.

residents, on the map. Mister Jack (as he is locally known) founded his business in 1866 and received the first federal license ever issued for a distillery. If you want to take a tour, make sure you wear comfortable shoes: There's a lot of walking and hill climbing. This is true history and Americana at its finest.

One of the highlights of the tour is the visit to Daniel's office, left virtually the way it was when he died. Make sure you ask the guide to show you where Mister Jack lost his temper one day, eventually causing him to experience a slow, painful death.

Start your tour at the visitor center, located in the hollow. It's a huge stone building with a magnificent front porch; you can't miss it. Inside, you'll learn just about everything you'd ever want to know about Mister Jack, plus you'll see some great exhibits of rare bottles and jugs and a reproduction of his first-ever still. Tours leave every 15 minutes or so 9 a.m. to 4:30 p.m. daily and last for approximately 75 minutes.

There's a great deal of charm in the nearby village of **Lynchburg,** where Daniel lived his entire life. Today, surrounding the 1855 redbrick courthouse, the square is chock-full of gift shops, general stores, arts and crafts outlets, and stores selling Jack Daniel merchandise. Among the shops that are fun to visit is the **Lynchburg Ladies Handiwork** (931-759-7919), on the north side of the square at 18 Short St. The shop features handmade items, mostly needlework, by people in Moore County. The ladies working the shop spend their time quilting, sewing, and crocheting.

Used whiskey barrels, Jack Daniel memorabilia, and antique reproductions can be found at the **Lynchburg Hardware and General Store** (931-759-4200), on the east side of the square. Pop open a cold drink and listen to the locals discuss the latest news. Maybe you can challenge someone to a game of checkers. Jack Daniel's nephew Lem Motlow opened the store to earn a living during Prohibition. A full line of Jack Daniel's merchandise is available alongside historic general store and hardware items that are just for display.

The best-known place to eat in these parts is **Miss Mary Bobo's Boarding House** (931-759-7394) in the southwest corner of downtown at 295 Main St. Miss Mary began serving meals in 1908 and served many of them to Mister Jack, who had lunch here quite often. Of course both Mister Jack and Miss Mary are gone now, but the tradition lives on. Specializing in southern traditional foods, they serve their meals family style.

Each meal is different, and the usual offerings include your choice of two meats, six vegetables, bread, beverage, and a totally awesome dessert. Reservations are a must, since the popular eatery seats only 65 people. During most of the year, seatings are at 11 a.m. and 1 p.m., Mon through Sat. They are closed on Sun. During the slower periods, especially on Mon, there may be only one seating. It's best to be flexible when you call for reservations, and if you're looking for a Sat seating, you'll probably have to call several months in advance! Meals for adults are $19; $8 for children under 10.

Lynne Tolley, Mister Jack's great-grandniece, is now the proprietress of Miss Mary Bobo's and can be found in the kitchen daily preparing the noontime meal. However, on Fri afternoon she runs off to her part-time job—as an official taster at her great-uncle's distillery, where each week she tastes the latest aged batch of the famous whiskey. Try a visit!

If you're hungry for the best barbecue in the country, make plans to come to Lynchburg in late October. That's when the *Jack Daniel's World Championship Invitational Barbecue* (jackdanielsbarbecue.com) takes place. Participation is by invitation and qualification only. In order to compete here, your team must have won a championship cook-off of 50 or more participants or be the designated champion of a state competition. There are also international teams involved. Of course there are a lot of food booths for sampling, as well as games and music. Check the website for dates and times.

The *Tennessee Walking Horse Museum* (931-359-1574; twhbea.com) is located along the square, about a block from Miss Mary Bobo's. Among the fun things in here are photos of all the world champion Tennessee Walking Horses from 1939 to the present. In addition, there are hundreds of other photos, memorabilia, and tools of the trade. Owned by the Tennessee Walking Horse National Celebration in nearby Shelbyville, the museum is open 10 a.m. to noon and 1 to 4 p.m. Tues through Sat.

As you head west across the mountain from Monteagle on US 41A/64, you'll pass the beautiful *University of the South* in *Sewanee.* Founded in the late 1850s, the 10,000-acre mountaintop campus is known for its shady lawns and Gothic sandstone buildings patterned after Oxford University in England.

Farther down the mountain you'll enter the village of *Cowan,* where you'll find the *Cowan Railroad Museum* (931-967-3078; cowanrailroadmuseum

.org) along the still-busy railroad tracks at 108 Front St. The museum is housed in the large circa 1904 depot that once served as the busy passenger station.

People would come from all over the South to visit the Sewanee area and the **Monteagle Assembly.** They would disembark from the passenger train in Cowan and take the Mountain Goat, a smaller train, up the mountain to their destinations. The Mountain Goat track, built in 1853, is no longer in use as a railroad track. It has been converted to a mountain bike trail.

Today the museum is full of railroad antiques and memorabilia of those early days. Outside there's a steam engine, a flatcar, and a caboose. Run by volunteers, the facility is open May through Oct on Mon and Thurs through Sat 10 a.m. to 4 p.m. and on Sun 1 to 4 p.m.

Hang on, we're really going off the beaten path on this one. The **Cumberland Tunnel** is the longest and steepest railroad tunnel in the US. Built in 1852, it's 2,200 feet long, 21 feet high, and 15 feet wide. It's still used today and is listed on the National Register of Historic Places.

To get there is a somewhat tedious, albeit fun and adventurous trek. Across the track and the small park from the museum is Tennessee Avenue. Take it south to the first right possible and go over the tracks. Make an immediate left turn onto a gravel road next to the track. The tunnel is nearly 2 miles up that road. Go slowly, and if you have a low-rider, forget it. The road is bumpy, uneven, and when it rains, a bit muddy in spots, but it's worth the trip once you're there.

The gravel road crosses about 25 feet above the track, just 50 feet from the tunnel entrance. Before you come up, get a train schedule and plan on watching a few trains go through—it's quite fun. Pack a lunch, and between trains take a hike into the raw mountains that surround you. The working rail yard in Cowan has a pusher locomotive operating 24 hours a day to help trains climb up to the tunnel and then help them through it.

Remember when you could buy a house from Sears & Roebuck? The company sold a great many for several years, and a few are still standing, including the one at 518 W. Cumberland St. (US 41) here in Cowan. The house was ordered from the catalog in the early 1900s.

Do not pass through **Winchester** without first going to visit the **Old Jail Museum** (931-967-0524). Built in 1897, the structure is now open only to those who really want to be here. After having served as the county jail for more than 75 years, the museum now preserves the various elements of the jail, including the cell area and maximum-security block. Six additional rooms have exhibits highlighting the county's history, from the frontier days through the Civil War to the present. The Old Jail Museum is located at 400 Dinah Shore Blvd. at Bluff Street, a few blocks from the Winchester Courthouse. Open mid-Mar through mid-Dec, Tues through Sat 10 a.m. to 4 p.m. Admission for adults, $1; children, 50 cents.

In 1987 a group of Mennonite families migrated to mid-south Tennessee in search of farmland and with a desire to start a Mennonite church in an area that had none. Among those in the group was the Miller family, who saw the demand for homemade breads and pastries. The **Swiss Pantry** (931-962-0567; swisspantry.net) had its beginning in the kitchen of Mrs. Miller, who sold her products to friends and neighbors. In 1989 Mrs. Miller was joined by her three sisters, and they moved the business into the present building, located along US 64 just west of Belvidere at 10026 David Crockett Hwy. In 1999 Mrs. Miller's brother, Enos Miller, and his family purchased the store from the ladies and now run the business.

Not only will you find 10 different types of fresh-baked breads but also rolls, cookies, pastries, homemade salad dressings and relishes, a large selection of fresh herbs and spices, more than 30 different cheeses, smoked bacon and sausages, nuts, snacks, dried fruits, homemade candies, and a selection of baking and cooking supplies. Outside, a small garden center has been established. They are open Mon through Sat 9 a.m. to 5 p.m.

When you leave the Swiss Pantry, continue west on US 64 and head into Davy Crockett country. You'll be going by a roadside marker designating Kentuck, the homestead that he left in 1812 to go off to the Creek War. He and his first wife, Polly, and their children settled near here when he came back from the war. She died in 1815 and is buried in an old cemetery overlooking nearby Bean's Creek.

If you want further information on Davy Crockett's ties with this part of Tennessee, stop by **Falls Mill** (931-469-7161; fallsmill.com) near Belvidere at 134 Falls Mill Rd. and talk with owner Janie Lovett. In addition to her duties at the mill she owns with her husband, John, she's active in the local historical association and seems to know everyone in the area.

The Lovetts bought the mill in 1984 and have been busy restoring it ever since. Built in 1873, the mill has operated as a cotton-spinning and wool-carding factory, a cotton gin, a woodworking shop, and a grist and flour mill through the years. Since 1970 it has also served as a sort of museum. But it wasn't until the Lovetts bought it that it started realizing its true potential.

Make sure you take a walk down to the river behind the mill to get a good view of the falls and the 32-foot overshot waterwheel, which is the largest still in operation in the country.

Grain is still ground and is available at the mill store, along with other local items. There's a weaving exhibit upstairs in the mill. An 1895 log cabin was moved here and reassembled and serves as a bed-and-breakfast for up to five persons. Rates are $110 per night for two people, $5 for each additional person. The mill and picnic grounds are open every day but Wed. Admission is $4 for adults, $3 for senior citizens, and $2 for children under 14.

Farther south on US 231 is **Fayetteville,** the seat of Lincoln County. The downtown area around the county courthouse is probably one of the busiest in the state. There's nary a building vacancy on the square, and it can be hard to find a parking spot at times.

Start your visit at the chamber of commerce welcome center at 208 S. Elk Ave. (931-433-1234; vallnet.com/chamberofcommerce), where you'll be able to pick up a walking tour map of the historic downtown area, use their restroom facilities, and obtain a welcome package containing coupons and free gifts. That's what I call southern hospitality. Find out for yourself!

While downtown, visit the **Lincoln County Museum** (931-433-7182, ext. 130; flcmuseum.com) at 521 Main Ave. South. Located inside the old Borden Milk Plant, numerous displays and exhibits highlight the town's past. There's a great agricultural exhibit and an amazing display of arrowheads.

During the second weekend of November, the town features a Christmas celebration and festival. There are trolley rides, strolling musicians, a candlelight walking tour, and an old-fashioned high tea.

One block off the square at 114 Market St. West, you can have lunch or dinner at **Cahoots** (931-433-1173), located in an old firehouse and city jail. Sit out front or in back in one of the rugged limestone cells. Built in 1867, the building was the city's jailhouse until the 1970s. Menu items include burgers, chicken, a variety of sandwiches, and Mexican, seafood, and pasta dishes. For dessert try the French silk pie. Yum! Open Mon through Sat. Hours vary.

Western Heartland

The bell that was cast in 1858 and hangs in the **Giles County Courthouse** on the public square in Pulaski still strikes on the hour, each hour, every day. The sound coming from the cupola is just one of the beautiful elements of this neoclassical building built in 1909. Outside, tall Corinthian columns mark the architecture. Inside, a balcony encircles the third floor and 16 caryatids (female figures) hold up the arched vault of the rotunda, with its stained-glass skylights. The courthouse is open Mon through Fri during business hours. Out in front of the courthouse, on the south side of the public square, is a statue of Sam Davis, the young Confederate scout who was captured and executed in Pulaski. He was caught behind enemy lines with damaging information in his possession, and instead of betraying the source of that information, he chose to be hanged. The **Sam Davis Museum** (931-363-2720) now stands on the spot where the "Boy Hero of the Confederacy" was executed on November 27, 1863. The museum contains Civil War memorabilia as well as the leg irons worn by Davis. Located on Sam Davis Avenue, the hours are sporadic, so call the chamber of commerce first if you want to visit.

onestop graveyard

The Old Graveyard Memorial Park in Pulaski is a city park, cemetery, and historic monument all rolled into one. It's a great example of how an old, neglected cemetery can once again be useful while preserving the respect due those buried there. It's a well-lit area where one can stroll and truly absorb the area's history. The monuments have all been restored, with inscriptions dating back to 1753. Located at the corner of Cemetery Street and US 31.

The chamber of commerce publishes a driving tour guide map of Giles County's top antiques, crafts, and collectible shops. Pick up a copy at the chamber's office, 100 S. Second St. Contact them at (931) 363-3789, or log on at gilescountychamber.com.

While there are few, if any, physical reminders, there's one part of local history most residents would like to forget—the Ku Klux Klan was founded in **Pulaski.** Resentment against the move toward black equality fueled the creation of white supremacist groups throughout the South. The most enduring of those, the KKK, was founded in 1866 by six Confederate officers.

Historic **Lynnville,** population 408, has quite the history as a railroad town, and to help preserve that grand heritage, a reproduction of the circa 1877 depot was built in 1997 to house a local museum of railroad artifacts and vintage railroad equipment. The town's history as a railroad town is unique in that the city was originally located 1 mile away from where it is now.

After the Civil War the city fathers decided to move everything to make it more convenient to the railroad. Today the entire town of 59 buildings is listed on the National Register of Historic Places. Contributing to the quaint factor of the downtown business district are several craft and antiques shops and **Soda Pop Junction** (931-527-0007), an old-fashioned soda shop inside the old Lynnville Pharmacy building at 141 Mill St., built in 1860. You'll find much more than ice cream here, though. A few years ago, their hamburger was voted best in the state and their milk shakes, second best. "I think they cheated when they counted the votes for the shakes; we're definitely the best," kidded the owner. Open daily; hours vary.

The **Lynnville Railroad Museum** (931-478-0880) is open May through Oct, Thurs through Sun until 5 p.m. Lynnville is located on Highway 129, 7 miles from exit 27 off I-65.

Although his legacy is divided among several areas in the state, David (aka Davy) Crockett only helped in the organization of one of the counties in which he lived, Lawrence County. He was working as a justice of the peace in the area in 1817 when it was ceded by the Chickasaw Indians to the US. He helped get things organized and was instrumental in getting Lawrenceburg named as the county seat of government.

In 1922, during the dedication of a large monument that still stands on the south side of the square in Lawrenceburg, officials gave Crockett the title of Father of Lawrence County.

Davy Crockett was truly a Tennessean. He was born in the eastern part of the state, ran a gristmill, was elected to Congress in 1821 from Lawrenceburg, and went off to fight in the Alamo from the west. Over his lifetime, Crockett was a pioneer, soldier, politician, and industrialist.

While serving as justice of the peace, Crockett established a diversified water-powered industry consisting of a powder mill, a gristmill, and a distillery. His entire complex and his financial security were washed away in a flood in 1821, causing him to move farther west a few years later.

Treasures & More on Route 64

If some can get their kicks on Route 66, Tennesseans surely can see more on Route 64. Running from I-24 in the Heartland into the Memphis area, this US highway skirts the bottom of the state through 10 counties. Five of those counties have gotten together to create a map of the attractions, accommodations, and events that can be found along the route in their counties. Call (931) 967-6788 for a copy.

Today, on the site along the river where Crockett lived and worked, Tennessee has created **David Crockett State Park** (931-762-9408; lawrenceburg.com/crockettpark). The 1,100-acre park has an interpretive center, which is staffed during the summer months and has exhibits depicting Crockett's life here and a replica of the gristmill he once owned. Other facilities in the park include a swimming pool, 107 campsites, and the **David Crockett Restaurant** at (931) 762-9541, one of the best eateries in this part of the state. The park is located on US 64, just west of Lawrenceburg.

During the second full weekend of Aug, the park hosts **David Crockett Days,** a fun and educational festival featuring a bevy of frontier-type activities, from tomahawk throwing to long rifle gun making. There's a Crockett film festival, snake shows, and bluegrass music concerts. An arts and crafts festival takes place the first weekend in Sept each year, featuring a wide variety of exhibitors. Additional unusual events run throughout the year.

By the way, the county was named in honor of Captain James Lawrence, who commanded a ship in the War of 1812. Mortally wounded, it was he who shouted out the famous command: "Don't give up the ship."

The pace in the **Ethridge** area, just north of Lawrenceburg, is definitely life in the slow lane. More than 200 Amish families call this community their home. The Amish, known as the Plain Folk, have a reputation for being productive farmers and expert craftspeople. Many families sell their wares from their front porches, but the best place to start your shopping is the **Amish Country Galleries** (931-829-2126), a 5-room antiques store/gallery featuring the works of nearly 200 local craftspeople.

Among the locally produced items you'll find here is the hickory bent rocking chair, a wonderfully comfortable rocker made and used by the

Amish in their homes. There is also a great selection of Amish baskets. Located 5 miles north of Lawrenceburg on US 43, the shop is open Mon through Sat 9 a.m. to 5 p.m.

The **Natchez Trace** is truly a road trip back in time. The 450-mile road has been a major highway between Nashville and Natchez, Mississippi, since the late 1700s. It is preserved today as a scenic 2-lane parkway with few intersections, no commercial activities of any kind, and numerous pull-offs at historic stands (resting areas usually placed one day's travel from the other). The parkway ends on Highway 100, across from the Loveless Motel and Cafe, in Davidson County.

One of the early travelers on the trace was **Meriwether Lewis,** the famed leader of the Lewis and Clark expedition. In 1809 he met a violent and mysterious death at **Grinder's Stand.** His grave is marked by a broken column, symbolic of his broken career. The monument is located near the intersection with Highway 20 here in Lewis County, east of Hohenwald.

The trace is overlooked by those in a hurry because the speed limit (50 mph or less) is monitored quite closely. Make sure you have a lot of gas before you set out. For a map and other details, call (800) 305-7417.

The village of **Hohenwald** is a junker's paradise. The downtown streets are lined with junk and secondhand clothing shops, and people come from miles away to do their bargain hunting here. Used clothing is brought in from the Midwest and Northeast in bales and dumped on the floors of the shops. The bales are broken open at most of the shops each Wed, Sat, and Sun, the

The Candy Bar Farm

Frank Mars, the founder of Mars Candy Company, may have made his millions elsewhere, but he came to the rolling hills of Tennessee in 1922 to build his dream mansion and farm. For his gem, he chose a site in Pulaski, south of Nashville on Route 31. Milky Way Farm is nestled among one of the stateliest stands of grand magnolias in the South, and the Tudor mansion has 21 bedrooms and 15 baths.

During its heyday, the Milky Way Farm consisted of 2,800 acres, 38 barns, numerous houses, the grand mansion, and its own railroad. The farm produced prizewinning cattle and horses, including a Kentucky Derby winner. The mansion is listed on the National Register of Historic Places.

days to be there for the best selection. If you're knowledgeable about brands and clothing quality, some real bargains await you here. There are tales about people finding money and even diamond rings in the old clothes.

German immigrants created Hohenwald (which means "high forest") in 1878 as they developed a lumber industry in the area. With the help of the railroad, an organized colony of Swiss immigrants settled in 1894 and built New Switzerland, just south of Hohenwald, and the two towns later merged. A great deal of the German architecture is still evident throughout the community.

The *Lewis County Museum of Natural and Local History* (931-796-1550; lewiscountymuseum.com), located at 108 E. Main St., houses one of the largest collections of exotic animal mounts in the US, including one example of each species of North American sheep. There are also skins of lions, Bengal tigers, and tundra grizzlies. The museum serves as the local history museum and has several displays on the county's past. Open Tues through Sat 10 a.m. to 4 p.m., Sun 1 to 4 p.m. Admission for adults is $5, for seniors $4, and for students $2.

Carol Buckley and her elephant, Tara, traveled and performed with circuses for years, and then Buckley decided Tara would be a lot happier away from show business and in an environment more natural and more fitting for elephants. She moved the two of them to Hickman County, where she set up the *Elephant Sanctuary* (931-796-6500), the country's first official elephant retirement home. "It's for the old, sick, and needy," she said, "There are many elephants out there that need a place like this. I have a strong feeling that we're going to be the first of many such homes." Through donations, special events, and a lot of help from concerned friends, Buckley has been able to raise the money to build the necessary facilities. The sanctuary is not open to the public, but if you'd like to see Tara, Buckley, and any other residents who may be living here, sign on to elephants.com and you can watch them on the ELECAM.

While many of the communities in the state have groups who sit around outside near the courthouse and spit and whittle their days away, you'll find the old-timers in *Centerville,* the county seat, playing checkers while they spit.

In Hickman County, nicknamed the Keg County, there's still a lot of moonshine made in these hills. If you're interested in sampling some, just put out the word. It has a way of finding you.

And speaking of tasty things, make sure you stop by **Breece's Cafe** (931-729-3481), on the square in Centerville. In business since the 1940s, it offers country cooking at its finest. A different plate lunch is offered each weekday, and they always have a selection of home-baked pies on hand. Ask for the blackberry; it's especially good. Open Wed through Sat 6 a.m. to 8 p.m. Breakfast is served anytime with country ham and red-eye gravy a favorite.

Head out Highway 100 toward Nashville, and as soon as you cross the Duck River, look to your right and you'll find the hottest spot in town for a catfish dinner. The **Fish Camp Restaurant** (931-729-4401), located next to two ponds, features Tennessee River catfish, and people come from all over to sample it. In addition to the fish, they have a full menu, including some great barbecue they smoke right on-site. No alcohol is served or allowed due to city regulations. Open 7 days a week for lunch and dinner.

The strangest name of any community in the state is probably here in Hickman County. Out on Highway 50 south of Centerville is the small community of **Who'd A Thought It.** Story goes that a schoolhouse was being built out in the middle of nowhere, and a man pulled up in his buggy and asked what they were building. They told him, and he was last seen shaking his head and mumbling "Who'd a thought it" as he pulled away. Other interesting names in the county are Defeated Creek, Little Lot, Only, Pretty Creek, Ugly Creek, Spot, and Grinders Switch.

Up in Nunnelly, behind the Church of Christ where Highways 48 and 230 split, you'll find a monument marking the birthplace of **Beth Slater Whitson,** the writer of poems, songs, and short stories. Her best-known song lyrics were "Let Me Call You Sweetheart" and "Meet Me Tonight in Dreamland." She lived here from her birth in 1879 to 1913, when she moved to Nashville. She died there in 1930.

The coal miner's daughter not only lives in **Hurricane Mills,** she owns it. When country music's most-awarded female vocalist, Loretta Lynn, and her husband, Mooney, were house shopping back in 1966, she was searching for a big old "haunted looking" place. When she saw this century-old mansion, she knew this was her dream. She wanted it immediately, not knowing the entire town and old mill came with it. The **Loretta Lynn Ranch** (931-296-7700; lorettalynn.com), on Highway 13 in Hurricane Mills, is her home as well as her museum and special place to welcome fans.

In 1975 a campground was developed, and since then numerous other attractions have been added to the ranch, including Loretta's personal museum, a replica of the coal mine her father worked in, a replica of her Butcher Holler house, a western store, and a gift shop.

Tours of her antebellum plantation mansion are given daily. Make sure you ask the guide about the haunted aspects of the building. Lynn now lives in a house behind the mansion. You can look out the windows of the mansion and see her home. There is no charge to enter the ranch, but there is for the tours, museum, and other activities, including miniature golf and canoeing. There are dances every Sat night during the summer, and Lynn schedules a few concerts during that time also. Located 7 miles north of I-40; open Mar through Oct with limited attractions open Nov through Feb.

Charlotte, the seat of Dickson County, looks much as it did in the mid-1800s. The circa 1834 courthouse is considered the oldest such building still in use in the state. Pre–Civil War buildings line the downtown square, and the old-timers still gather at the drugstore on the square to solve the world's problems.

But it could have been so different! The now quaint and quiet town was two votes short of becoming the capital of Tennessee. Only Nashville received more votes.

Northern Heartland

The 170,000-acre peninsula between **Kentucky Lake** and Lake Barkley owned and operated by the Tennessee Valley Authority is aptly called the **Land Between the Lakes** (800-525-7077; lbl.org), or LBL, as locals refer to it. About a third of it lies in Tennessee and the rest in Kentucky.

The area is an awesome display of nature. The Trace, the main north-south road, is 60 miles long, with southern entry just west of Dover off US 79. There's plenty to do here, and according to the rangers, most of the area is underutilized.

In addition to all the hiking trails and water activities, there are more than 100 miles of paved roads for biking. The **Homeplace** is a 19th-century living history museum with 16 restored structures that were moved from other LBL locations and rebuilt. Costumed personnel work the farm, and most will take time from their chores to talk history with you.

Homeplace employees eat here, with all food prepared over the open fires and in the kitchens of the restored buildings. While walking through the kitchens, talk with the cooks. They have some great stories to tell about their past cooking experiences. The Homeplace is open Mar through Nov.

There is a fee for many of the attractions, and there are several special events during the year that the free LBL newsletter available on the website covers in detail.

Although it has to share honors with Kentucky, Montgomery County is the home of the famed 101st Airborne Division—Air Assault of the US Army. The **Fort Campbell Military Reservation** covers more than 100,000 acres on the state line and is the county's largest employer.

The base is open, which means visitors are welcome as long as they pick up a pass at Gate 4 on US 41A. Located near the gate is the visitor center and the ***Don F. Pratt Memorial Museum*** (270-798-3215). Named for Brigadier General Don Pratt, who was killed while leading the 101st Airborne's legendary glider assault into Normandy during World War II, the museum traces the history of the division from World War I through the present. Exhibits also depict the history of Fort Campbell and the land it occupies.

Probably the most interesting exhibit in the place is the replica of the fragile-looking glider that the members of the 101st Division used in France

Big Art in Public Places

Tennessee artist Al Keim has some big art in the Tennessee Welcome Center on I-24 at the Kentucky border, just north of Clarksville. Entitled *The Man in the Wind and the West Moon*, the bright blue-and-yellow abstract sculpture could possibly be imagined as phases of the moon. The artist notes that the branching off of colorful lines in space on the sculpture is similar to the improvisations in jazz music.

Keim's artwork is one of 11 large outdoor sculptures in Tennessee Welcome Centers, thanks to a public arts program created by the Tennessee Arts Commission in 1982. These works of art stand as visual ambassadors for the state and are quite cool to look at while stretching your bones and picking up a few maps and information. A brochure showing each of the 11 pieces of large artwork is available by writing the Tennessee Arts Commission, 401 Charlotte Ave., Nashville 37243. For additional information call (615) 741-1701.

during the D-day invasion of 1944. More than 14,000 of the canvas-covered cargo gliders were built during the war, with such unlikely businesses as the Steinway Piano and Heinz Pickle companies contributing to the effort. Across the street from the large indoor portion of the museum is a lot with a large collection of tanks, artillery field pieces, and airplanes. Open every day but Sun 9:30 a.m. to 4:30 p.m.; free admission.

Clarksville is the state's fifth-largest city, with a population of about 104,000, but it probably has the largest selection of architectural marvels of any one city in the state. "Anyone interested in architecture will have a field day in Clarksville," maintains the curator of the *Customs House Museum & Cultural Center* (931-648-5780; customshousemuseum.org).

Any tour through the city should start at the Customs House, at the corner of Commerce and Second Streets at 200 S. Second St. Originally constructed as a US Post Office and Customs House in 1898, its eclectic architecture consists of Italianate ornamentation, an Asian-influenced slate roof, Romanesque arches, and Gothic copper eagles perched at each of the four corners.

Olympic star Wilma Rudolph was a Clarksville native. A bronze life-size statue of her is now on display inside the Customs House. It's a great tribute to the late, three-time Olympic gold medal champion.

Attached to the post office, the museum has a 53,000-square-foot cultural center complete with a 200-seat auditorium, several different art galleries, classrooms, exhibit halls, and the state's best artisan gift shops. If you can't find something here, maybe you're too picky!

Exhibits include one on the local tobacco industry and a salute to the local firefighters. This is one of the finest local museums in the state. Area tour maps can be picked up here. Open Tues through Sun with free admission on the second Sat of the month. Otherwise, admission is $7 for adults, $6 for seniors, $5 for teachers and students, $3 for children 6–18. Free admission on the second Sat of every month; (931) 648-5780 or customshousemuseum.org.

There are two self-guided tours of the city and county—a 2-mile (25-site) walking tour of the downtown architectural area and a 14-mile (50-site) driving tour.

Clarksville has a proud river heritage, and to celebrate the relationship between the city and the mighty Cumberland River, the city fathers have created the *Cumberland RiverWalk* (931-553-8467; larksvillecvb.com), a meandering riverfront promenade. Along the path you'll experience river overlooks, a playground, picnic areas, and a wharf. During the winter holidays, *Christmas on the Cumberland,* with dozens of colorful displays, takes place along the RiverWalk.

As The River Flows is the name of an exhibit in the *RiverCenter,* located along the RiverWalk. The center offers a great view of the river, and among its exhibits is a 12-panel chronological history of the Cumberland River and its significance to the development of Clarksville. The entire RiverWalk area is open daily.

McGregor Park, located along the RiverWalk, is home to the annual *Riverfest* (931-553-8467), a 3-day arts, music, and food celebration in early Sept. There is a visual fine arts competition, which means you'll find some great, original regional art for sale. There are four stages with continuous musical performances and performing arts presentations. Plenty of food, ethnic culture, and youth activities can also be found. This is one of the more fun festivals in this part of the state!

Remember the Monkees' big hit "The Last Train To Clarksville"? Some say it was inspired by the *L&N Train Station* (931-553-2486; mchsociety .org) here in Clarksville at Commerce and Tenth Streets. Built in 1890, the once-busy depot is now open as a museum and art gallery. Open Tues, Thurs, and Sat 9 a.m. to 1 p.m.

There are several buildings high on the hill on the public square where advertising painted on their river-facing exterior walls years ago is still visible. Originally painted to be seen by river traffic, most of the ads have faded over the years. However, the ad on the circa 1842 Poston Building on the square can still be seen and appreciated. It was painted back when the Uneeda Biscuit Company was selling their product for a nickel a package.

For fun entertainment, the local professional theater group, the *Roxy Regional Theatre* (931-645-7699; roxyregionaltheatre.org), offers up 10 productions a year, all staged in the renovated Roxy Theater at 100 Franklin St.

Annually judged as one of the Top 20 March Events in the Southeast, the *Old-Time Fiddlers' Championships* (931-552-1113; tnfiddlers.com) is a great time to visit for some authentic old-time music. It takes place at the Northeast High School and, with a large cash purse for the winners, attracts some great nationally known entertainers. One nice thing about this contest is that it takes place before the myriad outdoor music festivals are held during the summer throughout the state. It's like a warm-up to get you excited about great Tennessee music. Categories include Dancing 30 and Under, Harmonica, Dobro, Bluegrass Banjo, Mandolin, and Beginner Fiddler.

More information about Clarksville and Montgomery County can be found by calling (931) 647-2331 or at clarksvillecvg.com.

Just outside Clarksville is **Historic Collinsville** (931-648-9141; historic collinsville.com), an authentically restored 19th-century log pioneer settlement that's a lot of fun to visit. It's a great glimpse into what it was like living in this area of the state 200 years ago. The buildings have all been saved, moved to the village, and lovingly restored by JoAnn and Glenn Weakley. There are now 15 buildings, including a dogtrot house and several outbuildings. Annual events range from a quilt show to a Civil War encampment. Located off Highway 48 South at 4711 Weakley Rd. Admission is $5 for adults, under 5 free. Open mid-May through mid-Oct, Thurs through Sun 1 to 5 p.m.; don't miss it!

Montgomery County's answer to California's Napa Valley can be found at the **Beachaven Vineyards & Winery** (931-645-8867; beachavenwinery .com), a few miles off I-24's exit 4 at 1100 Dunlop Ln. Co-owner Ed Cooke thinks his winery can offer as good a tasting tour as do his counterparts in California. "We offer the same thing, but we add southern hospitality," he said.

Beachaven's tasting concept is a great plus for those needing a little education before buying a wine. Cooke or one of the employees will be glad to give you a taste of all their varieties. Tours are given year-round for those who would like to see how the fruit of the vine becomes so divine. And these wines are really divine. Wine judges across the country think so, too. Look at all those ribbons awarded to the various products of Cooke and his family lining the walls. Their champagne is of "world renown," having been written up in the major wine books.

The most exciting (and aromatic) time to visit is in the fall while the crushing is taking place, but there is always something going on. During the summer, special concerts are presented in the vineyard's picnic area. They can't sell by the glass, but they would be glad to sell you a chilled bottle to enjoy with your cheese during a concert.

The **Dunbar Cave State Natural Area** (931-648-5526) is 110 scenic acres of true history and legend. The activities on this site range from when the local Native Americans inhabited the cave entrance 10,000 years ago to when country music legend and Grand Ole Opry star Roy Acuff owned the property and held weekly country music shows in the cave entrance.

A stately old bathhouse now serves as a visitor center and museum. If you want to take a cave tour, you have to call ahead and see when the group tours are being held. Even if you don't take the tour, the museum and the nature trails make this a fun place to visit. Fishing is permitted on the lake. Located just off US 79, 4 miles from I-24 (exit 4) at 401 Old Dunbar Cave Rd. Open 7 days a week; call for hours and events.

There have been ghosts and there have been legends, but the **Bell Witch of Adams** is probably the most documented story of the supernatural in all of American history. This witch is unique because of the large number of people who have had direct experience with it.

John Bell was a well-respected and influential member of the **Adams** community. He and his family lived on a 1,000-acre plantation along the Red River. The trouble started in 1817 when bumping and scratching sounds were first noticed in the house, but the Bells passed them off as being caused by the wind. The big problems started in 1818, when continuous gnawing sounds were heard on each member of the family's bedposts each night. When someone would get up to investigate, the sound would stop. The sound would go from room to room until everyone was awake. Then it would stop until the candles were blown out and everyone went back to bed, when it would start all over again.

Things grew from there. People came to town to witness the occurrences and weren't disappointed. Gen. Andrew Jackson came up to Adams from his Nashville home to investigate the matter but turned around when the wheels on his carriage mysteriously locked.

This has gone on through the decades. A few years ago, several reporters came to Adams with plans to stay in the Bell cave, where many of the experiences have occurred. They lasted a few hours before fleeing.

Today the **Bell Witch Cave** (615-696-3055; bellwitchcave.com) is open to those who think they are brave enough to possibly face the witch herself. Many have. Off US 41 at 403 Keysburg Rd., the cave is open May through

Oct but is closed during rainy periods due to possible flooding. Check for hours. Admission is $12 per person. No one under 18 is allowed without parental permission. All the Bell buildings are gone now, except for a small, log slave building. It has been moved to the grounds of the old elementary schoolhouse and is open for viewing. You can't miss the graves of the Bell family at the Bellwood cemetery. There's a magnificent tower marking them—and a stone fence keeping the Bell Witch out.

The historic Red River is an easy river to experience by canoe. Where US 41 crosses the river in Adams, you'll find **Red River Valley** (615-696-2768 or 800-762-8408; canoetheredriver.com), where you can both rent a canoe and get river information. Open weekends Apr through Oct, daily from Memorial Day to Labor Day.

Springfield is the county seat of Robertson County, and its past is told nicely in the restored circa 1915 US Post Office, now the **Robertson County History Museum** (615-382-7173; rchsonline.com), just off Court Square at 124 Sixth Ave. West. One of the exhibits points out a facet of the county that few people realize today: At one time it was home to 75 whiskey distilleries. That's a lot of booze, especially for the state that's considered the buckle of the Bible Belt!

Since 1820 the county has been known for its tobacco crops and is widely acknowledged as the dark-fired tobacco capital of the world. An exhibit chronicles those 180 years of agricultural significance. Open Wed through Fri 10 a.m. to 4 p.m., Sat by appointment. Admission is $4 for adults, $2 for seniors, $1 for students. A unique site!

The county courthouse on the Springfield square dates back to 1879. Along Main Street you'll find several interesting stores and shops located in the old distillery warehouses, dating back to the early 1900s.

Cross Plains was the first settlement in Robertson County when it was founded in 1779. Today there's a great deal of charm in the community of 1,353 people. The houses that line Main Street and the side streets are beautifully framed by big, mature trees, and there are plenty of friendly shops to keep you busy.

Pharmacist Dan Green is now caretaker of a bit of history in Cross Plains. He and his wife, Debbie, are the owners of **Thomas Drugs** (615-654-3877; thomasdrugs.com) and its historic black-and-chrome antique soda

The Catholics of Tennessee

The state's oldest Catholic church still in use is St. Michael's, located in the Flewellyn community near Cedar Hill. The church was built in 1842, and in the late 1890s a structure from the nearby Glen Raven Estate was moved and attached to the original church to make it larger. Today the white-clapboard church sits serenely among the trees in this rural area, surrounded by a cemetery.

St. Michael's is a mission church, which means it doesn't have a resident priest. Father Joseph Desmond of Our Lady of Lourdes in nearby Springfield administers to the congregation of approximately 70 families and makes the drive out from town every Sunday morning to say the 8 a.m. Mass.

As you walk in the front door, look immediately to the right and you'll see a cut-away that shows what the original construction looks like behind the walls. Also of interest is the outdoor altar, built at the bottom of the cemetery. It was built with the stones from the original foundation of St. Michael's Academy for Boys, a long-defunct educational adjunct of the church.

To get to Flewellyn, take Highway 49 South from Springfield for 4 miles. At the Highway 49 Market, turn right (west) onto Highway 257. Go another 4 miles to Catholic Church Road, which is the first paved road to the left. Turn left and go another 4 miles until you reach the fork in the road; go right and you'll soon see the church. It's locked up during the week, but you are invited to enjoy the grounds and the exterior and to join the congregation for Mass on Sunday. Call for their schedule at (615) 384-6200.

fountain. While Green tends to the business of the pharmacy, his soda jerk mixes up his own concoctions, from milk shakes to vanilla Cokes to ice-cream sundaes. Lunch is served Mon through Fri 10 a.m. to 2 p.m. and includes an array of fresh sandwiches and soups.

In addition to the "regular" drugstore stuff, the store features antique reproduction toys and books, and local crafts including quilts and coverlets. You'll find it at the corner of Main and Cedar Streets at the four-way stop sign at 7802 Hwy. 25 East. Open Mon through Sat 8 a.m. to 6 p.m.; admission is free.

In the **White House** (615-672-0239; cityofwhitehouse.com), on Highway 76, 1 mile east of I-65 at exit 108, next to the firehouse, is one of the most distinctive library and museum buildings you'll find anywhere in the state. It's a reproduction of the original White House Inn, which gave the area its name. The inn was a major stopover between Nashville and Louisville during the horse and buggy days.

The community library is on the first floor, the museum is on the second, and the chamber of commerce is out back in the bachelor's quarters. For a small community, they've done a splendid job in presenting a local history museum. Make sure you take a look at the firehouse next door, and don't miss the fun statue of a Dalmatian out front. Nice touch! Open daily except Fri and Sun. Enjoy this unique site.

Up in northern Sumner County, **Portland** (615-325-9032; portlandtn .com) has a long history and today has one of the longest-running commodity festivals in the state. Strawberries became an important crop for the area in the 1920s and soon became a major export item. Today the **Middle Tennessee Strawberry Festival** is a salute to both the present and the past strawberry business. The festival has been held each mid-May since 1941, and the weeklong roster of activities ends on a Saturday with a Rotary Pancake Breakfast, a parade, and the Lion's Club Bluegrass Festival.

There's plenty of food, crafts, entertainment, and of course strawberry delicacies. Check out the town website for more details on the festival as well as a list of local farms where you can pick your own berries.

If you're into the quaintness of one-room schoolhouses, check out the **Cold Springs School.** Constructed in 1857, the building is now a museum of local history with a great deal of Civil War memorabilia. It was moved into Richland Park in Portland in 1975 and restored. Originally built in an area of the city that was a military training camp for Civil War soldiers, the little school was used as an infirmary during the war. It's run by the Highland Rim Historical Society.

Another crop that is making a name for itself since the mid-1990s is the grape. That's when the **Sumner Crest Winery** (615-325-4086; sumnercrest winery.com) was founded by two brothers at exit 117 off I-65 at 5306 S. Old Hwy. 52. Tours and tastings are available, and there's a nice little antiques gallery. Some of the wines they specialize in are Tennessee blackberry, Merlot, Cabernet, and Summer Queen.

Open daily at 9 a.m. and on Sun at noon. Closes at 5 p.m. on Sun, the rest of the week at 6 p.m. during the summer months, 5 p.m. during winter. During the summer, evening concerts are held on the grounds, plus some spiffy antique cars are on display, including a stunning 1957 Corvette.

The downtown commercial area of **Gallatin** is quite the historic area. With more than 25 restored buildings, many of which predate the Civil War, the area has been listed on the National Register of Historic Places. Occupying some of those buildings are antiques shops and restaurants.

A block off the main square area, you'll find the **Sumner County Museum** (615-451-3738; sumnercountymuseum.org), behind the historic Trousdale Place. The museum, at 183 W. Main St., is the keeper of nearly a quarter million artifacts that tell the history of the county. Included in that collection are 475-million-year-old fossils and several displays featuring Native American and African-American life in the area. Open seasonally and by appointment. Admission is $3 for adults, and $1 for children 6–12. Go back in time at this historic site.

Trousdale Place (615-452-5648; sumnercvb.com) was home to Tennessee governor William Trousdale, who served the state from 1849 to 1851. The home has been restored and contains period antiques as well as a small Confederate library. Open by appointment. Admission is charged.

In Castalian Springs, what may be the largest log structure ever erected in Tennessee still stands. **Wynnewood** (615-452-5463) was built in 1828 as a stagecoach inn and mineral springs resort, and by 1840 a row of cottages adjoining the inn had been built, as well as a horse racetrack.

The main house is 142 feet long with a dogtrot through the middle. Some of the logs, mostly oak and walnut, are 32 feet long. All the rooms have outside doors and are entered from a gallery that extends 110 feet across the back of the building. A stairway in the dogtrot goes to the second-story rooms.

Owned by the state, Wynnewood is located 45 miles northeast of Nashville, 8 miles east of Gallatin at 210 Old Hwy. 25. It's open daily Apr through Nov. Admission is charged.

About 100 yards east of the entrance to Wynnewood is a stone monument marking the location of a giant, 9-foot-diameter sycamore tree in which Thomas Sharp Spencer lived during the winter of 1778–79. Spencer, the first white settler in middle Tennessee, called the tree home while he was building a cabin nearby.

Also located along Highway 25, about 5 miles from Gallatin, is **Cragfront** (615-452-7070), one of the finest examples of federal architecture in the state. Built between 1798 and 1802 by General James Winchester of

Revolutionary War fame, the limestone house has been restored and is open to the public. Open daily except Mon, mid-Apr through Oct, 10 a.m. to 5 p.m. Admission is $5 for adults, $4 for seniors, and $3 for children 6–12.

More information on Gallatin and the rest of Sumner County can be found at sumnertn.org. You can also contact **Sumner County Tourism** (615-230-8474 or 888-301-7866; sumnercvb.com).

Places to Stay in the Heartland

CLARKSVILLE

Lylewood Inn Bed & Breakfast
110 Camp Lylewood Rd.
(931) 232-4203
Built in 1892, this Greek Revival-style
home overlooks the Cumberland River

DICKSON

East Hills Bed & Breakfast
US 70
100 E. Hills Ter.
(615) 441-9428
easthillsbb.com
Quiet country inn, close to the city;
bountiful southern breakfast

LAWRENCEBURG

Davy Crockett State Park (camping)
Highway 64
(931) 762-9408 or
(877) 804-2681
lawrenceburg.com/
crockettpark
Swimming, restaurant, boat rentals, fishing

MANCHESTER

Tims Ford State Park
Off Highway 50
570 Tims Ford Dr.
(931) 962-1183
Cabins and campsites; waterskiing, boat rentals, swimming, hiking

MURFREESBORO

Country Inn & Suites
2262 Armory Dr.
(615) 890-5951
countryinns.com
Indoor pool, exercise room, continental breakfast

NASHVILLE

Hermitage Hotel
At Sixth Avenue and Union Street
231 Sixth Ave. North
(615) 244-3121
thehermitagehotel.com
Beaux Arts design

Nashville KOA
2626 Music Valley Dr.
(615) 889-0282
koa.com
435 sites, 25 cabins
Free country music shows

Union Station Hotel
1001 Broadway
(615) 726-1001
unionstationhotelnashville
.com
Vintage Nashville train station; gold-leaf mirrors, Tiffany windows

TULLAHOMA

Ledford Mill Bed & Breakfast
1195 Shipman's Creek Rd.
(931) 455-2546
Rural setting next to natural spring waterfall;

1884 gristmill is on historic registers

Places to Eat in the Heartland

ADAMS

Thomas Drugs
On corner of Main
and Cedar Streets
(615) 654-3877
thomasdrugs.net
Soda fountain serving
lunch; vanilla Cokes
Lunch Mon through
Fri 10 a.m. to
2 p.m.

ASHLAND CITY

Riverview Restaurant
110 Old River Rd.
(615) 792-7358
riverviewrestaurant
andmarina.com

BELL BUCKLE

**Bell Buckle Cafe
and Music Parlour**
16 Louisville & Nashville
Railroad
(931) 389-9693
bellbucklecafe.com
Hickory-smoked
barbecue, hand-squeezed
lemonade
Food served 7 days a
week, live music 3 nights
a week

CENTERVILLE

Breece's Cafe
On the square
111 S. Public Sq.
(931) 729-3481
Country cooking,
homemade pies
Wed through Sun 6 a.m.
to 8 p.m.

CHRISTIANA

**Miller's Grocery and
Country Cafe**
7011 Main St.
(615) 893-1878
millersgrocery.com
Meat and vegetables,
bluegrass music Fri
Blue plate lunch Tues
through Fri 11 a.m. to 2
p.m., dinner Fri and Sat 5
to 9 p.m., Sun 11 a.m. to
2 p.m.

FAYETTEVILLE

Cahoots
114 Market St. West
(931) 433-1173
In old firehouse and city
jail; eat in a limestone cell
Mon 10:30 a.m. to 2 p.m.,
Tues through Thurs 10:30
a.m. to 8 p.m., Fri and Sat
10:30 a.m. to 9 p.m.

FRANKLIN

Dotson's Restaurant
99 E. Main St.
(615) 794-2805
Popular local eatery; family
owned; southern cooking,
bountiful breakfasts
Open daily at 7 a.m. for
breakfast; also serves
lunch and dinner

LYNCHBURG

Iron Kettle Restaurant
On the square
177 Main St.
(931) 759-4274
ironkettletn.com
Plate lunches daily, home
cooking
Mon through Sun, 6 a.m.
to 4 p.m.

**Miss Mary Bobo's
Boarding House**
295 Main St.
jackdaniels.com
Southern traditional foods
served family style
Two seatings Mon
through Sat, at 11 a.m.
and 1 p.m.
For reservations, a must,
call (931) 759-7394

NASHVILLE

The Bluebird Cafe
4104 Hillsboro Pike
(615) 383-1461
bluebirdcafe.com
Country superstar
hangout
Hours vary

**Bongo Java
Coffeehouse**
2007 Belmont Blvd.
(615) 385-5282
bongojava.com
Great nontraditional food,
home of the NunBun
Open daily for all 3
mealtimes

Boscos Nashville Brewing Co.
1805 21st Ave. South
(615) 385-0050
boscosbeer.com
Brewpub known for its pizza, sandwiches
Open daily for lunch and dinner

Cheeseburger Charley's
4510 Harding Pike
(615) 297-6929
cheeseburgercharleys
.com
Healthy fast food
Veggie, turkey, black bean burgers
Open daily, 11 a.m. to 8 p.m.

Fido
1821 21st Ave. South
(615) 777-3436
bongojava.com
Mon through Fri 7 a.m. to 11 p.m., Sat and Sun 8 a.m. to 11 p.m.
Veggie paella, homemade ratatouille, veggie lasagna

Jack's World Famous BBQ
416 Broadway
(615) 254-5715
jacksbarbque.com
"A Nashville Institution"
Tennessee pork shoulder, Texas beef brisket, St. Louis–style ribs

Open 10:30 a.m. Mon through Sun; open for dinner Thurs through Sat till 8 p.m.; Sun till 6 p.m.

Loveless Motel and Cafe
8400 Hwy. 100
(615) 646-9700
lovelesscafe.com
Fried chicken, country ham, fresh biscuits
Open daily 7 a.m. to 9 p.m.

Monell's
1235 Sixth Ave. North
(615) 248-4747
monellstn.com
In historic Germantown
Southern home cooking
Lunch Mon through Fri; dinner Tues through Sat; country breakfast Sat, 8:30 a.m. to 1 p.m.; and Sun brunch, 10:30 a.m. to 3 p.m.

Nashville Farmers' Market
900 Rosa L. Parks Blvd. adjacent to Bicentennial Mall
(615) 880-2001
nashvillefarmersmarket.org
Fifteen restaurants inside as well as the market.
Open 8 a.m. to 6 p.m.

Nashville Palace
Music Valley Drive, across from Opryland Hotel
2611 McGavock Pike
(615) 899-1540
musicvalleyattractions
.com
Live music nightly with delicious menu
Open daily 3 p.m. to 3 a.m. (Food service 4 to 11:30 p.m., Fri and Sat 11 a.m. to midnight)

Sole Mio
311 Third Ave. South
(615) 256-4013
solemionashville.com
Italian cuisine
Open Tues through Sun for lunch and dinner.

NORMANDY

Cortner Mill Restaurant
200 Cortner Mill Rd.
(931) 857- 3018
parispatch.com
In historic mill, part of Paris Patch Farm
Steak, ham, chicken, quail, ribs, trout, beefalo
Reservations required
Open Tues through Sat 5:30 to 9 p.m., Sun buffet 11:30 a.m. to 1:30 p.m.

THE WESTERN PLAINS

→

History on the Plains

Nathan Bedford Forrest, the notorious hard-riding Confederate cavalry officer known for his unexpected and often offbeat tactics, pulled off one of the Civil War's most interesting victories along the Tennessee River here in the fall of 1864. It was probably the first time in military history that a cavalry force attacked and defeated a naval force. High atop *Pilot Knob,* the highest point in this part of the state, Forrest secretly assembled his troops. He had his eye on the Union army's massive supply depot, directly across the river.

At the time the depot had more than 30 vessels, most fully loaded and waiting to head out to Union forces. Stacks of supplies lined the wharf. Forrest attacked and caught the Yanks off guard. Within minutes all 30 vessels and the various warehouse buildings were on fire, and within 2 hours everything was destroyed. By nightfall Forrest's troops had vanished into the dense woods.

The land surrounding Pilot Knob is now known as the *Nathan Bedford Forrest State Park.* Atop the hill is a

monument to Forrest. Also at the top is the ***Tennessee River Folklife Center*** (731-584-2128), "designed to explore the relationship between the river and the people who use it."

Most of the exhibits incorporate segments of oral histories taken from the locals who "lived the life." Separate accounts recall the early industries and the music, religion, and community events of the area.

The most colorful audio presentation highlights the days when folks would gather at the river to welcome the big showboats to their landing. The biggest exhibit is ***Old Betsy,*** an entire workboat from the early musseling industry along the river. The most visual representation of early river life is from the Brownie camera of Maggie Sayre. She lived on a houseboat for more than 50 years and photographed everyday life around her.

lotsoffish,too

With more than 2,300 miles of shoreline, Kentucky Lake is the second-largest man-made lake in the world.

Most rural areas throughout the South have their own version of the liar's bench and the spit and whittle club. The view from the porch or from under the tree may be different from town to town, but the plot is the same. A story is told, then retold, then exaggerated to the point where it becomes a modern-day myth. A typical riverfront liar's bench has been reconstructed here at the center, with a breathtaking view of the Tennessee River far below. Walk up, push a button, and sit down and relax. The series of taped stories (from original spit and whittlers) will keep you in stitches.

The center is open every day 8 a.m. to 4:30 p.m. Admission is free. As you enter the park, the visitor center is to your right. Inside are several exhibits, including artwork and tanks containing local fish. Check here to see if the folklife center is open; if not, ask and they will probably send someone up with you. The historical park area offers camping, hiking trails, and picnic areas. Both areas are at the end of Route 191, about 10 miles out of Camden.

It has been found that the Tennessee River and Kentucky Lake provide the perfect environment in which to grow freshwater pearls. It is warm year-round, unpolluted, and high in lime content.

AUTHOR'S TOP TEN PICKS

Buford Pusser Home & Museum	Tennessee River Freshwater Pearl Farm and Museum
Danny Thomas Grave & Gardens	Trenton Teapot Collection
Dixie Gun Works and Old Car Museum	West Tennessee Strawberry Festival
Mindfield Outdoor Sculpture	World's Largest Fish Fry
Sun Studio	
Tennessee River Folklife Center	

That's what John and Chessy Lantendresse discovered when they were perfecting the process of growing freshwater pearls that are today worn by the likes of Hillary Rodham Clinton, Tipper Gore, and Kathleen O'Brien.

The ***Tennessee River Freshwater Pearl Farm and Museum*** (731-584-7880; tennesseeriverpearls.com) at 255 Marina Rd. is located in the Birdsong Resort and Marina, along the river just outside Camden. There are pontoon boat tours of the operation and a jewelry shop inside the marina that features the cultured pearls. The story behind the procedure—how river mussels are implanted with pieces of shell and how those pieces grow into pearls inside the mussels through a "secret process"—is explained by the experts.

Talented country music star ***Patsy Cline*** was killed on March 5, 1963, when her airplane crashed about 2.5 miles northwest of Camden. Today there's a small monument marking the spot, way off the main road, down a gravel path. The monument was set up to honor Cline and those killed with her: Cowboy Copas, Hawkshaw Hawkins, and Randy Hughes. Next to the monument is a mailbox where fans can drop off letters. There's also a gazebo with newspaper articles describing the careers of the stars and the monument itself.

The monument is located deep in the woods 12 miles north of I-40, off US 641. Just north of US 70, turn west on Mt. Carmel Road at the Shell gas station; go 3 miles, and turn right onto a gravel road. Be careful and don't go too far—there's a big dropoff at the end of the path. Country music fans, call (731) 584-8395 or visit bentoncountycamden.com.

There's no place better than an organized wildlife refuge to observe that area's wildlife population, and the **Tennessee National Wildlife Refuge** (731-642-2091) is no exception. Nature trails, paved roads, and observation points are plentiful in this 80-mile-long stretch along the Tennessee River. The area is an important resting and feeding place for migrating waterfowl each winter.

Beginning about mid-Oct, up to 100,000 Canada geese and 250,000 ducks start their annual fall trek to the refuge, where they will spend the winter safe and warm—and well fed. The major attraction here for the animals is the farming program, which provides them with a great deal of food all winter long.

In addition to the waterfowl, the refuge is home for more than 200 species of birds, a fact that brings in serious birders from all over the country. Maps, brochures, and specific wildlife information are available. Open Mon through Fri year-round. Don't miss this refuge.

For more information on Camden, Holladay, and the rest of Benton County, call (731) 584-8395 or log on to bentoncountycamden.com.

In nearby **Paris** the self-proclaimed **world's biggest fish fry** (worlds biggestfishfry.com) is held each Apr. Since the early 1950s the city has hosted the event at the fairgrounds and has achieved a well-deserved

OTHER ATTRACTIONS WORTH SEEING

Britton Lane Battlefield
Jackson
(731) 935-2209
brittonlane1862.madison.tn.us

C.H. Nash Museum
Chucalissa Archaeological Site
Memphis
(901) 785-3160
memphis.edu/chucalissa

Fire Museum of Memphis
Memphis
(901) 320-5650
firemuseum.com

Memphis Botanic Garden
Memphis
(901) 576-4100
memphisbotanicgarden.com

Oaklawn Gardens
Germantown
(901) 757-7375

reputation for the quality of its catfish dinners and the traditional Tennessee way of preparing them.

Each year more than 10,000 pounds of fish are cooked in black pots containing more than 250 gallons of vegetable oil. The 4-day event also includes a rodeo, a carnival, a 3-hour parade, and a fishing rodeo.

Here it is, a sugar heaven if ever we tasted one! With more than 100 varieties of freshly made candies, *Sally Lane's Candy Farm* (731-642-5801; sallylanes.com) is a stop well worth making in the Paris area. Founded in 1958, the store has customers who regularly drive up to a couple of hours to get here. In addition, people in 48 states use mail order to receive their treats, which range from hand-dipped chocolates to hard candies to the famous Kentucky Lake Frog—a chocolate, caramel, and pecan concoction. Make sure you try the divinity; it's made from scratch and is totally awesome, as are most of the goodies. It's the store's pink and green mints, though, that put them on the map. "We literally make tons of mints each year," said candy makers and store owners Bobby and Shelby Freeman and Pan and Rick Rockwell. The candy is sold locally at 2215 Gum Springs Rd.

And what would Paris be without the *Eiffel Tower?* There's a 65-foot scale model of the famous structure standing at the entrance of Memorial Park on Volunteer Drive, east of downtown between Highway 69A and US 79.

The *E. W. Grove–Henry County High School* was the first privately funded public high school in the state. Known locally as the school "that came out of a bottle," the building was funded from the proceeds of "Grove's Tasteless Chill Tonic." Today the tower building houses the Henry County Board of Education and is located on Grove Boulevard, at the highest elevation in West Tennessee. Turn off Veterans Drive onto Dunlap Road, just north of US 79. Turn right onto Grove Boulevard and go to the top of the hill.

If you'd like to get a closer look at some of the historic structures in West Tennessee's oldest incorporated community, an audiotaped walking tour is available. CDs and maps can be had at the chamber of commerce, W. G. Rhea Library, and the Paris–Henry County Heritage Center at no charge. The chamber is located at 2508 E. Wood St. Call them at (731) 642-3431 or visit paristnchamber.com.

Gordon Browning's first driver's license is on display at the *Gordon Browning Museum* (731-352-351; tn-roots/com/GordonBrowning) in the old post office building at 640 N. Main St. in downtown **McKenzie** in Carroll County. What makes that license so special is that it is Tennessee's first driver's license.

Browning got it because he happened to be governor of the state in 1938, when licenses were first required. In all, Browning served three terms as governor. He was also a US congressman and a chancery court judge, and he served in both world wars. By the looks of the quantity of the memorabilia on display, he never threw anything away. A flag that he brought back from World War I is on display, as are various other patriotic mementos.

The museum is a great small-town collection dedicated to the life of the county's favorite son. It gives a good perspective on the values that he and the curator of the museum deemed important.

The museum is open Mon, Tues, Thurs, and Fri 9 a.m. to 4 p.m. Admission is free.

Actress **Dixie Carter** was born and raised in **McLemoresville,** population 311. Even though she left town and became a successful star, she would come back home each year for several weeks to enjoy Tennessee and her family and friends. She died April 10, 2010. Her house is just off the little business section, and just about anyone around can point it out to you.

The **Billy O. Williams Museum** (731-986-4563) is on Main Street on the square. Run by a spirited group of volunteers, the museum highlights the history of the community, as well as the entire county. The facility is dedicated to the late Billy O. Williams, who was Carroll County's poet laureate and an associate poet laureate of the state. An exhibit honors his literary contributions and displays some of his printed as well as unpublished poetry, according to his sister, Rachel McKinney, who helps run the museum. Open Wed and Fri 10 a.m. to 4 p.m. If you get there and no one is around, call the phone number posted on the door; someone will come over and let you in.

When bare-knuckled pugilism was popular and legal in America during the first half of the 19th century, one area of Gibson County was well known for its unique version of prizefighting sans gloves. **Skullbone** and the surrounding **Kingdom of Skullbonia** hosted a type of fighting that became known as skullboning. All bare-knuckled punches had to be delivered to the head. Hits below the collar were not permitted and were considered fouls. To "play," fighters would stand opposite each other and take turns trading blows. Each round lasted until one fell to the ground. The match lasted until one was satisfied that he had had enough. After bare-knuckled fighting became illegal in America and communities went "underground" for the excitement, matches in Skullbone continued to be held in the open. When adoption of standard rules for prizefighting occurred in 1866, non-gloved activities died out just about everywhere except Skullbone, where it continued well into the 20th century.

Today just about all that remains of Skullbone is the general store, built in 1848. It has been owned since 1964 by Landon and Ruby Hampton and is known locally as ***Hampton's General Store*** (731-742-3179), widely as the Skullbone Store. The busy little store serves what is left of the "king-dom." Yellowed newspaper clippings of the area's heyday hang on the wall. Outside, the building is quite a landmark. With its map of the Kingdom of Skullbonia painted on one side and various soft drink signs and paintings on

TOP ANNUAL EVENTS

JANUARY

Elvis Presley Birthday Celebration
Memphis
(800) 238-2000
elvis.com

APRIL

Teapot Festival
Trenton
(731) 855-2013
teapotcollection.com

MAY

Memphis in May International Festival
Memphis
(901) 525-4611
memphisinmay.org

Tennessee Iris Festival
Dresden
(731) 364-5101
tennesseeirisfestival.com

West Tennessee Strawberry Festival
Humboldt
(731) 784-7770
wtsf.org

JUNE

Shannon Street Blues & Heritage Festival
Jackson
(731) 427-7573

JULY

Savannah Bluegrass Festival
Savannah
(800) 552-3866

SEPTEMBER

Saltillo River Day
Saltillo
(731) 687-3822

the front, it makes it impossible for any stranger to drive by without stopping to investigate. Across the street a stacked row of directional road and mileage signs points the way to worldly centers such as Singapore 9,981 miles; Anchorage 3,320 miles; and Shades Bridge 1 mile. In addition to the regular fare of a country store, the Hamptons sell souvenir T-shirts. Skullbone isn't on most maps, but the Hamptons are trying to get Tennessee's governor to put it on the official state map. It's located on Highway 105 about 3 miles from Bradford. Open every day.

It's amazing that just 3 miles away from the skullbone capital of the world one can find the *Doodle Soup Capital* of that same world. What is Doodle Soup? It's a spicy, cold-weather dish. It's actually more of a sauce or gravy than it is a real soup. One of the most popular methods of eating it is by pouring it over a plateful of cracker crumbs or homemade biscuits and letting it soak in for a while before eating.

Here is one of the "official" recipes. Be forewarned: There has been a battle going on for years as to which of the myriad recipes floating around should be considered official. Take a large broiler chicken. Melt butter and run it all over the chicken. Put in broiler pan, split side down; salt to taste. Put in oven at 375 degrees; let cook until brown and tender; take chicken out of the drippings that were cooked in the pan. Add 11 cups of water, 1 cup vinegar, plenty of hot peppers, and 3 tablespoons of cornstarch so it won't be just like water and will stay on the biscuits. Let cook until it gets as hot as you want. Taste it along. Although Doodle Soup is a local tradition, most locals haven't eaten it, saying it sounds too greasy.

At the municipal building in *Trenton* at 309 College St., you'll find the world's largest collection of 18th- and 19th-century night-light teapots (*veilleuses-théières*). A New York doctor, originally from Trenton, was going to give his multimillion-dollar collection of 525 pieces to the Metropolitan Museum of Art in New York City, but his brother convinced him to give them to his hometown instead.

Originally displayed in the trophy cases at the local high school, the unique Trenton Teapot Collection found a permanent home when a new city building was built. The teapots now line the walls of the city building's chambers. If you get there during regular business hours between 9 a.m. and 5 p.m., you're welcome to walk around and study this one-of-a-kind collection. Admission is free.

The teapot website offers great photos of the collection and has information about the well-attended annual **Teapot Festival** (731-855-2013; teapotcollection.com).

No one seems to know why it was done in the first place more than 10 years ago, but there are no 30 mph signs in Trenton. They are all 31 mph signs. "I have no idea, but I think it's kind of cool. We get a lot of publicity out of it, like in *Off the Beaten Path: Tennessee,*" laughed one city official when asked about the signs.

Up US 45W from Trenton is **Rutherford,** where a former **home of Davy Crockett** (731-665-7253; goahead.org) is open to the public. David (as residents prefer him to be called) moved to the area in 1823. His original cabin, built 5 miles east of town along the Obion River, was dismantled and stored with the intent of rebuilding it at a later date near where his mother is buried. But before it could be rebuilt, some of the logs were used in fires by campers.

Some of the logs were saved, though, and are now a part of the reproduction of that original cabin. On display are tools, furniture, and utensils from the period, as are letters that Crockett wrote home during his years in Congress. The grave of Rebecca Hawkins Crockett, Davy's mother, is next to the log home.

The cabin is open Tues through Sat 9 a.m. to 5 p.m., Sun 1 to 4:30 p.m. from Memorial Day to Labor Day. It's located on the city's grammar school property on US 45N at 219 N. Trenton St. Open daily; admission is $2 for adults, $1 for children, and $5 for a family.

For more information on Trenton, Rutherford, and the rest of Gibson County, contact the chamber of commerce at (731) 855-0973 or gibson countytn.com.

Farther up US 45W you'll find an amazing colony of **white squirrels,** one of only a few such colonies in the world. As you enter **Kenton,** a town of about 1,500 residents, you'll be greeted by a big sign proclaiming KENTON: HOME OF THE WHITE SQUIRRELS. Although the exact number is hard to pinpoint, as most white squirrels look alike, the city's official stance is that about 200 of the critters live here. The squirrels are fed by just about everybody, and there's a $50 fine if you kill one.

A wildlife biologist explains that the animals are actually "albino gray squirrels who have survived for so many years because the people have taken such good care of them." They have inbred for so long that the normally recessive albino trait has become predominant.

Exactly how the first such squirrels came to the area about 120 years ago is the subject of a great many speculations. The most common theory is that during the early 1870s a band of gypsies spent the night on a local farm. The next morning, in appreciation of the farmer's kindness, the leader of the gypsies presented two white squirrels to the farmer. Thus it began.

The best time to see the flock (bevy? herd?) of white squirrels is in the morning and evening, when they are most apt to be scurrying from tree to tree. Stop by the city hall, which also informally serves as a white squirrel visitor information bureau.

Across Gibson County from Kenton is **Humboldt,** home of the **West Tennessee Strawberry Festival** each May. It features a big parade, which is promoted as the longest nonmotorized parade in the nation; a street dance; a checkers tournament; a strawberry recipe contest; and a carnival with all sorts of family and kiddie amusement rides, plus any kind of strawberry-flavored food you can think of.

A museum for a strawberry festival? Yep, this may be the only one of its kind. The **West Tennessee Historical/Strawberry Festival Museum** (731-784-7770; wtsf.org) is on the first floor of the 1912 restored neoclassical building that once served as city hall at 1200 Main St. The museum salutes local Humboldt history as well as the history of the popular festival, from its beginning in 1934 to its latest event. Open Mon, Wed, and Fri 9 a.m. to 4 p.m.

The **West Tennessee Regional Arts Center** (731-784-1787; wtrac .tn.org) is on the upper floors, over the strawberry exhibits. It represents works of regional artists throughout Tennessee as well as surrounding states, including Red Grooms, Paul Harmon, Carroll Cloar, and Gilbert Gaul. The valuable collection was owned by a local doctor who donated it in honor of his parents and for the aesthetic education of students of all ages.

The arts center is open Mon through Fri 9 a.m. to 4:30 p.m. Group tours on Sat and Sun are by appointment. Admission is free.

Crockett County was established in 1871 and named in honor of the famed Tennessee frontiersman Davy Crockett. The county seat of the 14,000 residents of the county is Alamo, where the *Crockett Times* newspaper at

46 W. Main St. has been published for more than 120 years. Get more info at (731) 696-4558.

Crockett had already been killed when the county was formed, so when it came to finding a name for it, locals thought naming an entire county for the man would be an appropriate tribute. Cageville was renamed Alamo and became the county's center.

Crockett never lived in the county, and there is no record that he ever visited here, but the people are proud of their living monument to one of the state's best-known sons.

Carl Perkins, Elvis Presley, Roy Orbison, and all the other rockabilly stars are honored in Jackson's *International Rockabilly Hall of Fame* (731-427-6262; rockabillyhall.org). The history of the genre is told on tape and film by the stars themselves. One of the most unusual objects on display might be the heart paddles and defibrillator said to have been used on Elvis before he was pronounced dead on August 16, 1977.

The founder of the facility, Henry Harrison, told me that Jackson is the only place in the world where this facility should be located. "West Tennessee is the birthplace of rockabilly. It all started here and spread through the world. The roots are right here," he said, adding that the attraction is "located halfway between Graceland [in Memphis] and the Grand Ole Opry [in Nashville]."

Each Aug the *Rockabilly Fest* is held at the fairgrounds, and entertainers from all over come to show off their rockabilly roots. The festival promotes itself as the "world's largest gathering of rockabilly entertainers and history makers."

Tennessee's Only Archeofest

A unique two-day festival takes place each fall deep in the heart of Pinson Mounds State Archaeological Park. *Archeofest* is a celebration of Native American culture and archaeology and features Native American dancers, haywagon tours, storytelling, Native American foods and crafts, wildlife programs, flint knapping, and artifact identification. And it's all free. Pinson Mounds is a 1,086-acre prehistoric Indian ceremonial center containing the second-highest mound in the US. The fest takes place the third weekend of September. Located off US 45, south of I-40, southeast of Jackson. Call (731) 988-5614.

During the festival you can meet and talk with the stars. A huge 28-foot-by-66-foot mural outside the Rockabilly Hall of Fame features Carl Perkins and his band members, brothers Jay and Clayton Perkins, and other rockabilly artists. Look closely and you can see Paul McCartney in the painting. The Beatle was a great fan of Carl Perkins, and Harrison said McCartney was honored to be included.

The museum is located at 105 N. Church St. in Jackson and is open Mon through Thurs 10 a.m. to 5 p.m. and Fri and Sat 10 a.m. to 2 p.m. A live band and line dancing classes are offered some evenings. Visit their website for a great video on the history of rockabilly music.

Right off Courthouse Square, the **West Tennessee Farmers' Market** (731-425-8308) features fresh-from-the-garden produce and flowers during the growing season. Located at New Market Street and North College, the covered market is open daily except Sun and features various activities and festivals during the year.

Jackson's original **Greyhound Bus Terminal** (731-427-1573) is still in operation and as beautiful as ever in its 1920s art deco glory! Several movies have been filmed here, and it's a popular spot for still photographers from all over the mid-South at 407 E. Main St across from city hall at North Cumberland.

A few blocks from downtown Jackson, on the left side of S. Royal Street just after you cross the railroad tracks, is the site of the city's first modern waterworks at 604 S. Royal St. During its construction in the mid-1880s, one of the area's most prolific underground mineral rivers was discovered. By the early 1900s thousands were visiting and drinking water from this artesian well, searching for a cure for their stomach, liver, and kidney ailments. Today the powerful **Electro Chalybeate Well** still bubbles forth inside a gazebo built adjacent to the city's restored art deco water plant. A small park separates the well from the railroad tracks. For information or directions contact the chamber of commerce at (731) 425-8333 or visit online at jacksontncvb.com.

On the other side of the tracks is a local railroad museum, created inside the restored century-old depot. The city purchased the depot from the railroad, which had not used it for 20 years and had plans to tear it down. Restoration was completed in 1994, and it was opened as a museum in late 1995. Inside are exhibits, photos, a model railroad, and other memorabilia that tell the story of the five different railroads that serviced Jackson through the years. Known locally as the *N.C. & St. L Railroad Depot* (731-425-8223), the museum is open Mon through Sat 10 a.m. to 3 p.m. Admission is free.

A very pleasant place to stay while you're in this area is the *Highland Place Bed and Breakfast* (731-427-1472 or 877-614-6305; highlandplace .com). Innkeepers Cindy and Bill Pflaum have created quite an elegant home that is convenient to downtown Jackson at 519 N. Highland Ave. It's a traditional colonial revival mansion, circa 1911, with 10-foot-wide hallways, towering ceilings, an elegant center stairway, and a warm, very studious-feeling cherry-paneled library. Old French Country pine furniture and comfortable couches dominate the huge living room. The modern rooms have private baths, TV-stereo jacks, Internet access, and a wide choice of books and CDs. No smoking or pets. Rooms run $119.50 to $165 per night, full breakfast included.

"Come all you rounders if you want to hear a story about a brave engineer." That's the beginning of the tale of Casey Jones, an engineer who became a legend after being killed in a much-publicized train crash. The *Casey Jones Home and Railroad Museum* (731-668-1223 or 800-748-9588; caseyjones.com) tells the story of that fateful night. Casey was at the throttle of "Old 382" when it approached a stalled train on the same track near Vaughn, Mississippi, on April 30, 1900. The fireman jumped and yelled to Casey to do the same, but instead he stayed on and valiantly tried to stop the train. He didn't succeed, but he slowed it down enough so that he was the only casualty of the wreck. The engineer immediately became a folk hero, and his story has been recounted for more than a century in story and song.

Casey was living in Jackson at the time of his death. His home has since been moved and now serves as the centerpiece of the museum, located in Jackson's *Casey Jones Village* on the US 45 Bypass, just off I-40. Open daily, year-round; admission is charged.

In addition to the museum, the village contains specialty shops and *Brooks Shaw's Old Country Store and Restaurant,* a country restaurant complete with an 1890s-style soda fountain and a large gift shop.

Walking into Brooks Shaw's Old Country Store is literally a step back in time to the 1890s. Brooks Shaw was an American picker before his time who would be right at home on the popular TV show. The walls are adorned with antiques. More antiques hang from the ceiling. It takes time just to stand and admire everything that is there. Shaw traveled around the back roads of West Tennessee in the early 1960s to collect his treasures. He found them in dilapidated barns, in antique shops all over the South, wherever his fancy took him. Shaw family outings often turned into treasure hunts for some little gem. It started as a relaxing hobby, turned into a passion, and resulted in one of the South's largest private antique collections. Opened in 1965 as an antique museum, the Old County Store evolved into an always-packed restaurant serving southern favorites.

When I first saw the dilapidated **Providence House** that the Shaw family had moved to Casey Jones Village, I wondered how in the world they could salvage it. Well, they certainly have. Opened in 2012, Providence House has seen a wealth of history and is now set for even more. Until 2010, this home stood in Trenton, Tennessee, 30 miles north of Casey Jones Village. Townspeople climbed to its roof in 1862 to witness the Civil War Battle of Trenton.

But in recent years, the house was fighting a losing battle of its own and seemed doomed for demolition. Then Clark Shaw and his wife Juanita stepped in. The couple had the house moved behind the Old Country Store and Restaurant and beautifully renovated. Now it can be used for special events and will be pivotal in living history reenactments. The house is also a favorite photo site for visitors.

The Shaws then added still another special spot. More than a century old, the **Village Chapel** has been relocated to Casey Jones Village from Haywood County. Formerly known as the Brown's Creek Primitive Baptist Church, the church now has a steeple, complete with an antique bell and is available for small weddings and other events. It also is open to the public as a place of prayer and contemplation. The restaurant has become quite famous for its three daily all-you-can-eat buffets. The breakfast buffet plus drinks costs $9.49 during the week, $10.49 on Fri, Sat, and Sun. The luncheon buffet plus drinks is $10.49 Mon through Thurs, $11.49 on Fri and Sat, and $12.99 on Sun; the dinner selection plus drinks is $10.99 Mon through Thurs, $13.99 on Fri and Sat, and $12.99 on Sun.

Outside, in addition to the Casey Jones Museum, there's a train store, a well-shaded and well-run miniature golf course, and a bunch of shops, including a tourist information center. Live bluegrass music is often offered free.

Covering 48,000 acres, the **Natchez Trace State Resort Park and Forest** (731-968-3742; tnstateparks.com) is Tennessee's largest state-run facility. It is cared for by three state agencies. The Division of State Parks cares for the people, the Tennessee Division of Forestry cares for the trees, and the Tennessee Wildlife Resources Agency cares for the animals. The massive park, with its lakes, trails, and heavily forested areas, is a success story for one of President Franklin D. Roosevelt's New Deal programs. When the US Department of Agriculture acquired the land in the early 1930s, the area was some of the most heavily abused and eroded land in the state. The area's occupants were relocated, and a "Land-Use Area" project was set up to demonstrate how wasteland could again be made productive through proper conservation practices.

This is an interesting place to explore, with its three lakes, miles of hiking and equestrian trails, and plenty of off-the-beaten-path solitude.

There are three active churches within the park's borders. One of them, Mt. Comfort Missionary Baptist Church, was founded in 1846 by the great-grandfather of Gene Autry, the singing cowboy. Tombstones in the adjacent cemetery date back to 1830. In all, there are 25 cemeteries in the park. All are marked and allow visitors.

There are plenty of lodging opportunities here. The **Pin Oak Lodge** (800-250-8616), located next to the 700-acre Pin Oak Lake at 567 Pin Oak Ln., offers 47 modern rooms. Nearby are 10 new 2-bedroom villas, offering great views of the lake. There are also 17 rustic cabins, 5 camping cabins, a new RV campground with full hookups, and plenty of rustic camping throughout the park.

On May 5, 1999, a windstorm leveled 7,200 acres of trees, but Mother Nature is slowly reforesting the area. The roads were cleared, but the forest areas are being left alone to reforest themselves.

Each April coon hunters gather at the Decatur County fairgrounds just south of Parsons on Highway 69 to take part in an event that is billed as the **world's largest coon hunt.** Depending on the year and the weather, about 600 hunters from 35 states come here to hunt for the state's "official" animal, the raccoon.

This is basically a competition for dogs, so no guns are allowed and no coons are hurt. The hunter with the dog who does the best "tracking and treeing" goes away as the winner. Since coons are nocturnal, most of the action on this weekend takes place at night. A country band plays until

3 a.m., and the local Jaycees (731-847-4202) keep their concession stands open around the clock for the entire weekend. The event is considered to be the biggest independent fund-raiser for St. Jude Children's Research Hospital in Memphis. More than $100,000 is raised and donated each year. Over $2.3 million dollars has been donated from this event in 25 years.

Down the road apiece, where Highway 100 meets US 412, is the little riverside community of **Perryville**. In town, up on the very top of Pentecostal Hill, the **Tennessee River Antiques-Flea Market** (731-847-9383) does business year-round every Fri through Sun. Lloyd Privitt has taken over an old church camp that now features more than 50 dealers within the 12,000-square-foot building. There's a big collection of antiques in here as well, including a lot of glassware. What a collector's heaven this is! You'll find some great stuff, and the best part, it's off the beaten path. Follow Pentecostal Camp Road to the top at 545 Pentecostal Campground Rd.

Southern Plains

The **Shiloh National Military Park and Cemetery** (731-689-5696; nps .gov/shil), 12 miles south of Savannah on Highway 22, is a grim reminder of how bloody the Civil War really was.

On April 6 and 7, 1862, the North and South fought the first major battle in the western theater of the war here, just a few miles north of the Mississippi state line. More than 23,000 soldiers died, about one-fourth of the total forces that fought. The casualties in this one battle exceeded the total American casualties from the nation's three preceding wars: the Revolutionary War, the War of 1812, and the Mexican War.

Known as **Bloody Shiloh**, the battle went down in the history books as one of the most gruesome in all American warfare. The park was established in 1894 and includes the battlefield and environs. A 9-mile self-guided auto tour highlights the battle and explains the various monuments that have been erected. The visitor center has a library and a museum complete with relics and maps and a movie explaining the battle. Open daily, year-round 8 a.m. to 5 p.m. Don't miss this historic site.

For a month prior to Shiloh, the Union forces, under the leadership of Gen. Ulysses S. Grant, used the grounds of **Cherry Mansion** (731-607-1208),

101 Main St. in nearby Savannah, as Union headquarters. Tents were set up in the yard, and Grant slept in the house and dined with the Cherry family. He was eating breakfast on April 6 when he got word of the battle of Shiloh. Built in 1830, the house is the oldest structure in Savannah and is currently a private residence. Tours are now offered at $10 for adults and $5 for students. There's a monument to General Grant 1 block east of the mansion.

The **Tennessee River Museum** (800-552-3866; tennesseerivermuseum .org) in Savannah is a tribute both to the Tennessee River—from Paducah, Kentucky, to Muscle Shoals, Alabama—and to the influences it has had on the people who lived and worked along it. Several exhibit areas include displays on the early steamboats that plied the river, paleontology, archaeology, the Civil War, and a great collection of locally made musical instruments. Several gunboats are on display. Officials say their ceremonial Shiloh Effigy Pipe is world famous. Located in the old post office building at 495 Main St., the museum is open daily year-round. Admission is $3 for adults, free for children.

Both **Saltillo** and **Cerro Gordo** were named for Mexican communities by soldiers returning to their Tennessee farmlands following the Mexican War. Homes throughout the area date back to the 1840s and include an eclectic assortment of architecture, from early farmhouse to Greek Revival. Several cemeteries predate the Civil War. A brochure listing 17 points of interest in Saltillo is available from city hall.

The signs along US 64 outside **Adamsville** proclaim the community to be the **biggest little town in Tennessee.** A lot of that obvious pride may come from the fact that the town was home to one of America's most celebrated lawmen, Buford Pusser.

Pusser, who died in an auto accident in 1974, is immortalized in the **Buford Pusser Home & Museum** (731-632-4080; bufordpussermuseum .com), located at 342 Pusser St. He was sheriff of McNairy County from 1964 to 1970 and had the reputation of a no-nonsense, hard-nosed lawman. The exploits of this 6-foot, 6-inch tall, 250-pound "legend" were the basis of the three *Walking Tall* movies.

Today in the quiet residential area that he called home, his brick ranch house is overflowing with artifacts of his life. Following his death, his mother allowed nothing to be removed. Opened officially in 1988 as a museum, the facility is owned and operated by the city. Everything from his credit cards to his toothbrush to the roll of $100 bills he had in his pocket when he was killed are on display. An advertisement from a mattress company rests on his bed. "Big Buford Bedding, designed to honor a man who walked tall in Tennessee."

The years he spent as sheriff were hard ones on this "soft-spoken country gentleman." He was shot eight times, knifed seven times, and gunned down in an ambush that killed his wife. Many residents believe the flaming auto crash that took his life was no accident.

According to the museum's hostess, Pusser was constantly on guard and often remarked that he was "on borrowed time." His home is a reflection of that attitude. He had a special entrance built on the lower level, where his underground bedroom and living quarters were. He slept with his head against the earthen wall to help protect himself against the continuous threats.

In addition to his personal belongings, numerous scrapbooks of newspaper clippings, a videotape of television interviews, and a copy of his 1956 high school yearbook are on display. Admission to the museum is $7 for adults, $5 for seniors, $3 for ages 12–18, and $2 for ages 6–11. For extra fun, plan your visit for the last weekend in May. That's when the **Buford Pusser Festival** takes place, with live music and a carnival.

Up Highway 224 near Leapwood at 2985 Hardins Graveyard Rd., the **Coon Creek Science Center** (901-320-6320; cooncreek.ontheinter.net) reveals that this whole area was under a sea about 70 million years ago. The center, opened in 1989, is owned and operated by the Memphis Museum System, although it is more than 100 miles from that city.

When emptied, the warm, shallow ocean left behind an abundance of unusual and significant geological treasures. The marine shells found here in the bottomlands are not actually fossils but the real things, since they have not undergone the process of mineralization and have not turned to stone. The clay of the area has preserved the shells in their original form.

Known as the Coon Creek fossil formation, the entire area attracts geologists from all over the world. The center has been established to preserve the area and to provide an educational facility for the study of the earth sciences.

Various educational exhibits and programs have been established and are available for groups of 15 or more. If you're not in a specific group and want to see the place, the center sponsors several "family days" during the year when individuals can sign up for a program.

The hog is king at ***Pappy Johns Original Barbecue*** (731-645-4353) on US 45 South a few miles outside Selmer. Here you've got to be hungry for pork or chicken, because that's all they have. No burgers, no fries. Open daily except Sun, pork ribs are cooked up three nights a week—Wed, Fri, and Sat—while the rest of the hog is available all the other times. A good deal of the business here is takeout, but if you enjoy eating near the hickory pits where the cooking is done, there are tables inside.

little-knownfacts
abouttennessee

One of the toughest-fought elections in the state took place in 1933 during the election to determine which bird should be the Tennessee State Bird. More than 72,000 votes were registered, with the mockingbird edging out the robin by 450 votes.

Hardeman County's first courthouse, now known as the ***Little Court House Museum*** (731-658-6554), was built in 1824, making it one of the oldest original courthouses in western Tennessee. Located at 116 E. Market St. in Bolivar, the restored structure now houses the county museum.

The original part of the existing building was a 2-story log structure that served as the courthouse. In 1827 the building was purchased and moved to its current site, where additions were made to the log structure. It was converted into a family residence in 1849 and more additions were made, turning it into a large federal-style home.

The building itself is worth the stop, but some of the items inside highlighting this county's past are fascinating in themselves. Open every second and fourth Sat 10 a.m. to 2 p.m.

Another historic structure in Bolivar is ***The Pillars*** (731-518-7148), former home of John Houston Bills, one of the original settlers of West Tennessee. Built prior to 1826, the building at 522 S. Washington St. saw the likes of James K. Polk, Davy Crockett, Gen. Ulysses S. Grant, and Sam Houston. Open by appointment or chance; admission is charged. Visit in April for the annual ***Historic Home Tour*** during the ***Hardeman County Spring Fest.*** The tour features seven sites.

The **Magnolia Manor** (731-658-6700; magnoliamanorbolivartn.com) is this area's premier bed-and-breakfast. The 1849 structure at 418 N. Main St. has been completely restored to its early splendor with wooden floors throughout. Owner Elaine Cox currently runs the five-guest room antebellum inn. Rates range from $110 to $150, including a choice of meals. In the hallway you'll find portraits of four famous generals who stayed here many years before you found out about the place. Commissioned by the Cox family, the portraits feature Ulysses S. Grant, William T. Sherman, John A. Logan, and James B. McPherson.

Over on US 64 in Somerville, you'll find a real gem. The **Tennessee Pewter Company** (901-465-2609; tnpewter.com) is the only commercial producer of a full line of pewter products in the South. Pewtersmith Kathleen Armour Walker works to create new items while preserving traditional pieces. Pewter was widely used from the Middle Ages to the 19th century until glass and porcelain began to be mass produced. After that, pewter was used more for heirlooms and decorative items. An alloy of tin, copper, and antimony, pewter is completely lead free and never tarnishes. No more silver cleaning with pewter.

The small community of Grand Junction, located near the point where Highway 57 is joined by Highway 368, is known throughout the world as the home of the **National Field Trial Championships.** Held nearby at the 18,600-acre **Ames Plantation** since 1896, the annual Feb event is often called the Super Bowl of Bird Dogs.

The competition lasts 8 to 10 days, with the winning dog earning the title of World Champion Bird Dog. Hunting mostly for quail, the dogs and handlers are followed by a large gallery of spectators on horseback. Ames Plantation, located 4.3 miles off Highway 18 just north of Highway 57 at 4275 Buford Ellington Rd., is not only synonymous with the quest for canine excellence, it also plays an integral part in the University of Tennessee's livestock and agriculture program. The facility is one of the 11 branch experimental stations in the university's system. Built in 1847, the magnificent **Ames Manor House & Plantation** (901-878-1067; amesplantation.org) is open for tours on the fourth Thurs afternoon of each month, Mar through Oct, 12:30 to 4 p.m., with a $2 admission charged. Adjacent to the manor house is a small collection of original log cabins that have been moved here to create a small farmstead, which is open daily.

Across the street from Dunn's is the ***Field Trial Hall of Fame*** and ***National Wildlife Heritage Center*** (731-764-2058; birddogfoundation .com). It was created by the Bird Dog Foundation; the dedication plaque reads: DEDICATED TO PRESERVING THE PAST, PROTECTING THE FUTURE FOR SPORTING DOG FANCIERS THE WORLD OVER.

Films, paintings of some of the most famous bird dogs of the past hundred years, artifacts, literature, photography, and other memorabilia are featured here and help tell the story of the talents of well-trained bird dogs. If you're not familiar with any of this, don't worry; the folks working here are more than eager to share their love of the sport and of the dogs with you. Closed Mon; admission is free.

Heading toward Memphis on Highway 57, you'll find ***LaGrange,*** a quaint little village that has been able to avoid the commercialization that the others have fallen to along this busy highway corridor. In addition to a couple of antiques shops, the streets are lined with a plethora of well-kept little white cottages with green shutters and trim. Settled in 1819 on the site of an Indian trading post, the town was named for General Lafayette's ancestral home in France. Translated to mean "beautiful village," it was occupied by Union forces from 1862 to 1865. It was an antebellum center of wealth, education, and culture, having had two colleges, four academies, two newspapers, and 3,000 residents in 1862.

The best way to get into Memphis from this part of the state is to continue west on Highway 57. If you do that, you'll go through ***Collierville,*** a neat little community with a historic town square and a countless number of antiques shops and unique eateries. Along the square, which serves as a gathering place for the locals, the ***Fair on the Square*** takes place the first weekend of May each year, a free ***Sunset Concert Series*** is held every Thurs evening during June and July, and a first-class juried art competition is the centerpiece of the ***Mulberry Festival*** in Oct. For more information on this sleepy little suburban community, call the chamber of commerce at (901) 853-1949 or go to colliervillechamber.com.

The Delta Region

With a population of about 650,000, ***Memphis*** rests along the Mississippi River and is one of the river's largest inland ports. Among many other things, the city is famous for its impact on the development of popular American music as well as the blues. For a good overview of the area call (888) 633-9099 or visit memphistravel.com.

The history of music in the Memphis area revolves around the King of Rock 'n' Roll, **Elvis Presley.** Although he died in 1977, Elvis is even more popular today than when he was alive, and his estate is worth much more now (more than $100 million) than it was when he died ($4.9 million) because of his home (Graceland Mansion), souvenir and tourist shops, and museums. Estate revenues were topping $15 million annually by the late 1980s, more than the singer made in any one year of his career.

Graceland Mansion (901-332-3322 or 800-238-2010; elvis.com), at 3765 Elvis Presley Blvd., is one of the many unique places in the state where the beaten path catches up with the unbeaten one. There's nothing like this anywhere else in the world, and it shouldn't be missed. Elvis and members of his family are buried here in the Meditation Garden, and tours of the mansion are run daily year-round, except for Christmas, Thanksgiving, and New Year's Day. Closed Tues in Nov and Dec.

You'll get a chance to walk the grounds, see Elvis's private recording studio, and tour his private jet, the *Lisa Marie,* named for his daughter. You'll also have the opportunity to add to his estate at a variety of merchandise shops across the street from the mansion. It would be a good idea to make reservations, because the lines can get very long, especially during the summer months. Admission is charged.

Each year in mid-August Memphis hosts **Elvis Week,** an annual gathering of friends and fans from around the world celebrating Elvis's life and music career during the week surrounding the anniversary of his death on August 16, 1977. During Elvis Week, visitors experience concerts, tribute artists, movies, tours, Elvis insiders' conferences, and the famous Candlelight Vigil on the lawn of Graceland.

A funky place to spend the night while in Memphis is the **Heartbreak Hotel** (877-777-0606; elvis.com), based and themed on Elvis's big hit of the same name. It's a fashionable boutique hotel with 128 rooms and suites and, located at 3677 Elvis Presley Blvd., it's convenient to everything else Elvis. Rates range from $115 for a basic room to $601 for a themed suite (and boy is it themed!). Several money-saving packages include a room, meals, and tickets to Elvis attractions. Their website is really cool—plenty of music, fun dialogue, and unexpected diversions.

Sun Studio (800-441-6249; sunstudio), where Elvis recorded a song for his mother for $4, is open to the public. Founded by disc jockey Sam Phillips, Sun was the first studio to record such musicians as Presley, Jerry Lee Lewis, Carl Perkins, and Johnny Cash. The studio is located at 706 Union Ave., just a few blocks from Baptist Hospital, where Elvis was pronounced dead. Open 7 days a week 10 a.m. to 6:15 p.m., with tours scheduled every hour on the half hour; longer hours during the summer. Admission is $12 for adults and $5 for children 5–11. Children under 5 are not permitted. The website has a wealth of information and some really great sounds recorded, of course, in Sun Studio.

A great way to travel between Graceland, Sun Studio, and the Rock 'n' Soul Museum is a free shuttle. You can pick up the shuttle at any of the three locations, but it might be best to park your car in the free lot behind Sun Studio and catch the shuttle there.

Beale Street, in downtown Memphis, is considered the spiritual home of the other type of music the city is famous for, the blues. During its heyday in the twenties and thirties, there wasn't a tougher, more swinging street in America. The zoot suit originated here, and Machine Gun Kelly peddled bootleg on the streets. Always a mecca for musicians, the street's nightclubs were frequented by the country's best blues artists, including the man known as the Father of the Blues, the legendary William Christopher (W. C.) Handy.

Today the street is once again a hot nightspot with numerous clubs, restaurants, and shops. And the best part is that the sound of the blues has not been forgotten. Several clubs now offer traditional blues and jazz, including the *Rum Boogie Cafe* (901-528-0150; rumboogie.com) at 182 Beale and *B. B. King's Blues Club* (901-524-5464; memphisbbkingclubs .com) at 143 Beale.

Virtually unchanged through the years is *Schwab's* dry goods store (901-523-9782) at 163 Beale St., where a sign still hangs in the window proclaiming if you can't find it here, you're better off without it. The clerks still offer old-time service with a written receipt for each item purchased.

The Schwab family has created a museum, and having been on Beale Street since 1876, they have been able to collect quite a few memories of the "good ole days" to display. Upstairs, the store sells all sorts of items, from dream books to straw sailors to crystal balls to size 74 men's pants. Forty-four kinds of suspenders are kept in stock.

The new **Memphis Rock 'n' Soul Museum** (901-205-2533; memphis rocknsoul.org) is a true treasure and an intimate salute to the early soul music that permeated Memphis culture. The museum features the Smithsonian Institution's *Rock 'n' Soul: Social Crossroads* exhibit. Seven different galleries within the museum present a chronology of the hearts and souls that created the Memphis sound.

Those who helped create the Memphis Sound include Elvis Presley, Otis Redding, B. B. King, and Jerry Lee Lewis. The city's recording studios produced more than 120 top 20 hits. Many musicologists call Memphis the Holy Ground of American Music. In fact, when the Smithsonian began putting this exhibit together, an official of the National Museum of American History was quoted as saying: "In our quest to identify an American popular music, all roads led to Memphis."

The exhibits feature artifacts, pictures, and, of course, music. With each admission purchased, you get an audio gallery guide with more than 300 minutes of information, more than 100 songs, and interviews of dozens of soul music pioneers. The audio guide lets visitors move at their own pace through the galleries featuring three audiovisual programs, more than 30 instruments, 40 costumes, and other musical treasures.

Located at 191 Beale St., the museum opened in 2004. Open daily, 10 a.m. to 7 p.m. Admission is $11 for adults and $8 for ages 5–17.

Two white marble lions guard the entrance. A large bronze bell gongs every 90 seconds. With its 50-foot pagoda, tinkling waterfall, goldfish pond, bamboo stands, and strutting pheasants, the home of the giant pandas at the **Memphis Zoo** (901-276-9453; memphiszoo.org) seems like China's Forbidden City. The 3-acre, $16-million China exhibit immerses visitors in the history, culture, and wildlife of China.

The Memphis Zoo at 2000 Galloway Ave. has come a long way from its simple beginnings with a bear named Natch. The black bear was a mascot for the Memphis baseball season. After the baseball season ended, Natch was chained to a tree in Overton Park. Col. Robert Galloway took pity on him and began lobbying for funds in 1904 to build Natch a real home. In 1906, the Memphis Zoo opened with 23 simple cages and a row of concrete bear dens. In the 1990s zoo officials and local folks organized a tremendous fund-raising drive to turn the facility into a world-class zoo. Open all year, the zoo is home to over 3,500 animals representing more than 500 species.

A new taste treat awaits at **Dyers Burgers** (901-527-3937; dyersonbeale .com) featuring deep-fried hamburgers, and the grease they are cooked in has not been changed since 1912! It has been strained, but the same basic grease has been used all these years, and officials say it has never been allowed to cool and has never been solidified. When the restaurant was moved to 205 Beale St. from another part of town, the truck with the hot grease was given a police escort to make sure they could make it before the grease got cold. Open daily.

For a listing of all the clubs, restaurants, and shops on Beale Street, as well as a listing of concerts and events, visit bealestreet.com.

If it's history you came to Memphis for, take the short trip out to Mud Island, in the Mississippi River across from downtown. The city has developed this area to display its rich river heritage. The **River Walk** is a 5-block-long scale model of the entire Lower Mississippi's 1,000 miles from Cairo, Illinois, to the Gulf of Mexico. Every twist, turn, and split that the river makes is shown on the model. Each step equals 1 mile along the mini-river, where each bridge and town is also depicted. Markers along the way point out interesting facts and figures. Water flows down the model into a one-acre Gulf of Mexico.

The 18-gallery **Mississippi River Museum** (901-576-7241; mudisland .com) is also on the island and a showcase for the people and the history of the river, with exhibits ranging from Indian arrowheads to a replica of the pilothouse of a modern diesel towboat.

One of the galleries traces the 1865 wreck of the steamboat *Sultana,* which burned and sank nearby, killing 1,547 people. It is considered the worst maritime disaster in US history.

A visit to the **Peabody Hotel** (901-529-4000; peabodymemphis.com), at 149 Union St. in downtown, is a must. Built in 1925, the grand hotel has been restored and carries on a tradition started back in the mid-thirties. Each morning at 11 o'clock, five ducks are transported by elevator from their penthouse facilities to the lobby of the hotel.

As the doors slowly open, a red carpet is unrolled from the big fountain to the elevator as the "King Cotton March" is played over the sound system.

A SAMPLING OF HISTORIC AFRICAN-AMERICAN SITES & ATTRACTIONS

Afro-American Museum & Research Center
200 E. Martin Luther King
Blvd., Chattanooga
(423) 266-8658
caamhistory.com
Portrays history and culture of the
city's African Americans and their
contributions to society

Beck Cultural Exchange Center
1927 Dandridge Ave., Knoxville
(865) 524-8461
beckcenter.net
Archives, research, and museum for
the city's African-American citizens

Bethlehem Cemetery
US 51 North, Henning
(731) 738-2240
Alex Haley's family burial plot; where
Chicken George is buried

Fisk University Historic District
1000 17th Ave. North
Nashville
(615) 329-8720
Founded in 1887 as "free school"
for blacks; area consists of vintage
buildings, theaters, galleries

Highlander Research Foundation
1959 Highlander Way, New Market
(865) 933-3443
highlandercenter.org
An important training center for
the modern civil rights movement;
graduates include Dr. Martin Luther
King Jr. and Rosa Parks

Meharry Medical College
1005 Dr. D. B. Todd Blvd.
Nashville
(615) 327-6111
mmc.edu
First medical education program in US
for African Americans

National Civil Rights Museum
450 Mulberry St., Memphis
(901) 521-9699
civilrightsmuseum.org
Housed in Lorraine Motel, where Martin
Luther King Jr. was assassinated

W. C. Handy Home & Museum
352 Beale St., Memphis
(901) 527-3427
wchandymemphis.org
Where W. C. Handy penned his many
famous songs; memorabilia and
artifacts

WDIA Radio Station
47 Union Ave., Memphis
(901) 529-4300
mywdia.com
Founded in 1948 as first African-
American formatted radio station in
the US

With official Duck Master Anthony Petrina in control, the ducks waddle to the fountain, where they will spend the day. At 5 p.m. the action is reversed, and the ducks go back to their duck palace on the roof. During the day, if you visit the roof home of the ducks, you'll find a sign on their door proclaiming: GONE TO WORK IN THE LOBBY. BE BACK AT 5 P.M.

To get a prestigious gig like this, a duck first has to be lucky enough to be recruited from a duck farm in Arkansas. Mostly three-year-olds get the job. The lucky duck gets sent to Memphis, where he spends two weeks in training, learning from the veterans already working there. Once he becomes a part of the first team, he'll work for about three months before being returned to the farm.

The penthouse is open to visitors, but that's not all you'll find up there. You'll also find a very impressive view of the river and downtown Memphis. Lots to see!

I hope the irony isn't lost that Peabody's famous ducks live just across town from the **Ducks Unlimited National Headquarters** (901-758-3825; visit ducks.org) on One Waterfowl Way. Founded in 1937, the international organization's mission statement reads: "To fulfill the annual life cycle needs of North America's waterfowl by protecting, enhancing, restoring, and managing important wetlands and associated uplands." The headquarters is open for tours Mon through Fri 8 a.m. to 5 p.m., with no tours during lunch. Along the way you'll see exhibits of DU memorabilia and displays of wetland ecosystems.

Metalsmithing, everything from delicate gold jewelry to massive wrought-iron fencing, is the subject of one of the area's most unusual museums. In downtown Memphis on a bluff overlooking the Mississippi River, the **National Ornamental Metal Museum** (901-774-6380; metalmuseum .org) was opened to the public in 1979 as a memorial to metalsmithing.

Changing exhibits form the basis of the museum, but its permanent collection contains a variety of items from jewelry to handmade nails to large outdoor sculptures to ancient iron locks. In the museum's smithy (anyplace where metal is worked) work is done daily by resident artists and members of museum classes. On the third weekend of October each year, Repair Days are held. People from all over the South bring in their broken metal items to be fixed. On average, 60 craftspeople are available during that time to repair "broken, bent, or otherwise mutilated metalwork."

Make sure you pay attention to the front gates as you enter. Known as the Anniversary Gates, the tall metal gates contain nearly 200 specially designed rosettes, each made by a different metal craftsman. Each was submitted as part of the museum's tenth anniversary project and placed in an S scroll on the gate. Designs range from the traditional to contemporary, abstract, and whimsical. This is a great piece of unique art, and in no way should you visit Memphis without seeing it.

The grounds immediately surrounding the museum are also unique. Talk about artistic yard art! Wonderful metal sculptures and doodads are placed throughout. In the gazebo, you can see the Mississippi River from high above.

The museum grounds, at 374 Metal Museum Dr. (formerly known as West California), are a part of what was once known as the Marine Hospital, with the oldest of the three large brick buildings dating from 1870. That building was used in the extensive Memphis research that led to a cure for the yellow fever epidemics that once swept the area. The museum's main exhibit building was constructed as a Works Progress Administration (WPA) project in 1932 and once served as a nurses' dormitory for the hospital complex. Admission is charged.

At **Huey's** restaurant and bar (901-527-2700; hueyburger.com) you are encouraged to use your straw to shoot toothpicks into the ceiling! Name another eatery that permits that. The menu consists mostly of burgers, salads, pitas, and other sandwiches. Make sure you bring your Sharpie— you're also allowed to write on the walls. Opens daily at 11 a.m. and closes well after midnight; located at 77 S. Second St., across from the Peabody Hotel.

Tad Pierson owns **American Dream Safari** tours (901-527-8870; americandreamsafari.com). Pierson also owns a pink 1955 Cadillac. "Well, it really isn't pink," Pierson said. "Cadillac calls it Pecos Beige, but I call it pink, and the power of suggestion makes everyone think it's pink!"

This guy knows his Memphis and environs. Book a tour with him and he'll load you into his classic auto and take you on a fun and informative journey. He has several different tours to choose from. His Greatest Hits tour takes 3 hours and includes what he calls "lots of Elvis, Beale Street, Mississippi River lore and legend, the Lorraine Motel, and southern mansions on tree-lined boulevards." It's $200 for a 5-person vehicle. His Juke Joint tour starts at 9 p.m. and lasts until it's over. The tour takes you deep into the Memphis juke joint culture, and it's a real hoot!

Pierson says there are only two reasons to go to a juke joint full of blues. Either you feel good or you feel bad. He said that most of his tours are booked before the people get to Memphis, so calling ahead is a good idea. He'll pick you up at your hotel.

Soul music was practically invented in Memphis, mostly in a small neighborhood just south of downtown known today as *Soulsville, USA.* Stax Records and Hi Records were both located in this area in the late 1950s, and this is where the greatest soul singers of all time were born, lived, or recorded. Aretha Franklin was born in the neighborhood, and the likes of Al Green, Ann Peebles, Rufus Thomas, Maurice White, Isaac Hayes, and Booker T. and the MGs spent countless hours here.

The center of attraction was the Stax Records studio, where the hottest soul records of all time were recorded between 1959 and 1975. During that 15-year period, Stax released 300 LPs and more than 800 singles. An incredible 167 singles made it to the top 100 Pop Chart, and 243 made it to the Top 100 on the R&B charts.

The *Stax Museum of American Soul Music* (901-942-7685; staxmuseum.com) is now on the same corner where Stax Records once stood. Run by a nonprofit group for inner-city youth, the museum showcases an amazing collection of more than 2,000 artifacts, photos, and exhibits. Along with a running historical commentary and the legendary Stax Sound, the museum also spotlights the music of Muscle Shoals, Motown, Hi, and Atlantic Records.

The "real-cool" exhibits include Isaac Hayes's 1972 gold-trimmed, peacock blue "Superfly" Cadillac, Phalon Jones's saxophone recovered from the lake where the airplane of Otis Redding and the Bar-Kays crashed, and Albert King's famous purple "Flying V" guitar.

you'llfretover thistour!

One of the factories making famous Gibson Guitars is located in downtown Memphis. Knowledgeable tour guides lead you through 16 of the workstations, creating a unique factory tour. Located near Beale Street, at 145 Lt. George W. Lee Ave. Your contacts: (901) 544-7998 and gibson.com.

It's open daily year-round Tues through Sat 10 a.m. to 5 p.m., Sun 1 to 5 p.m. Closed Mon. Admission is $12 for adults, $11 for seniors; and $9 for children 9–12. Children 8 and under and museum members get in free. The gift shop has a super selection of music to buy! Located at 926 E. McLemore, at the corner of College Avenue, less than 3 miles from Beale Street. A good website to surf for additional Memphis music attractions and links is memphislocal.com.

The **National Civil Rights Museum** (901-521-9699; civilrights-museum.org) is the nation's first museum dedicated to documenting the complete history of the American civil rights movement. Constructed around the Lorraine Motel, where Dr. Martin Luther King Jr. was assassinated on April 4, 1968, the center features an interpretive education center, audiovisual displays, interactive exhibits, and civil rights memorabilia. Large exhibits portray several memorable moments in the movement, including the arrest of Rosa Parks for not moving to the back of the bus when requested, the sanitation workers' strike in Memphis, and the assassination of Dr. King.

King used to stay in Room 307 at the motel when he came to Memphis, and it was outside that room on the balcony that he was shot. Visitors can now look into that room and be immersed in the assassination story. It's quite moving, and if you see nothing else, this is the one exhibit you shouldn't miss. Located at 450 Mulberry St., the museum is open daily year-round. Admission is $10 for adults, $9 for seniors, $8 for ages 4–17.

The *Commercial Appeal,* the daily newspaper of Memphis, has prepared an extensive archive of articles written through the years about the civil rights movement, Dr. Martin Luther King Jr., and the city's favorite son, Elvis. It's all free and a good way to get some background on what made Memphis the city it is before you get here. The website is gomemphis.com.

Danny Thomas, entertainer, humanitarian, and founder of **St. Jude Children's Research Hospital** (901-495-3508; stjude.org), is buried in a memorial garden in front of the hospital, next to a beautiful pavilion that features his life, his career, and his love for his fellow man. There are videos of his *Make Room for Daddy* television series and a wall full of photos of Thomas posed with other legendary stars. In addition, there are hundreds of personal items and most of the trophies and awards he won during his illustrious career. Located in downtown Memphis at 332 N. Lauderdale, the pavilion and gardens are open 7 days a week during summer, Mon through Fri during winter. Admission is free.

There's nothing off the beaten path about the **Sleep Inn at Court Square** (901-522-9700; sleepinn.com/hotel-memphis-tennessee-TN451), in downtown Memphis. In fact, it's on the path as well as on the trolley line. It's the best place for your dollars if you want to stay within a 5-block walk of most of the downtown attractions listed in this chapter, including Beale Street and Mud Island. On one side of the hotel at 40 N. Front St. is the riverfront Confederate Park; the other side is the trolley line and the historic Court Square. A great continental breakfast is included.

The **Crystal Shrine Grotto** (901-767-8930), inside the **Memorial Park Cemetery,** is a must-stop if you're looking for the unusual in unusual locations. A unique cave was constructed by cemetery founder Clovis Hinds and Mexican artist Dionicio Rodriquez during the period of 1935–38. The cave and exterior environs were built of concrete in imitation of rocks, boulders, and trees. The entranceway appears to be through a tree trunk.

Natural rock and quartz crystal collected from the Ozarks form the background for nine different scenes from the life of Christ. Because of those scenes, the local kids often call the cavern the Jesus Cave. It's beautiful and quite an unusual work of naturalistic art. The shrine is open daily 8 a.m. to 4 p.m. at 5668 Poplar Ave., just off I-240 east of downtown.

In **Mason,** just across the Tipton County line at 342 Hwy. 70, is **Bozo's Hot Pit Bar-B-Que** (901-294-3400). Look for one of those tiled cafe buildings that dotted America's landscape in the 1950s, and you'll find Bozo's.

Founded in 1923 by Bozo Williams, the restaurant stayed in the family until 2001, when Hayne Ozier purchased it from Bozo's great-grandson. Famous for its pork shoulder barbecue sandwiches and plates, Bozo's has a full menu that has not changed since shortly after World War II. Save room for a piece of Ms. Perry's famous pie. Having never advertised, the restaurant's 100 seats are filled by longtime customers and newcomers who have heard about the place from a friend. On weekends about 50 percent of the business comes from Memphis, 35 miles away. Bozo's is open Tues through Sat 10:30 a.m. to 9 p.m. and offers the same menu items all day.

Farther north on US 51 in Tipton County is **Covington,** where you'll find an eclectic architectural area known as the **South Main Historic District** (901-476-9727). In all, there are more than 50 different structures reflecting "architectural styles that were sought by the emerging, affluent members of society in the late 19th and early 20th century," reads the historic marker. Among the styles represented: American four-square, prairie bungalow, colonial revival, and Queen Anne.

The restored ***Ruffin Theater*** (901-290-8225; ruffintheater.org) at 113 W. Pleasant Ave. is part of the historic district. Built in the art deco style in 1937, it now serves as a performing arts center for the community.

Over in ***Brownsville,*** West Tennessee's most unusual outdoor sculpture is located 3 blocks from the courthouse on W. Main Street. Reaching heights of 75 feet, ***Mindfield*** is a work in progress by local artist and welder Billy Tripp, who lives in his welding shop behind the sculpture. The huge, eclectic steel structure symbolizes life and the process of growing up, and it's up to all who see it to interpret it for themselves. He

andthebelltolls

The bell on top of the gingerbread-enhanced Carpenter Gothic Cottage, inside the Elmwood Cemetery, tolls for each interment today, just as it has since 1870. The 80-acre, circa 1852 cemetery is now the eternal home to two governors, four US senators, 22 mayors, soldiers from all US wars, including 19 Confederate generals, and an array of jazz singers, madams, suffragists, and beer drinkers. Purchase a map or rent an audio car-tour tape at the cottage and take a tour of this beautiful parklike facility. It's located at 824 S. Dudley St. Call (901) 774-3212, or visit elmwoodcemetery.org.

adds to it constantly and says he will do so for as long as he physically can.

Nestled among the old structures in Brownsville College Hill historic district is the College Hill Community Center. Situated at the top of the hill at 129 N. Grand Ave., the center houses the ***Morton Felsenthal Lincoln Collection.*** Now the property of the city, the large collection of books and memorabilia concerning the 16th US president is an all-encompassing exhibit.

The ***Haywood County Museum*** is also located at College Hill and features a good view into this part of the Mississippi Delta region. Adjacent to the museum is the ***Haywood County Sports Museum,*** featuring high school sports in the county dating back to the early 1900s. The three College Hill facilities are open Mon through Fri 10 a.m. to 4 p.m. and on Sun afternoon. Call them at (731) 772-4883.

A walking tour of the historic homes in this area is available; brochures can be obtained at the Brownsville-Haywood County Chamber of Commerce at 121 W. Main St.

The blues music heritage is alive and well and in good hands around here. The annual **Brownsville Blues Fall Fest** (731-772-2193; haywood countybrownsville.com) is held in late Sept or early Oct and features live blues music all day, a barbecue contest, a scarecrow contest, and various children's activities. The **West Tennessee Delta Heritage Center** (731-779-9000; westtnheritage.com), at exit 56 off I-40 at 121 Sunny Hill Cove, is the state's newest and probably coolest visitor center. Not only can you obtain information for the entire Western Plains area of Tennessee here, but there's also a museum with four major exhibit areas, a gift shop offering the work of regional artisans, an ATM machine, the Sleepy John Estes house, and an outside amphitheater, where concerts are held to promote the arts and musical heritage of the area.

The four exhibit areas are the Tennessee Room, which showcases West Tennessee towns and attractions; the **West Tennessee Music Museum,** highlighting such area talent as Tina Turner, Eddy Arnold, T. J. Shepherd, and Carl Perkins; the Scenic Hatchie River Museum, explaining the entire river watershed and ecosystem; and the Cotton Museum, which shows how cotton has affected the lives of West Tennesseans and its economic impact upon the area.

onthebeatenpath

Interstate highways—you know, those concrete ribbons that cross the state and all look the same? Well, there are 1,074 miles of them in Tennessee, and although they can save time, they certainly aren't the way to go if you want to see more than cows and billboards. Want to avoid truck traffic? Stay off the interstates! In 2012, more than 12.5 million semi trucks and commercial vehicles stopped at the state's five interstate weigh stations.

The house where **Sleepy John Estes** last strummed his guitar is part of the center. This is where the blues legend was living when he died in 1977. There are photos and memorabilia, and blues music fills the house. Open Mon through Sat 9 a.m. to 5 p.m., Sun 1 to 5 p.m.

Up Highway 19 from Brownsville, in the small community of **Nutbush,** Anna Mae Bullock was born on November 26, 1939, to sharecropper parents. She was a young girl surrounded by cotton fields and plenty of dreams. With a few lucky breaks and an immense amount of talent, this young lady moved away, got married, and became Tina Turner, Queen of Rock 'n' Roll.

She immortalized her hometown in her 1973 hit, "Nutbush City Limits," and she was inducted into the Rock and Roll Hall of Fame in 1991. The sharecropper's shack in which she was born has long since disappeared, but the farm where that shack stood is still there. A sign now marks the farm, located on Highway 19 adjacent to the cotton gin. The high school she attended in Brownsville and the elementary school she attended in Ripley are both still in service.

The **Brownsville-Haywood County Chamber of Commerce** (731-772-2193; brownsville-haywoodtn.com) can be contacted for more information on the area.

Henning, the boyhood home of the late author Alex Haley, is a picturesque town of Victorian homes and turn-of-the-20th-century storefronts. The town probably would have progressed quietly like many small towns had it not been for native son Haley.

His 1976 Pulitzer prize–winning novel, **Roots,** and the subsequent TV miniseries, based on the family stories his grandmother and aunt told him, brought international fame to Henning, where Haley's family home is now the **Alex Haley House Museum** (731-738-2240; alexhaleymuseum.com).

Those stories inspired Haley to research his family members who were brought to America as slaves, and the book came as a result. He recalls sitting on the front porch of his boyhood home and listening for hours to the stories.

Haley's museum by description is a "tribute to Kunta Kinte's worldwide family." Built in 1918 by a Kunta Kinte descendant, the house has been restored and serves not only as a tribute to Haley but also as a good example of rural small-town life in West Tennessee. It is also the first African-American state historic site and the only writer's home open to the public in Tennessee.

Following his death on February 10, 1992, Haley was buried in the front yard of the house, and his grave site is available for viewing at any time.

In 2010, the new Alex Haley Interpretive Center was dedicated. The center showcases a new exhibit gallery that has a large model of a slave ship, Haley's iconic eyeglasses, his childhood violin, genealogical charts, a video interview with Haley, a replica of the Haley home front porch where family stories were passed down, and more. Located at 200 S. Church St. at Haley Avenue, the museum is open Tues through Sun 10 a.m. to 5 p.m. Admission charged.

In a bright red caboose in downtown Henning on Main Street, adjacent to the city hall, the area's historical society has its records and artifacts on display in its heritage museum. If you'd like to visit, go into city hall and someone will come out and unlock the doors for you. Open hours are scarce and sporadic. To be sure not to miss it, call first at (731) 738-5055.

North of Henning, just off US 51 is *Ripley,* the seat of Lauderdale County. Believe it or not, this place has a wonderful array of interesting buildings, including two magnificent structures created by the Works Progress Administration in the 1930s. On Court Square is the Lauderdale County Courthouse, which is listed on the National Register of Historic Places. The center of the lobby has a colorful map, made of tile, of the county.

At 117 Jackson St. is the Ripley post office. In the lobby of this WPA structure, which is listed on the National Historical Register of Post Offices, is a beautiful oil mural, worth a stop even if you don't need stamps. Phone them at (731) 635-9691. The *Sugar Hill Library* (731-635-1872), at 123 Jefferson St., is inside the first wood-frame house built in town. The bell in use when the First Presbyterian Church (731-635-9751) opened in 1892 is still in service today and is made of the silver dollars donated to the bell fund. Hear it at 130 N. Jefferson St.

believeitornot!

Remember the 1986 Hands Across America effort to help raise awareness and money for the homeless? Americans joined hands from New York to Los Angeles, and the halfway point was at the intersection of Cleveland Street and US 51 in Ripley, Tennessee.

Farther north on US 51 is Halls. Among its interesting structures is its public library, housed in an original 1930s-era art deco building, formerly a Sinclair service station. Call for hours open: (731) 836-5302. More than 20,000 bales of what the locals call White Gold are processed each fall at the Halls (cotton) Gin Company. Located at 1279 Industrial Rd., this modern, computerized gin is adjacent to the Halls Dyersburg Army Airbase, where an exceptional air show takes place each year.

While in Halls, stop by and meet Murray Hudson, who owns and operates **Hudson's Antiquarian Books & Maps** (800-748-9946; murrayhudson .com). It's a collector's paradise where you'll find maps, globes, and books. It's kinda cool to see all those globes when you first walk in, and Murray, a former English teacher, certainly looks the part of a map and globe collector! It's located at 109 S. Church St.

Here's one for the "engineers" who are looking for off-the-beaten-path mechanical wonders. Outside Dyersburg is the world's only surviving "swing span, pony Pratt through truss bridge." Known for the town from which it came, the **Lenox Bridge,** as it is now called, was built in 1917 and moved and restored in 1985. The bridge was positioned for land travel. When a ship would need to go through, it would blow its whistle to alert the bridge tender, who would come down, walk out to the center pier, and crank the bridge open by hand. The bridge would turn away from both riverbanks and line up out of the way of the ship in the middle of the river, parallel with the shores, supported only in the center.

The bridge is 150 feet in length and 14 feet wide, and the pier is 18 feet in diameter. Jere Kirk, whose grandfather helped with the construction of the original bridge, bought and refurbished it. It is now on display over a body of water in the Lakewood subdivision. Take Highway 78 north out of Dyersburg. From I-155, go 2.7 miles and turn left on Highway 182 South. Go 1 mile and turn left into Lakewood. Stay right; the bridge is on your right, just past the lake.

Delta Flyway

Opened in 2013, the $10 million **Discovery Park of America** (877-885-5455; discoveryparkofamerica.com) in Union City at 830 Everett Blvd. is a 50-acre complex offering education and entertainment. The complex has more than 70,000 square feet of exhibits focused on nature, science, technology, history, and art. The focal point of the new park is Discovery Center, a 100,000-square-foot building with 10 exhibit galleries—Children's Exploration, Energy, Enlightenment, Military, Native Americans, Natural History, Regional History, Science/Space/Technology, and Transportation.

You can feel a theater simulation of the 1811–12 earthquakes that shaped the land in this region. Marvel at a planetary tour in the starship theater. Glimpse underwater life of Reelfoot Lake in a 20,000-gallon aquarium. Zoom down a 30-foot slide that is part of a 60-foot replica of a human body.

On the grounds of Discovery Park is a 100-year-old church as well as a train station with a locomotive and various cars. Visitors also can see a replica of the Liberty Bell, along with log cabins, farm buildings and equipment, and family items that illustrate rural life in the 1800s.

A water feature flows north to south, bisecting the site. Starting at a circa 1800s gristmill, the feature include waterfalls and bridges, plus a heap of lovely landscaping. Japanese, European, and American gardens allow visitors to enjoy nature and learn about plants and flowers from around the world. Gun collectors worldwide probably already know about this city's **Dixie Gun Works and Old Car Museum** (731-885-0561; dixiegunworks .com), while noncollectors across town may have never heard of it. Founded by the late Turner Kirkland in the early 1950s, the business is now considered the world's largest supplier of antique guns and parts. The firm sells about 80,000 guns a year, including antique reproductions.

At any given time a walk through the Dixie Gun Works' showroom at 1412 W. Reelfoot Ave. is like walking through an antique firearms museum, except that you can buy most of the guns you see here. Usually, more than 1,500 guns are on display. Kirkland's other passion, antique automobiles, is also in evidence. Adjacent to the gun showroom is an auto museum with 36 old cars, including a 1908 Maxwell.

A small log cabin gunshop is a part of this attraction. Originally built in this area around 1850, the shop contains two rifling machines and more than 1,000 gun-making tools. The complex is located on the Highway 51S Union City Bypass. The museum is open Mon through Fri 7:30 a.m. to 5 p.m., Sun 8 a.m. to noon. Admission is charged for this interesting museum.

Adjacent to the county courthouse, in the center of Union City, is the **Flame of Freedom,** an eternal flame dedicated to "all veterans of Obion County in all wars and conflicts, past, present, and future." It was dedicated in 1971. Along the railroad tracks on South Depot Street next to the municipal building, Kiwanis Park offers a nice place to rest for a spell. Make note of the Confederate monument in the park. It's one of the few in the South that looks north. There's a band shell, fountains, playground equipment, and plenty of huge shade trees.

At the end of Edwards Street is the first monument erected in honor of the unknown Confederate soldier. It was dedicated on October 21, 1869.

If it's architecture you like, don't overlook the **First Christian Church** at W. Lee and S. Second Streets. The circa 1912 domed church is the third to be built on the site. The bell that is on display on the church lawn was the first bell of the brick church built on this site after the 1862 destruction of the 1857 frame church by Union forces. Check out the beautiful stained-glass windows of the church.

The **Masquerade Theatre Company,** a community theater group in Union City, raised the money to buy and has now restored the beautiful circa 1927 **Capitol Theater,** at 118 S. First St. Through the years, it was used as a film house, a stage for traveling legitimate theater, and a vaudeville stage. The theater group will produce several shows a year in the 364-seat venue and will host a bevy of local entertainment events such as recitals. If you're hungry for what a lot of people around here consider the best cheeseburger in the world, stop by **P.V.'s Hut** (731-885-5737). It's open Tues through Sat 11 a.m. to 7 p.m. and is located at E. Florida and S. Perkins Streets at 209 E. Florida Ave.

Following World War II, housing was in demand throughout the US, and as a result many all-steel prefabricated homes were built. They were quick to put up and reasonably inexpensive for the returning servicemen. Only one remains in Obion County. It's at 1020 Church St. and has been maintained quite nicely through the years.

A couple streets over in the oldest residential neighborhood in town, and the home of Lexie Parks still stands at 822 E. Main. The house contains the first elevator in town—and the ghost of the wealthy Mr. Parks. He was

little-known food facts about tennessee

Every Pringle potato chip ever eaten anywhere in the world was made in Jackson.

Like Christie Cookies? All the cookie dough and all of its wholesale cookies are made in Nashville.

Coors Brewing Company is in Colorado, but all its nonalcoholic and malt drinks are brewed in Memphis.

killed in the house by his butler, who was never convicted of the crime. Residents who have lived here since have documented Parks and his congenial hauntings as he walks through the house. It seems he is upset that the butler got away with the murder.

Additional information about Union City and Obion County can be had by contacting the chamber of commerce at (731) 885-0211 or obion county.org.

Reelfoot Lake is the result of a true quirk of nature. The worst earthquake ever measured in American history took place in this area in 1812. On February 7 the quake hit, and the lands of northwest Tennessee near the Mississippi River dropped as much as 20 feet.

The "Real Legend" of Reelfoot

Once upon a time in the early 1800s, there ruled a mighty Chickasaw chieftain whose only son had a deformed foot. The son ran with a rolling motion, so the tribe nicknamed him Kaolin, meaning "Reelfoot." When the son became chief and was to be married, he found he had no feelings for any maidens in his tribe.

He went searching for a wondrous beauty and found her among the Choctaws. She was the daughter of the chief. Reelfoot immediately fell under the spell of the princess and asked her father to allow a marriage.

The old chief replied: "It is true that my daughter is enchanting, and she will only be given in wedlock to a Choctaw chieftain. I will not ever permit her to join a tribe which is so unfortunate as to have a clubfooted chieftain." Reelfoot was more determined than ever, but the Great Spirit had a few words for him. "An Indian must not take his wife from a neighboring tribe, and if you disobey and take the princess, I will cause the earth to rock and the waters to swallow up your village and bury your people in a watery grave."

Reelfoot chose not to believe the Great Spirit, and within months he had captured the princess and brought her back to West Tennessee. As the marriage rites took place, the earth began to roll, and Reelfoot cried out for mercy on his people. The Great Spirit answered, "I will show you and your people mercy, but you will have to pay for your disobedience. I will form a lake where I stamp my foot, and you and your people will forever watch over the lake, for I will rest your souls in the cypress."

The 1812 earthquake continued, the lands dropped, and the Mississippi River filled the new basin. Cypress trees became abundant and Reelfoot Lake was formed.

For 15 minutes the river's water flowed backward to fill this major void, which had been a swampy forestland. Now the area is a 13,000-acre shallow lake, an average of 5.2 feet deep, with the remains of the forest just under the surface, which makes boating quite an adventure. The water is a dark green color, with visibility never more than a few inches. The area surrounding the lake is now a state park, and a journey through here is truly a trek into unspoiled nature. The combination of shaggy cypress trees, some of them centuries old, and water lilies is most unusual for this state.

Reelfoot Lake is the winter home to more than 100 American bald eagles. The birds, with wingspans of 6 to 8 feet, come here from their northern summer homes to spend the winter in a warmer, ice-free environment. The park provides numerous eagle programs, including bus tours of the area, during winter.

The park's museum offers the chance to experience an earthquake first-hand. The 1812 quake has been reproduced, to a lesser degree, and allows guests to feel and hear what took place during those 15 minutes. You can also sit in a stump jumper; learn about its creators, the Calhoun family; see Native American artifacts; and read firsthand accounts of the creation of the lake. The museum is also the loading site for the lake's sightseeing cruises. The museum is open daily 8 a.m. to 4:30 p.m. Call (731) 253-9652.

Deep Swamp Canoe Trips are offered by the museum every Mar and Apr on Sat and Sun at 1 p.m. Cost is $10 per person. Reservations required. Join park naturalists for canoe trips into the old growth cypress forest of Reelfoot Lake. As the canoe glides around huge cypress trees, watch for a variety of birds, including a nesting pair of bald eagles.

wildlifegalore

Reelfoot Lake is an oasis for wildlife because of its shallow, pristine waters, marshlands, and dense stands of bald cypress trees. In addition to the 100-plus American bald eagles that winter there each year, more than 60,000 geese and a quarter million ducks visit the area annually. There are also 54 species of fish in the lake, and there have been 53 mammal species spotted in the area. Who counts these things anyway? What a job!

The park has camping sites, a camp store, and hiking trails. Guided "swamp tromps" are offered during the year. The entrance to the park is located off Highway 21.

An annual calendar lists the best times, month by month, to see the various wildlife around the lake. A copy can be obtained by calling the ranger's office at (731) 253-7756. A 3-day arts and crafts festival is held each October at the park.

A fantastic place to stay while you're in this area is the ***Blue Bank Resort*** (877-258-3226; bluebankresort.com), on Highway 21 a few miles east of Tiptonville at 813 Lake Dr. Located on the water's edge, the rooms are rustic in style but are new and offer great views of the lake. The water practically comes up to your door! Rates are about $100 per night, per room. Special hunting and fishing packages, which include lodging, boat, motor, bait, and ice, are available and can save you quite a bit of money.

The ***Blue Bank Fish House & Grill*** is closer to Tiptonville, (731-538-2112) at the Blue Bank Motel, and is owned by the same people. The restaurant opens early each morning with a hearty breakfast and has steaks, quail, frog legs, crappie, country ham, ribs, and chicken for dinner.

Places to Stay in the Western Plains

BOLIVAR

Magnolia Manor
418 N. Main St.
(731) 658-6700
magnoliamanor
bolivartn.com
Antebellum
bed-and-breakfast

CAMDEN

Birdsong Resort and Marina
255 Marina Rd.
(731) 584-7880
birdsongresort.com
RV campground and rental cottages on Tennessee River/Kentucky Lake

COUNCE

Hampton Inn — Pickwick
(731) 689-3031
90 Old South Rd. and Highway 57
Three stories, outdoor pool, meeting rooms

Little Andy's Sportsman's Lodge
7255 Hwy. 57
(731) 689-3750
littleandysmotel.net
1950s-era motel with knotty-pine rooms

DYERSBURG

Hampton Inn
2750 Mall Loop Rd.
(731) 285-4778
Close to all northwest Tennessee attractions

JACKSON

Highland Place Bed and Breakfast
519 N. Highland Ave.
(731) 427-1472
highlandplace.com
Circa 1911 mansion

MEMPHIS

Heartbreak Hotel
3677 Elvis Presley Blvd.
(877) 777-0606
elvis.com
Boutique hotel convenient to everything Elvis

Madison Hotel Memphis
79 Madison Ave.
(901) 333-1200
madisonhotelmemphis.com
Luxury boutique hotel in downtown Memphis

Memphis Graceland RV Park & Campground
3691 Elvis Presley Blvd.
(901) 396-7125
elvis.com
Laundry, showers, pool, store

Peabody Hotel Memphis
149 Union Ave.
(901) 529-4000
peabodymemphis.com
World-famous historic landmark

PARIS

EconoLodge
1297 E. Wood St.
(731) 642-8881
econolodge.com
Pool

PICKWICK DAM

Pickwick Landing State Park Inn
Highway 57
(800) 250-8615
Pool, tennis, restaurant

TIPTONVILLE

Blue Bank Resort
Highway 21
813 Lake Dr.
(877) 258-3226
bluebankresort.com
Rustic rooms with lake views

Blue Basin Cove B&B
Air Park Road
100 Blue Basin Rd.
(731) 253-9064
bluebasin.com
On shore of Reelfoot Lake in old fishing lodge

WILDERSVILLE

Pin Oak Lodge and Restaurant
In Natchez Trace State Resort Park and Forest
567 Pin Oak Lodge Rd.
(731) 968-8176
Cabins, swimming, hiking, fishing, camping
Open year-round

Places to Eat in the Western Plains

DECATURVILLE

Emilee Kay's Cafe
158 W. Main St.
(731) 852-2657
Down-home cooking

HORNBEAK

P.V.'s Hut
At E. Florida and S. Perkins Streets
209 E. Florida Ave.
(731) 885-5737
Yummy cheeseburgers
Tues through Sat 11 a.m. to 7 p.m.

JACKSON

Brooks Shaw's Old Country Store and Restaurant
Casey Jones Village
I-40 at US 45 Bypass
(800) 748-9588
caseyjones.com
Bountiful, all-you-can-eat breakfast, lunch, and dinner buffets every day

Redbones Grill & Bar
584 Carriage House Dr.
(731) 660-3838
redbonesgrillandbar.com
Steaks, chicken, seafood

MASON

Bozo's Hot Pit Bar-B-Que
342 Hwy. 70
(901) 294-3400
Pork shoulder barbecue
sandwiches
Tues through Sat 10:30
a.m. to 9 p.m.

MEMPHIS

Arcade Restaurant
540 S. Main St.
(901) 526-5757
arcaderestaurant.com
Breakfast all day; plate
lunch specials; since
1919, neon signs, vinyl
booths
7 a.m. to 3 p.m.

Automatic Slims Tonga Club
83 S. Second
(901) 525-7948
automaticslims.com
Southwestern and
Caribbean cuisine and
decor; coconut mango
shrimp, Caribbean voodoo
stew
Lunch Mon through
Fri 11 a.m. to 4 p.m.;
dinner Mon through Sun
4 to late; Sat and Sun
brunch 9 a.m. to 3 p.m.

Charles Vergo's Rendezvous
52 S. Second
(901) 523-2746
hogsfly.com
World-famous barbecued
ribs; a Memphis tradition
since 1948
Tues through Thurs 4:30
to 10:30 p.m.; Fri and Sat
11 a.m. to 11:30 p.m.

Chez Phillippe
149 Union Ave.
(901) 529-4188
peabodymemphis.com
Opulent room, decadent
dining in the Peabody
Hotel

Dyers Burgers
205 Beale St.
(901) 527-3937
dyersonbeale.com
Delicious deep-fried
hamburgers cooked in
grease not changed since
1912
Open daily at 11 a.m.;
closes when everyone
leaves

Huey's
77 S. Second St.
(901) 527-2700
hueyburger.com
Allowed to write on walls
and shoot toothpicks into
ceiling
Open daily at 11 a.m. or
noon until after midnight

Restaurant Iris
12146 Monroe Ave.
(901) 590-2828
restaurantiris.com
A culinary gem

SAVANNAH

The Worleybird Cafe
990 Pickwick St.
(731) 926-4882
Black Angus beef,
homemade chicken salad,
fried green tomatoes

SELMER

Pappy Johns Original Barbecue
On US 45 South
(731) 645-4353
All pork and chicken menu
Open daily except Sun

TIPTONVILLE

Blue Bank Fish House & Grill
Highway 21
(731) 253-6878
bluebankresort.com
Steak, quail, frog legs,
crappie, country ham
Open for breakfast, lunch,
and dinner

Boyette's Dining Room
Highway 21
10 Boyette Rd.
(731) 253-7307
Famous for catfish,
country ham, and family-
style meals since 1921;
adjacent to Reelfoot Lake
Open daily 11 a.m. to 9
p.m.

Index

Already "Been There, Done That"?
Then Get Off the Beaten Path!

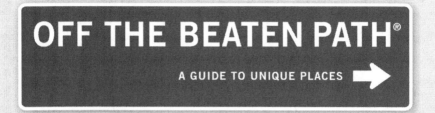

"For the traveler who enjoys the special, the unusual,
and the unexpected."—*The Traveler* newsletter

Alabama	Kansas	New Hampshire	Rhode Island
Alaska	Kentucky	New Jersey	South Carolina
Arizona	Louisiana	New Mexico	Southern California
Arkansas	Maine	Metro New York	Tennessee
British Columbia	Maritime Provinces	Upstate New York	Texas
Colorado	Maryland & Delaware	North Carolina	Utah
Connecticut	Massachusetts	Northern California	Vermont
Dakotas	Michigan	Ohio	Virginia
Florida	Minnesota	Oklahoma	Washington, D.C.
Georgia	Mississippi	Oregon	West Virginia
Hawaii	Missouri	Pennsylvania	Wisconsin
Idaho	Montana	Philadelphia	Wyoming
Indiana	Nebraska	Puerto Rico	
Iowa	Nevada	Quebec	